ROCKING
THE
GODDESS

ROCKING THE GODDESS

Campus Wicca for
the Student Practitioner

Anthony Paige

CITADEL PRESS
Kensington Publishing Corp.
www.kensingtonbooks.com

CITADEL PRESS BOOKS are published by

Kensington Publishing Corp.
850 Third Avenue
New York, NY 10022

All Kensington titles, imprints, and distributed lines are available at special quantity discounts for bulk purchases for sales promotions, premiums, fund-raising, educational, or institutional use. Special book excerpts or customized printings can also be created to fit specific needs. For details, write or phone the office of the Kensington special sales manager: Kensington Publishing Corp., 850 Third Avenue, New York, NY 10022, attn: Special Sales Department, phone 1-800-221-2647.

Citadel Press and the Citadel Logo are trademarks of Kensington Publishing Corp.

First printing: September 2002

10 9 8 7 6 5 4 3 2 1

Printed in the United States of America

Library of Congress Control Number: 2002104317

ISBN 0-8065-2356-5

In loving memory of
G.C.
1921–1998
Strength. Honor. Compassion.

Contents

· Book Three ·
A WITCH'S PARTY
Independent Study

Acknowledgments

Sincere and heartfelt thanks to my literary agent, Jane Dystel: your faith, guidance and unshakable strength are the most important mainstays of my writing life. To Miriam Goderich, whose creative vision always lights the way. A shout-out to Stacey Glick and Michael Bourret, who so graciously dealt with the occasional, crazed e-mail.

Bob Shuman, my awesome editor (and High Priest of Publishing), worked his own magic with Francine Hornberger and copy editor Susan Higgins on these pages. Thanks for believing in me. I couldn't have done this without you.

To the great people at SUNY Purchase College: John Forrest, professor, mentor and friend—thanks for making a difference; Eileen Holt, Registrar; my academic advisor, Joseph Fashing; Matthew Immergut, adjunct lecturer; and to my fellow Purchase buddies who walk in the Mysterious Realm, especially: Elizabeth Pyrih, Diana and Melanie Bayard, Jennifer Swallow, Danny Gong, Eduardo Saponara and, of course, the beautiful Jennifer Arena.

To the many college and university students who shared with me their thoughts, opinions, experiences and personal stories: you know who you are—Rock On. Special thanks to Seamus McKeon, Aradius, Evelyn, Moona, Jimmy B., Silver K. and Shadow. Several professors agreed to answer my questions, and their expertise is greatly appreciated. I especially thank John Simmons, Western Illinois University and Chas Clifton, University of Southern Colorado.

Kudos to Margot Adler, who agreed to answer my questions with such warmth and good cheer.

To the very good friends who never mind that I'm always on deadline: Amanda Juszczak, Jennifer Damiano, and Oni Kabir.

And to my nearest and dearest: my parents, Rose and Nunzio, who encourage and support my endeavors; my brother, Joseph, in love and honor of a past well-shared; my sister, Maria, for her dauntless efforts on my behalf; and my aunt, Antoinette, who listens to and always believes in me.

Till next time . . .

Preface

The Goddess has summoned you.

Her voice is alive in your mind, whispering like a treasured secret. You have been listening to it for some time now. It strengthens when you glimpse a candle burning in a window or breathe the scent of morning dew dripping from the grass. It gathers as you tread the lonely path into the woods at twilight. On those chilly moonlit nights—the sky glittering with stars, the trees haloed by silver—her voice speaks to you with the cadence of an old friend, and time is lost to the magic of a single moment. You have beheld the Mystery: it is invisible but present, indescribable but visceral. The Goddess is nearby.

Think of the feeling that seized you as you watched the sun set over the mountains, the sea, the desert. In all its simplicity, Earth thrilled you. When did you last question the unexplained? You are doing it at this very moment, the covers of this book resting against the palms of your hands. Other experiences led you here, too. Maybe it was the vivid dream of years ago that proved eerily prophetic. Maybe it was your questioning of God and a faith that left you unfulfilled. Maybe you have always believed that Nature is the most powerful religion, the combined rhythm of the seasons a creed in itself. In the chill blue of dawn you heard birds singing, rivers rushing, and awakened to greet the day with an inexplicable sense of awe. At dusk, the embracing darkness reminded you that what ends will only begin again in a circle of rebirth. Ill or despondent, you retired to a quiet corner and knew healing through meditation, your mind an antidote to pain. You listened, and the Goddess spoke.

In thought and spirit, you traveled back to centuries past and saw yourself standing amid a ring of stones. Images flooded you: of sired herbs, dripping wax, winds stirred by sleight of hand. Did you heed the ringing bells that called you to a burning? The stories of those bygone eras entranced you. In the Roman ruins and the temples of Egypt you found inspiration and familiarity. It is in the mystical that your psyche dwells—that limitless place between the worlds, where shadows breathe and spells are cast and the forgotten dead speak. You feared nothing, and the Goddess claimed you.

And so it is not by coincidence that you have found this book. Indeed, this book found *you*. Turn the pages. Listen. Learn. Live what you feel. On the threshold of discovery, there is no turning back.

You are already fluent in the wordless language of the Witch.

Author's Note

Even before beginning *Rocking the Goddess*, I knew I would not be able to cover every aspect of Wicca comprehensively. As a religion, Wicca is detailed in its various tenets and beliefs, and its non-dogmatic principles often vary from one practitioner to the next. Some have adopted the Gardnerian tradition of Witchcraft, for example, while others simply consider themselves "eclectic." There are differences, and I have tried herein to render them precise. Where requested, I referred to some as "Pagans," but otherwise I have used the word "Witch" when referring to those who follow the religion known as Wicca.

This book is about the widespread practice of Wicca on college campuses in the United States. Though it delves deeply into what Wicca is, it also encompasses the opinions, viewpoints, and experiences of a specific population and generation. Countless interviews and conversations comprise the heart of this book. In many instances, I met people in the flesh and attended rituals and workshops both on and off campuses. When distance became an issue, I conversed via e-mail or telephone. I agreed to listen to anyone but, inevitably, certain students, professors, and campus organizations did not make it into these pages. Some may disagree with the stories or opinions contained herein. I can only say that I spoke to countless individuals and included what I thought to be the most representative voices.

At the request of several people, I changed names to protect the privacy of certain individuals. While many students are public about their spiritual beliefs within the university setting, some still fear being stigmatized by greater society and want their personal lives protected. I altered names and identities to the extent I deemed appropriate.

New campus groups are forming all the time. Some do it with the support of their college or university and others choose to go at it alone. Thus, the directory at the back of this book is not necessarily complete. The colleges and universities listed either have their own student Wicca/Pagan groups or represent educational institutions from which students spoke to me.

Bonfires dot the rolling hillsides
Figures dance around and around
To drums that pulse out echoes of darkness
Moving to the Pagan sounds

Somewhere in a hidden memory
Images float before my eyes
Of fragrant nights of straw and of bonfires
And dancing till the next sunrise

Loreena McKennitt
"All Souls Night"
The Visit

Book One

•

A WITCH'S KNOWLEDGE

•

Core Requirements

· 1 ·

Wicca

An Old Religion,
a New Generation

Midnight waits for them.

It waits with a chill wind and a curious silence and a sky caressed by moonlight. It waits in mystery.

They move slowly around the consecrated space, four friends readying themselves for worship. The preparations have been made. The mood is set. Gone are the worries of the day. Months of practice will make the ritual effortless, but each takes great care in creating an atmosphere conducive to magic. They are modern-day Witches, offering their reverence and respect to the Goddess and God our long-dead ancestors once praised. Embraced by the realm of night, their celebration has begun.

I sit a short distance away, immersed in darkness. I listen to the soft ruffle of footfalls, the jangle of keys, even a furtive whisper. Forgetting my whereabouts is easy. The scent of incense transports me to a forest in late autumn. The air here is vaguely redolent of a bonfire. New Age music rises from a hidden CD player, and the precious notes lull me into relaxed contentment. Even so, I cannot help but think of the four young adults who have invited me into their world tonight—a world of altars, herbs, and spells. A world where ancient deities are invoked through nature's hidden door-

ways. A world, I remind myself, once forbidden and branded evil, and for which countless devotees died by fire.

Centuries ago, this very meeting would have incurred the possibility of fatal exposure. Now, however, there is no fear. Too many have already reclaimed the word and the way of the Witch. The religion known as Wicca is said to be the fastest growing in the United States. Centered around the Goddess and God, it is a system of beliefs and practices rooted in the Paganism of pre-Christian Europe. The earth is the Witch's temple. The elements are her accoutrements of praise. More than an enigma, she has become a staple of mainstream culture. Nonetheless, her true identity remains veiled in secrecy and misrepresentation. Who is the modern-day Witch? How has Wicca—a religion of simple, archaic ideologies— managed to penetrate the scope of our technological age?

The music dies away. Rustlings grate against the dark. I wait patiently, not wanting to disturb the calm. Questions continue churning through my mind, yet I respect my place as observer and, albeit loosely, participant. For I am no stranger to the Goddess.

"In honor, strength, and truth, we gather," a male voice murmurs suddenly. A match is lit, and a single flame knifes the inky void. The glare illuminates Mark's face. His eyes catch the wavering glint as he fires up three candles.

The light breathes. It lifts like a golden circle and encompasses the three young women who complete the coven. Justine closes her eyes. Lisa flexes her fingers above the dancing flames. Sara is smiling in the immediacy of the moment. Standing shoulder-to-shoulder, the four surround a small makeshift altar adorned with rose petals, a bowl of water, a cup of salt, and a spoon. The candles rest in the center.

"Tonight, we come together to give praise to the Goddess," Lisa says.

"We honor Her as maiden, mother, and crone," Justine chimes in.

"In doing so, we praise Earth, the Moon, and the universal wisdom." Sara motions for them to join hands. They do. Once again a

silence falls. Slowly they move clockwise, mentally casting the magic circle that will act as a barrier between the two worlds: that of spirit and that of form. This is also regarded as the bridge where limited human knowledge is conjoined with the unlimited possibilities of the supernatural realm.

They stop and close their eyes. They breathe in unison.

I can feel their collective concentration thrumming like electricity. I can hear the rhythmic beating of my own heart as the members of the coven cleanse and purify the confined space. They employ simple visualization techniques: a shimmering ring of light drawing them closer together, a blue energy field rising up from the ground. In moments, they are equally rooted and released.

Midnight draws near. The proverbial witching hour. Mark reaches for the bowl of salt and gathers a few grains in his palm. He sprinkles them on the ground, then across the altar. One by one, each calls a corner, inviting the elements to guard the rite: Earth, Air, Fire, Water. The circle is completed. They lower themselves into sitting positions and begin preparing for the matter at hand. On this, the eve of the Full Moon, they will cast a spell for good fortune. They will ask the Goddess to bestow upon them the strength to overcome imminent obstacles and avert negativity. But first, they will give thanks for the splendor that has already touched their lives: a happy relationship, a job promotion, good health, a multitude of sunny days and clear crisp nights.

"I'm thinking of the other day," Lisa says. "I went to the doctor because last week I found a lump in my breast. I meditated for hours, took long walks on the beach. In the end, I got good news. And so I offer up my gratitude." She lifts the silver spoon from the altar and clanks it against the bowl of water.

"The last month has been incredibly stressful," Sara tells her fellow siblings-in-spirit. "I managed to get through it all with a clear head. I give thanks." Spoon in hand, she repeats the step and passes it on.

Mark and Justine have much to be grateful for as well. They voice their own achievements before focusing on the spell. When the time comes, Justine plucks the burning green candle out of its holder. She digs a small pin from the bottom of the salt cup and carefully inscribes her name into the wax. They all follow suit. The candle is then replaced, but its purpose has been altered. Infused with the essence of their intention, it is now a sanctioned tool—ordained, revered, holy. It will act as the focal point of their magic, but the magic itself is carefully invoked from within. The magic is alive, glowing in their minds like a beacon. As Witches, they possess the ability to alter consciousness at will. It is not a feat of otherworldly sorcery; it is instead a boon of nature, a live wire of possibility and promise that runs through the course of everyday life. Thus, a Witch's power is derived from the universal forces that govern existence.

Turning, Lisa meets my fixed stare. She stretches her hand out, inviting me into the circle. I slowly make my way forward. Despite the autumn chill, I feel as if the candles are warming me from a distance. I step into the chasm of incense, smoke, and eerie firelight. An odd prickling pervades my senses. It is as if I'm being welcomed into an altered realm that inexplicably strips me of all worry and inhibition. I sit. I look around. The darkness seems to tremble.

Justine smiles knowingly. "We're raising energy," she says. "Inside the magic circle, anything is possible. That's what you're feeling right now. It doesn't matter that we're far away from the woods and not directly beneath the Full Moon."

"As Witches," Mark adds, "we can harness the natural forces of our surroundings regardless of location. The power comes from within." He points to the candle sitting in the very center of the altar. The flame shoots upright, erect. "I carved your name into the wax. Now you're part of the spell."

Part of the magic.

We join hands and close our eyes. "And so I summon the Goddess," Lisa says with conviction.

For the next several minutes we descend into a state of silent, steady meditation. There is no chanting. We do not dance around or attempt to draw down the Moon.

The Goddess is already present.

She comes in shadow and flickering pinpricks of light. She comes like a brisk wind into the circle, stirring the depths of our consciousness. She comes with blinding clarity. The sacred space in which we sit is transformed by a unity born of power, passion, and praise. And so the magic is done.

Or has it just begun?

Nearly an hour later, as the ritual draws to a close, I hear the familiar sounds: the soft ruffle of footfalls, the jangle of keys, a furtive whisper. None of it matters. I am lost in the tangle of this enchanted, mysterious place—a place where Witches gather and the Goddess walks and the darkness breathes in beauty. It is no ordinary destination. I can feel its seduction in the perfumed air snaking around my body. I can taste it on my lips, an elixir of the midnight hour. To what dwelling have I come?

Opening my eyes, I am assailed by the harsh glare of an overhead light. I blink, confused. I take in my surroundings—the bare walls, the twin beds, the little desk crowded into one corner—and smile unwittingly.

It is a college dorm room.

Witchcraft: Past and Present

For centuries, the word *witch* has held uncanny power. It prompts fear. It invites suspicion. It calls to mind a black-robed figure conjuring her tempest by the light of a Full Moon. Her accoutrements are many: a bubbling cauldron, the conical hat, the broom upon which she flies.

These vivid icons came to fruition during the infamous Burning Times, when countless women and men suffered the wrath of the Inquisitors. The widespread hysteria prompted gruesome forms of torture: mutilation, sustained drowning, and, of course, death by flame. To the Pagans of pre-Christian Europe, it surely came as a surprise. In small villages and seaside towns alike, the local midwife was revered as both a healer and, occasionally, a soothsayer. She

brewed tonics and cultivated herbs. She nursed the afflicted and ushered new life into the world. She foresaw storms by way of the wind.
Back then, these practices were a common part of everyday life.
People lived in accordance with Nature and adhered to the shifting
patterns of the seasons. They worshipped not a God but a Goddess,
and saw divinity as a female principle that governed the universe. It
was a sensible assertion. The female anatomy, biologically designed
to give life, was synonymous with the life-giving properties of
Earth. Just as the Moon fluxes through rigid cycles, so too does a
woman's body renew itself via the process of menstruation. No solid
proof exists that women were ever superior to men in class or social
structure, but prior to the Inquisition, women were certainly regarded with a sort of mystical esteem.

No single culture has escaped the mysterious lure of Paganism.
Ancient Phoenicians prayed to the goddess Astarte. Throughout the
Neolithic and Bronze Ages, the goddess Ishtar was an omnipotent
entity. In Italy, the goddess Aradia, daughter of Diana, was worshipped by *le strege* (the witches), who danced in the Florentine
hills to honor her. Egyptians built temples to adore the goddess Isis,
and the hieroglyph of her name was of a throne. Romans believed
that the goddess Cardea possessed the power to both protect and
destroy. In Greek mythology, Gaia remains the Mother Earth goddess, while Hecate lurks the shadowy crossroads of uncertainty. In
Africa, Oya was the goddess of the Niger River. The Indian goddess
of illusion, Maya, appeared in the shimmering image of a rainbow.
Examples are virtually endless, and each gives testimony to the historical significance of Paganism, or what is commonly referred to as
"Old Religion." Benevolent and rooted in the simplistic ideologies
of nature, Paganism was a way of life, a faith far removed from the
negative campaign with which it has become synonymous.

It was the rise of Christianity that gave Pagans a feared identity.
Women who once cured the sick were branded Witches, and the
startling and shocking claims thrust upon them prevailed. Nocturnal
trysts brought her to the devil's doorstep, where it was believed she
feasted on flesh and blood. Later, she cursed her foes into death. She

even possessed the rare ability to summon demons to do her bidding. Torrential rain, famine, the onslaught of disease—each was attributed to the Witch. A resistance to conversion was met with widespread slaughter. The role of women in Paganism was undoubtedly a threat to the male-dominated catechism of the Roman Catholic Church, and numerous scholars and historians have branded the horror of those times "the women's holocaust." Not even Joan of Arc, one of the most revered saints, escaped the hysteria: her religious ecstasy was deemed Witchcraft and the accusation escorted her to the funeral pyre. By the time the delirium reached across the Atlantic, the small town of Salem, Massachusetts, was steeped in turmoil. Witchcraft was the crime, ignorance the motive. Nineteen women and men were hung on Gallows Hill and hundreds more imprisoned.

In the United States, the Salem Witch Trials remain an enigma. The lurid details of the year 1692 are etched in books and have been immortalized in feature films and on television. It is the dark past. It is the spooky memory resurrected around the campfire on Halloween. With the dawning of Puritanism, Americans—people of various cultures, in fact—had long put to rest the possibility that Witches were real. After all, the majority of mainstream religions had evolved into monotheism, and the concept of God was overwhelmingly male. (Christianity, Judaism, and Islam subscribe to a wholly masculine Supreme Being. Even Buddhism, which does not recognize any superior mystical force, upholds the male Buddha as its central figure.) And so it was believed that the Goddess of ancient times—despite the grandeur of her gilded temples, the statues radiating her beauty—died with the ashes of her once devoted children.

But was the Goddess ever truly eradicated from human consciousness? Did she simply cease to exist? Unequivocally, she did not. The United States is a prime example of the timeless power the Goddess has long commanded. Nowhere else has she witnessed such a vibrant and phenomenal rebirth. The New Age resurgence that has gripped America began in the 1960s and flourished well into the 1970s. It was between these decades that the term *Wicca* became mainstream. The collective liberal mind-set of that time saw an uprising of interest in spirituality. Feminism was at the summit of America's political agenda. People were seduced by the idea of "freedom" in all forms. Eager to reconnect with nature and thirsty for religious liberty, women and men began reclaiming the Old Religion, combining various Pagan traditions with Moon worship and a deep reverence for the Goddess. Although most of those who converted to Wicca were women at odds with their Christian or Judaic roots, it wasn't long before men found themselves attracted to this seemingly radical and autonomous religion. From the very first, Wicca embraced the notion of sexuality as sacred; unlike other faiths, it did not discriminate against or exclude the homosexual population. Quite the contrary, Wicca presented itself to curious minds as a religion devoid of dogma and hierarchy. To be a Witch, one had to embrace Nature as a true life force and adopt the perspective of male/female equality within the boundaries of worship.

Today, Wicca is centered around the Goddess and her consort, the Horned God. It is the Goddess, however, who embodies the very heart of Wicca. She is the giver and taker of life, the abundance of fertility. She is Mother Nature, from the sprouting soil to the limitless sky to the elements that surround us every day. She is joy, sorrow, angst. She is emotional and intellectual depth. She is physical growth, pleasure, and demise. She is the mystical power of the Moon and the sustained heat of the Sun. She is all-knowing and infinite, the cycle of death and rebirth. Oftentimes, she is depicted with three faces; in this trinity aspect, she is maiden, mother, and crone. Witches of today worship the Goddess in various forms, though mainly as an omnipotent entity. She is symbolized by the Moon and its phases of waxing, waning, and full. The time of the Waxing Moon is when energy is building to a summit; Witches cast spells to attract positive energy, perform healing rituals, heighten psychical awareness. The Waning Moon is reserved for the banishing and destruction of negativity or bad luck. Once a month, when the Moon is full, Witches give praise to the Goddess at her most potent. Female Witches worship the Goddess because it is a way to reconnect to their own feminine power. For male Witches, the Goddess represents getting in touch with the feminine side that is often concealed behind the veil of staunch masculinity.

The Horned God in Wicca represents the male aspect of deity. As the Goddess's consort, he is ruler of the Underworld and also a giver and taker of life. He prevails over the forests and woodlands, his horns said to represent the various beasts that roam those paths. He exemplifies the hunt in nature and the vitality necessary for survival. The gods Cernunnos and Pan are examples of Wicca's Horned God, for they are often portrayed artistically as wrapped in leaves or bearing animal-like bodies. In worship, the God is symbolized by the High Priest, who works with the High Priestess in raising energy and creating rituals. The God is an image of raw sexuality and power. In laymen's terms, he is the perfect mate.

The last decade was particularly instrumental in propelling Wicca to the forefront of American culture. Media outlets surged with news stories, profiles and reports about the modern-day Witch. Major television networks delved into the religious boom, from CNN's *Larry King Live* to *60 Minutes* on CBS. Hollywood was quick to respond as well. Feature films like *The Craft* and *Practical Magic* were hugely successful at the box office, and television heeded the call with increasingly popular shows: *Charmed, Sabrina the Teenage Witch*, and *Buffy the Vampire Slayer*, to name a few. The publishing industry witnessed an explosion of books detailing Wicca's every thread: how to cast spells, how to form covens, biographies of the Goddess. The abundance of resources directly linked to Wicca continues unabated, just as the number of converts multiplies. Undoubtedly, Wicca is here to stay.

The nucleus of Wicca—the greatest strength and most important mainstay—is its burgeoning population of practitioners. Passionate and outspoken, the Witches of today have delineated their identities clearly. Gone is the image of the evildoer. Legally recognized since 1986, Wiccans have emerged as an international community built on the foundation of activism. They own businesses. They raise their children in the shadow of the Goddess. They represent all walks of life and an amalgam of cultures. Like Nature itself, the face of

Wicca is diversified and non-centralized. Those who denounce it as a true religion—scholars, theologians, politicians—view the principle of spiritual self-governance as a product of radical thinking unrelated to historical doctrine. To them, it is merely a facet of the liberal "New Age" invented to justify a certain lifestyle. But Witches believe otherwise. The proof lies in history, in the drawings etched on cave walls, in the Goddess sculptures unearthed throughout Europe and the Middle East, in the preserved texts of the great Roman Empire. Witches have roamed Earth since the dawn of time. What they practice and honor is an age-old tradition steeped in undeniable fact: the antiquated language of Paganism.

Wicca: The College Years

The majority of Wicca devotees "find" the Goddess in their late teens and early twenties. Why is this? Opinions vary. Many teenagers are admittedly attracted to the eclecticism of the Witch identity, the "cool" concept of praying to the Full Moon and casting spells. Others find comfort in the non-judgmental aspects of Wicca's tenets and beliefs. The college population has fostered Wicca consistently throughout the years: on campus, in dorm rooms, within the conservative realm of academe. They have formed covens and, when denied or shunned, have taken the Goddess underground. Interestingly enough, college students are also the only specified sect of Witches that have been ignored or, at least, greatly overlooked. And yet, college Wicca has thrived. Challenged by administrative authority, faced with discrimination, fearing exposure, students across the nation and around the world have transcended these steely boundaries and reinvented the image of the young Witch.

As a freshman at John Jay College of Criminal Justice in Manhattan, I did not expect to hear whispers of the Goddess. A school of several thousand commuting students, it is equipped with forensic laboratories and autopsy protocols and faculty members who have spent as much time on the firing range as in the classroom. Book-toting cops run up and down the hallways. Agents from the FBI and

DEA speak in the lecture halls. There is a conservative nature to the school because it was initially formed to train men and women as New York City police officers. Shortly after beginning my first semester, however, I noticed them. Standing outside smoking cigarettes or haunting the library: students wearing pentacles—the five-pointed star associated with Wicca and magick—and chatting about the New Age shops in Greenwich Village. I was admittedly shocked. I approached several of them and discovered that John Jay was home to a fairly large number of college Witches. They were majoring in forensic science and psychology, criminology and police studies. They aspired to enter the workforce as cops, scientists, or federal agents. Didn't they know, I asked myself, the dangers of living publicly as Witches in such a conventional environment?

Shortly thereafter I met Peter, a twenty-two-year-old John Jay student who had been born and raised in Brooklyn. The first time I saw him, he was sitting in the lobby of the Tenth Avenue building flipping through a notebook. He was dressed in jeans and a navy shirt emblazoned with the NYPD insignia. A pentacle hung from his neck, bright against the dark blue collar. Peter was completing the mandatory sixty college credits before entering the police academy.

Peter's father was a cop and their home had been traditionally Roman Catholic. In high school Peter discovered Wicca and felt as though he had "come home." Once in college, his beliefs strengthened. He found a small community of practicing Witches at John Jay that met twice a month to talk about Wicca. It was a "group," he told me, and not a coven. He favored practicing alone and reserved the nights of the Full Moon for worship. Peter wanted to be a cop, and he explained to me that "coming out of the broom closet" was a choice for him. He had faced some discrimination, but to him, Wicca was already mainstream and accepted and protected by the Constitution. He even believed that being a Witch would aid him in his career as one of "New York's Finest." What was more, Peter told me that he had already met several police officers who were practicing Witches. His message was loud and clear: no matter the environment or geographic location, Wicca was everywhere.

Two years later, upon my transfer to SUNY Purchase College in Westchester County, New York, I met up with more college Witches. That first October on campus, I attended a Samhain ritual held in a dorm room on Halloween. Later, I witnessed a solstice ritual in the woods that bordered the parking lot. Just down the road was Manhattanville College—private, costly, Catholic—where students held a pagan May Day celebration in the shadow of the church that sits in the middle of its lush grounds. A few minutes away, at Pace University, five roommates were beginning to form a campus coven. In time, I would meet others from SUNY Oswego, Cornell University, Connecticut College, Marymount College, Sarah Lawrence College, and Rutgers University in New Jersey. It wasn't merely a handful of Wicca devotees; it was a society all of its own, replete with tailored rituals and dorm room spells, faculty advisors and underground covens. What continued to amaze me was not the number of college Witches I encountered but the specificity of their practices. It gave testimony to the serious, intellectual depth of a generation branded indifferent to spirituality and idolatrous of popular culture—music, fashion, designer drugs. College Wicca was a significant movement happening all over the country and, I was soon to learn, all over the world. But was there, I began to wonder, a psychological component to the collegiate Witch, a combination of new surroundings and ideas sparking a desire for spiritual exploration? Was it simply the initiation into young adulthood that compounded identity?

Lady Espa, a high priestess who runs her own coven in Los Angeles, has been studying and teaching Wicca for nearly twenty-five years. She worked at two different universities, first as a secretary and later as a counselor. In the latter capacity, she acted as a mentor to students curious about exploring spirituality. "Wicca and college students have an interesting relationship," she told me when I first chatted with her. "It's a difficult time—packing up, leaving home, facing a world on your own. That can be scary. But it's also an incredibly liberating time, and students find themselves eager to explore the world from a different angle. That's what separates the teenage Witch from the college Witch—in college it's all about making your own decisions as an adult. You can form your own identity without the parental constraints."

As a counselor, Lady Espa often encountered students who were practicing Wicca, but with little guidance. A dedicated member of the Wiccan community, she felt it was her responsibility to lead them in the right direction. "A lot of the students I came across had heard the rumors about me, which floated around both of the campuses I worked at. I was never secretive about my religion, and that kind of inner strength serves as an example to younger practitioners. College students are dealing with a multitude of issues throughout their four academic years, and I showed many of them how to weave Wicca into their daily lives. They found the Goddess at all times— while writing difficult term papers or, in some cases, overcoming dangerous addictions. After graduating, they headed out into the real world with an educated sense of Wicca, and that serves as a foundation for the rest of their spiritual lives."

Lady Espa formed her first coven in 1990 with three friends. Two years later, the number doubled. It was a group that prided itself on experience and dedicated practice. The members were not looking to serve as role models for younger Witches, but in 1995, the coven initiated and admitted its youngest sibling-in-spirit: a twenty-year-old college student. "He was a remarkable young man," Lady Espa explained. "He had been studying Wicca for two years while at Columbia University, where he was a member of a student coven. By the time he found me, he was ready to move deeper into his spiritual quest. And I think that's true of a lot of college Witches today. They are very assured and serious."

Asked why she believes Wicca and the college years go hand in hand, Lady Espa replied, "I think the freedom Wicca represents mirrors the whole college experience. It's a new time, a new world. It's full of excitement and promise. Wicca is a mystery tradition, and as a Witch you are constantly learning. What better time to find yourself spiritually than while living in a community surrounded by scholarship and new ideas?"

John S., an adjunct professor at a major Midwestern university, teaches classes about the historical roots of Paganism, but also acts as a mentor to students finding their way into Wicca. A high priest of the Gardnerian tradition of Witchcraft, he became a Witch while studying abroad in the United Kingdom. "With every new semester I see more undergraduates pledging themselves to the Goddess," he said. "I think Wicca exploded among the younger generation—specifically college students—because it is a religion that seeks to liberate rather than isolate. There is no concept of grievous sin or suffering. Wicca hinges a lot on the supernatural, but it views the supernatural as feasible and characteristic of the Universe. That certainly attracts people to becoming Witches. On college campuses, everyone is really in the same frame of mind. You're there to learn about yourself and others, which automatically opens the door to acceptance among your peers. Students who might have been shunned by parents or friends back home come to college and find outlets that allow them to practice freely."

What is unequivocal about Wicca today is that it adheres to a single rede: "harm none, do what you will." It is the very motto of modern-day Witches, the concept serving to both ground followers and negate public misrepresentation. The creed is an umbrella under which float a multitude of equally significant beliefs. Witches are strong supporters of karma, or what is commonly known as "The Threefold Law": whatever energy a Witch sends out into the atmosphere returns with three times the initial intensity. Thus, they seek to cast spells and perform rituals with good intention. In keeping with the mind-set of pre-Christian times, they do not give credence to the existence of a "devil." Satan is a solely Christian construct. Witches believe in the power of the mind, and their abilities enable them to tap into a depth greater than that of the ordinary person. Simply put, what others view as "supernatural" is commonplace to the seasoned Witch.

Zachary, a twenty-four-year-old senior at the University of Wisconsin at Stevens Point, converted to Wicca in freshman year. He was raised in Judaism, but he felt an affinity with Wicca because it was the only religion that validated the multitude of psychic experiences he'd had since early childhood. The episodes ranged from simple intuitions, like knowing when the telephone was going to ring, to full-fledged premonitions, several of which came true. "When I was eight," Zachary told me, "I used to freak my parents out because the phone would ring and I'd say, 'Oh, that's Aunt Michelle,' and I'd be right. Mom and Dad didn't like it. I tried as much as I could to keep it hidden, but when I was about thirteen I started seeing auras around people—bright circles of color that were accompanied by very real feelings. Blue was depression. Yellow was happiness. And when I saw black, I knew a person was either ill or entering a final phase of life."

He then gave me a chilling example. "We were at a family function when I was about fifteen, and a friend of my dad's walked into the room. He was ebbed by a black shadow, and my stomach just about lurched. I told my mom about the feeling but she just scolded me. But I knew I was right—*I saw it,* clear as day. Dad was annoyed with me and asked me to leave. Later, the friend told my folks that he had been diagnosed with a terminal disease one week earlier and had opted against medical treatment. He died six weeks later."

The mysterious incidents continued. Zachary left home and entered college, where he first began exploring Wicca. He met other Witches on campus, who were quick to accept him into their secret society. "There were four kids who ran a coven on campus, but they weren't public about it. I found one of them by chance, and she was the first person who told me I wasn't crazy. They all just looked at me and said, 'Hey, that's cool.' It was that kind of openness and willingness that gave me confidence. I started casting spells in my dorm room with great success. I knew I was a Witch early on because Wicca was all about what I was feeling and experiencing. The Goddess and God taught me about nature, and about how energy exists on all levels. I never got that from Judaism. And the truth is,

I found myself completely in college—spiritually and intellectually. I think I'll always be a college Witch!"

His psychic experiences not withstanding, Zachary made a point of presenting himself as a "regular guy." He enjoys reading and working out. He listens to all types of music but favors Metallica, Aerosmith, and Creed. In June 2001, his coven from the University of Wisconsin organized a public Summer Solstice ritual in the greater Milwaukee area. They passed out flyers and pamphlets about Wicca and helped raise money for a number of local charities.

Although the supernatural plays a large role in Wicca, many Witches feel more at home with the environmental aspects of their religion. They view psychic phenomena and the spirit realm as secondary to the worship of nature. Watching a television show like *Charmed* does not necessarily paint an accurate picture of Witchcraft as both a religion and a practice.

When Marcy began her college career at the University of Nevada in Las Vegas, she had already consecrated herself to the Goddess. Being a Witch for her is all about loving, respecting, and caring for the environment. "I think of myself as a green Witch," she explained. "First and foremost is Nature—the air, the oceans, and the lakes, the realization that life is a lot like Earth because it lives and dies but renews itself. That's the Goddess to me. I view Wicca as a combination of science and metaphysics, a religion that combines it all. You connect spiritually with the Pagan deities but you marry it with the phases of the Moon and the Sun, the elements and even the Hermetic Principles. For me, worship is sitting in a quiet place on the night of the Full Moon and just recognizing that Nature moves and breathes all around me."

At twenty-one, Marcy does not belong to a coven, nor she does she feel the need to network within the Wicca community. She is a member of the campus National Interest Public Research Group (NIPRG) promoting environmental awareness and political change. Though admittedly a "young, calm college Witch," she favors activism and draws inspiration from the feminist movement of the 1960s. She believes that Wicca has gone from a reactive stance to a proactive stance. "I support the pluralism of religious liberty, and I make a point of educating the public about Wicca as a religion that is grounded in nature. College is a great place to be a Witch because mostly students back one another up a lot. I try my best to make people understand what it's all about. I focus on the fact that Witches don't believe in Satan and that spells are really prayers. But as a whole, I'm not as concerned with promoting the whole magical side of my religion—that's a very personal thing."

For Witches, magic has nothing to do with the modern concept of sorcery. It is not disappearing at the snap of one's fingers or moving objects at a glance. There is no trickery, no illusion. "Magick" is the practice of Witchcraft, the physical and mental doing of one's will. Lighting candles, gathering herbs and oils, and accessing the proper lunar and astrological correspondences all play a significant role in casting a spell. Living in a dorm room or campus apartment makes the task doubly difficult. The overwhelming majority of colleges and universities outlaw the burning of candles indoors, and a disagreeable roommate or even the girl across the hall who views Wicca with a stilted eye presents additional problems. Oddly enough, these hurdles have not hindered the practice of Wicca on campuses.

So how do college Witches go about practicing magic? Marcy at the University of Nevada utilizes the outdoors, where she lights a single votive candle and writes poetry. Scott, a nineteen-year-old junior at Carnegie Mellon University in Pennsylvania, favors a desk lamp affixed with colored bulbs to create certain moods when he is casting a spell. Listening to music also helps. When the sounds of Enya and Loreena McKennitt pierce the air, Scott's roommates know what he's doing. He told me: "Magick isn't only about the things you use. It's more about the power of your will and the concentration you put into it. If the Moon is waxing, I can sit in my dorm room, on my bed, and just meditate deeply. I use visualization and see the intended goal of my spell. Same thing if the Moon is waning. Being a Witch is a lot about transcendence, and a good Witch can find ways to practice magic without the candle and the incense. But when I do need it, I improvise. I use other tools and methods to invoke and worship the Goddess."

Genna, who frequently uses her Witch name, Moonstar, is a member of a small, student-run coven at the University of Texas at Dallas. She is one of many young Witches incensed by what she believes is a lack of respect for Wicca by school administrators. "At this point," she said, "everyone who's in college knows what Wicca is, and that includes the administration. They know candles and incense are a part of rituals but they deny us what I think is a basic right. We aren't allowed to do it in the privacy of our dorm rooms, so we have to find ways to skirt around those bogus rules, and we absolutely do."

But determination doesn't always work. Some college Witches have faced racism, discrimination, and even violence on campus. Such was the case with Shadow, a young man who contacted me using only a pseudonym. A twenty-two-year-old senior at a New England university he declined to name, Shadow has been a practicing Witch since high school. He grew up in a small Rhode Island town where, he says, he knew many Witches, young and old. When it came time to attend college, he chose his current school because it offered him a partial scholarship. It is a Roman Catholic university with "an excellent academic reputation" and a prestigious name. When Shadow arrived on campus, he kept his identity as a Witch concealed, but only because he was a solitary practitioner and didn't expect to find any other followers of Wicca.

"It's a jock school," he told me. "Frat parties are big, and so are drugs. Campus life revolves around the football field or one of the local bars. That was never my scene so at first I had a hard time fitting in, but I wanted to be there because I knew I'd be getting a great education." Throughout his freshman year, Shadow practiced Wicca "under stress," timing his dorm room rituals and spells around his roommate's schedule. Alone, Shadow invoked the Goddess and God, wore his pentacle on the outside of his shirt, and read through his vast assortment of Wicca books. It was a lonely time. He remained focused on his work and haunted chatrooms for support. But at the beginning of sophomore year, his life changed dramatically.

"Over the summer I had cast a spell for strength and guidance," he explained. "Then in September, while sitting in class, I took a glance at the girl sitting next to me—she was hot—and saw that she was wearing a pentacle ring. I got up enough nerve to question her about it, and sure enough, she was a Witch." The young woman would eventually become Shadow's girlfriend, and she introduced him to the four other Witches on campus. All were closeted about their identities. They formed a sort of support group and, by the following semester, a coven. Soon they approached the Office of Student Affairs and asked if they could receive funding for a student-run Wicca club. The response was anything but favorable.

"We were met with shock and horror and shame," Shadow said. "One of the deans, a Jesuit priest, told us we needed counseling. We walked away angered but all the more determined to live publicly and freely. There were students of all religious denominations on campus—Jewish, Muslim, Zorastrian. They got along fine, so why couldn't we? The six of us started wearing our pentacles and telling those who questioned us about it the truth. That's when things got rough."

One day while walking to class, Shadow was approached by three male students who accused him and the other five coven members of satanic worship. Tempers flared. Fists flew. Shadow left the scene with a bloody nose and a torn shirt. He filed a report with campus police, who were "aloof" about the incident. The taunting and abuse continued well into junior year, but the coven members remained steadfast in their beliefs. And instead of fighting for a recognized campus Wicca group, they took the coven underground. They used the woods bordering the university to perform rituals and, Shadow claimed, found a basement storage room in one of the buildings that protected them during the snowy, cold winters.

"A few people knew we were going into the woods," Shadow admitted. "Rumors started to spread on campus, and I guess we all went from being shunned to being feared. Students didn't bother us as much, but they didn't exactly talk to us either. We proved our point: that Witches are real and dedicated and that we're not going to be stopped." Shadow claimed that the air of mystery surrounding the coven members spawned interest, and soon other students curious about Wicca began making inquiries. He received e-mails, phone calls, and notes in his mailbox. "These were students who were Witches themselves, living on campus just like me. They were scared to do anything about it, but they also wanted to be part of a community. They wanted friends and the chance to practice seriously." Now in his senior year, Shadow acts as high priest of the underground coven, which is comprised of no less than fifteen members. The coven still goes out to the woods, and the little room in the basement continues to welcome them in the deep chill of night.

Tami, a recent graduate of Oberlin College, did not experience any such discrimination while a student. She began practicing Wicca in freshman year. When she was ready to meet other fellow college Witches, she posted a note on a cafeteria bulletin board and soon found herself bombarded with replies. "I met about thirty Witches who lived on campus within a week of putting out the word," she said. "It wasn't some big production, but we just started meeting and talking and exchanging ideas about Wicca and what we felt our religion was all about. There was a lot of support for us on campus. Many of us were open about who we are, and the professors and faculty members treated us with respect." Once, she and six others college Witches held a public Full Moon ritual on campus. A number of students showed up to watch and sate their own curiosities, but it was not a spectacle that garnered much attention. Tami believes that religious freedom is a basic perk at a school like Oberlin, which has a long and liberal history. Location can make a difference. "It would've been a lot harder for me and the other students if we were on a campus with Christian roots or very conservative politics. I'm not saying that Witches should stay clear of those types of schools, but I just think it's easier to be yourself in a place that you know will accept you. Not all colleges are going to embrace Witches, and fighting for rights can take as long as earning your degree. So if you're a Witch or Pagan who's thinking about being active on campus, choose the right one. In my opinion, it's just better to be safe than sorry."

Despite the New Age resurgence that has gripped America, people are still apt to associate Witches with ignorant images. Many—especially those living in small towns or attending universities with conservative political ties—go about their daily lives thinking of ways to conceal their identities. Reluctant attitudes and harassment, however, have not hindered the growth of Wicca on college campuses. For every college Witch who has experienced discord with roommates, professors, or fellow students, there are thousands living comfortably within the university setting. They are learning and exploring. They are casting spells and making magick. They are delineating the identity of the young modern-day Witch.

Drawing Down the Moon

In 1979, Margot Adler published *Drawing Down the Moon: Witches, Druids, Goddess-Worshippers and Other Pagans in America Today.* Painstakingly researched and brilliantly executed, this book continues to serve as an introduction to Wicca for curious minds; it is also a valuable historical account of the Pagan spiritual movement as seen through the eyes of an acclaimed journalist and Wiccan priestess. The overwhelming majority of students and professors I interviewed were quick to mention *Drawing Down the Moon* when discussing their ideas and opinions about Wicca and the identity of the modern-day Witch. Of all the books on Wicca, Witchcraft, and Paganism currently sitting on store shelves, *Drawing Down the Moon* is by far the most comprehensive—not to mention the most well-written. Adler interviewed Witches, Pagans, and various Goddess-Worshippers from across the country while simultaneously joining in on rituals and gatherings. The result is a colorful and informative odyssey into the heart of Witchcraft in America.

As a teenager growing up in New York City, I frequently browsed

SPOTLIGHT
University of Arkansas
Student Pagan Association
www.uark.edu/studorg/stpa

The Student Pagan Association at the University of Arkansas is one of the most impressive college organizations in the country. Their Web site contains a plethora of information about Paganism and includes several valuable links, from local businesses to the various Pagan traditions practiced all over the United States.

The organization was founded in 1993 and has grown steadily since then. According to the Web site, SPA attracts thirty or more members annually, and students conduct on-campus meetings on a weekly basis. They have been honored with awards for community service and service to the online Pagan/Wiccan community because of their dedication to negating misrepresentation about their religion. As a member of the University of Arkansas's Council of Religious Organizations, the Student Pagan Association maintains an official constitution and a listing of all its past rituals. They have been profiled in local newspapers and make a point of welcoming students of all religious denominations into the organization. The Web site can also be viewed in Latin.

One member of the SPA told me: "We try to hold lectures on topics of interest to our members every week, and we hold generic neo-Pagan ceremonies several times a year. We're open to both students and non-students, and we have members from many faiths. We try to offer support to our members in three main areas: intellectual (through weekly lectures), social (through open ceremonies, a list-serv, and get-togethers after meetings), and spiritual (through ceremonies, community volunteer projects, and the information gleaned through lectures). A lot of students say that we're kind of like a support group or a community for Pagans and Wiccans. We're pretty well accepted. We haven't had many problems over the years. Our meetings are advertised in the student newspaper, and we generally get an enthusiastic turnout."

In October 2001, the SPA held a Samhain ritual, which was open to anyone who had ever attended a meeting in the past. Nineteen students participated.

What advice does the University of Arkansas Student Pagan Association offer to those college students thinking about forming their own Student Pagan/Wiccan Group? "We would recommend having regular meetings and informal get-togethers at a coffee house or somewhere after meetings so that people can get to know one another better," one member told me. "Doing volunteer work and co-sponsoring projects with other religious and volunteer organizations also helps to foster acceptance."

---

bookstores seeking out the one text that I hoped would explain *something* about the people who called themselves Witches. More often than not, I came across books filled with spells and rituals and magickal practices. And then I found *Drawing Down the Moon.* It was my own introduction to Wicca and its vast pool of devotees. The book remains on my reading table.

WICCA
The Facts

- The Goddess and God are at the heart of all Wiccan practice
- The Threefold Law of Wicca forbids a Witch from using his or her magick negatively
- Magick is the ability to alter consciousness at will
- Witches can practice in covens or as solitaries
- Witches do not give credence to the notion of a devil or any other evil force
- Witches practice rites that attune them with nature
- Witches do not recognize an authoritative hierarchy
- A combination of the spiritual, the psychological, and the scientific grants Witches an intellectual depth exceeding that of the average person
- Witchcraft laws were repealed in England in the 1950s
- Wicca was legally recognized in the United States in 1986
- To be a Witch is to celebrate Earth
- Paganism dates back to Paleolithic times

When I started writing *Rocking the Goddess,* I wondered what Margot Adler would have to say about Wicca today, a little over two decades since she completed *Drawing Down the Moon.* I was fortunate enough to have the opportunity to ask her a few questions.

AP: Why do you think Wicca has grown in popularity and in the number of practitioners since *Drawing Down the Moon?*

MA: The reasons that have always made Wicca attractive still hold. It is a non-dogmatic religion that does not proselytize, that does not claim to have the one true way, that exalts Earth and the real world as opposed to seeing Earth as just a place we are passing through. It doesn't have a literal scripture, is in tune with scientific change, and allows an enormous place for creativity and liturgy creation. In addition, it allows women their rightful place in ministry, which is missing in Orthodox Judaism, Catholicism, and Islam. Wicca has always been a religion without a middle person, a religion that is anarchistic enough for a libertarian, yet has a value system. But at the bottom line, Wicca allows the juice and mystery of ecstatic experience while allowing a person to maintain his or her intellectual integrity. I like to say it like this: you can dance around a bonfire until dawn, yet still make your living as a scientist or computer programmer.

AP: Younger Americans are pledging themselves to Wicca now more than ever before. Do you think this has anything to do with the liberal mind-set of a generation, or does Wicca fill a spiritual gap because of its non-dogmatic principles?

MA: The truth is that lots of teens have entered Wicca because of movies, yucky movies like *The Craft,* and television shows like *Charmed* and *Buffy* and so on. The mind-set of this generation is not too liberal, but since Wicca is a self-made religion to a great extent, it fits in with the American spirit.

AP: In your opinion, how has the media presented Wicca to the public?

MA: Much better than before. There are actual serious articles on Wicca and they aren't always on or about Halloween. The problem Wicca still faces is that word *Witch* just has too many meanings for the average person or journalist to understand. *Witch* means power, means psychic ability, means fortune-telling . . . you name it, and it takes quite a long conversation to get around to the idea that Wicca is a religion. Let's face it: the moment you say 'Witch' to most people they say, 'I don't believe in that,' and so Wicca suffers from the notion that it is fanciful and silly more than it suffers from the notion that it is evil. However, things are getting better and better as more people come to understand the complex nature of Wicca.

AP: The practice of Wicca is widespread on college campuses all over the United States. Some have labeled student Wicca/Pagan groups a subculture. What are your thoughts on Wicca within the university setting?

MA: I haven't really spent a lot of recent time with college Wiccans, but all of Wicca is subculture to some degree. That doesn't mean we don't mingle in the 'real' world, but we are still an alternative.

AP: Who is the modern-day Witch?

MA: The modern-day Witch can be almost anyone, since people come to Wicca from so many different roads: people who like the magic, people who are deeply environmentally concerned, people who love the beauty and fantasy and imaginative aspects, women who love the idea of the Goddess, people who love ritual . . . we could go on and on. But if there are any truths about 'all' Witches—and there probably aren't—I would say that they are usually very self-directed people who want to learn the truth for themselves, are comfortable in a multifaceted world. They don't need their philosophy to be reduced to a single vision. In general, Witches are people who value liberty and free thought.

AP: What advice would you offer to college students studying or those who may be curious about it?

MA: First read a bunch of books, particularly if you enjoy books. And then, assuming that a student is reasonably social, I would recommend that she or he go to a good festival where they can meet a bunch of people and see rituals from a variety of traditions. At that point they can better make decisions of whether or not they should join a group or go at it alone.

The Academic View: What They Think of Us

Sometimes college professors and university administrators are our friends, and sometimes not. No matter the case, they educate us. They encourage and guide us through four rigorous years of exams and term papers and deadlines. Did you ever look at a professor in the middle of class and wonder: *What would he really think if he knew I was a Witch? What are her opinions on Paganism, magick, the Goddess?*

Professors are scholars in their chosen fields. They hold doctorate degrees in everything from history and science to English and sociology. Teaching is as much a professor's job as is mentoring students and offering academic advice. What do they think about the growing practice of Wicca on campuses?

Matthew Immergut is a Ph.D. candidate at Drew University. An adjunct professor within the SUNY system, he teaches a course titled "Psychology of Religion." His academic interests lay on the religious side of the environmental movement. He earned his undergraduate degree in outdoor education and wilderness skills from Prescott College in Arizona. He spent time working as a wilderness guide in Colorado, Utah, and Idaho, where he came in contact with many practicing Pagans. Though not a Pagan himself, his first truly religious experience grew out of his deep reverence for nature.

Immergut was raised in reformed Judaism, but faith left him early on. After college he experienced a need to reconnect with his religious roots. His spiritual and intellectual pursuits took him to Morristown Rabbinical College of America in Morristown, New Jersey, where he was indoctrinated into the Hasidic world. More study would follow—including time spent in Israel—but he eventually abandoned Hasidism and is today comfortable in a very secular life. He still enjoys studying the Torah, the Talmud, and the Cabala and employs that biblical scholarship in his teaching.

"People are seeking security in a world that is insecure," he said of the New Age movement in America. "Wicca and Paganism have been growing for years, and I've seen so much of it because of my involvement with environmental issues. When I was an undergraduate, I knew more Pagans than non-Pagans."

A topic of interest to many scholars, academics, and sociologists is that of conversion. Why have so many people chosen Wicca as their religion? Is it the magick? Is it the Goddess? Is it because Wicca has no inherent concept of sin?

"I think the reasoning behind conversion is profoundly complex," Immergut explained. "I think it's political, psychological, religious, and sociological. To say it is only one of these reasons would be misleading. There are dimensions to all of these, and not one of them is exclusively correct. People have valid political issues with religions that displace them. Wicca falls into these categories. Looking back, I think Modernity, as it was born from the sixteenth, seventeenth, and eighteenth centuries—the Protestant Reformation, the Industrial Revolution, the Scientific Revolution—made a great sucking noise in terms of the meaning structures we have to hold the world together. It dislocated the 'scared canopy' that was arching over all of us. You have a disintegration, and this is the secularization thesis or hypothesis. What's surprising, though, is that secularization predicted that religion would disappear—but in fact, it's back and it's stronger than ever. It's powerful. The bottom line is that people need meaning in their lives. They need a larger frame of reference in which to orient their actions on a day-to-day basis."

One constant factor for modern-day Witches is the claim that they are practicing a wholly historical religion, that the roots of Paganism outdate those of Christianity, Judaism, and Islam. As a scholar and a professor, Immergut cautiously agreed. "I think it's possible," he said. "But I also think it's a way for Witches to legitimize themselves. For social scientists, all religions are humanely constructed. They are made and maintained by humans. As soon you connect a primal past or a Goddess or any ancient history, you have in your hands a legitimacy that transcends the social world. It's a political movement, but it's just as valid as what we call 'religion.'"

Another area of Wicca prone to academic scrutiny is that of the Goddess. What and who is she from a scholarly perspective?

"In a patriarchal culture, I think the Goddess is wonderful," Immergut said. "In Freudian analysis, the father religion is about law, morality, and guilt. It's about Oedipal dynamics. What does a Goddess religion do? It all goes back to the mythological. It's about presence. It's about being held. It's about being nurtured and lifted up. It's about being loved. That divine acceptance is what a Goddess religion gives people from a psychoanalytical perspective."

Asked what he thought of Wicca playing a role in the lives of so many college students, he said, "I think it can be a good thing. If Wicca empowers and enables people, especially those who have been rejected by their dominant religions, it's great."

Chas Clifton, a professor of writing at the University of Southern Colorado, has written a number of books on Paganism and Wicca. Among his published credits are *Iron Mountain: A Journal of Magickal Religion* and *Sacred Mask, Sacred Dance.* He has also been practicing the Craft for twenty years. He believes there are several reasons that contribute to the popularity of Wicca today.

"That portion of young adults who is drawn to the 'counterculture' of the era (mesmerism and spiritualism in the nineteenth century, for example) is going to be drawn to the way in which Wicca inverts the characteristic of the mainstream religions. Wicca has no scripture," he explained. "Its leadership has a majority of women. It celebrates the seasonal rituals instead of those commemorating the events of the founder's life (Christianity, Islam) or those of ethic history (Judaism). Wicca is youthful and optimistic in its outlook, and it offers an alternative vision of power through magic, compared to the ways in which one gets power conventionally: working lots of years, accumulating investments, 'paying your dues.'

"In addition, the lifestyle aspects are important. Witches, at least in the popular stereotype, were 'goth' before there was such a thing as Goth. Wiccan ritual is openly sexual and at least some Witches openly advocate polyamory, sex magick and other fascinating ideas. For all that, the Craft community includes many people who lead lives that are completely conventional on the surface. It's also becoming known that we're fairly open to people who like misfits, whose gender identity is in flux and that sort of thing. Whether they stick around or not is another story. Thus, Wicca will attract the spiritual rebel, the psychic, the power-seeker, and the hedonist, and it's up to us to get them all sorted out, and hopefully, balanced somehow."

Many practitioners fear that the popularity of Wicca may shift it into a "fad religion." American pop culture is teeming with examples that hinge on the cool and controversial, and although prevalence sometimes paves the road to acceptance, it can also mitigate the factual.

"I do worry sometimes about Wicca becoming a fad religion," Clifton said. "But I don't think this a realistic fear. All of the categories that I mentioned earlier probably do not add up to more than 10 percent of the group we are discussing. Back in the late 1960s and 1970s, the so-called hippies certainly did not amount probably to even 10 percent if you look at the people who truly lived that life, if only for a summer or so, as opposed to those who just took on some of the trappings. Nevertheless, they had an effect on the culture, particularly on its food and recreational drug habits."

Clifton believes that media representations have fostered Wicca's popularity over the years.

"The media treatment has changed tremendously over the last twenty-five years," he said. "We're on the edge of becoming respectable, if not trendy—and I'm not sure that we all want that. I noticed that a recent episode of the ABC evening television show

Once and Again concluded with a variety of seasonal greetings filmed by the cast: Christmas, Chanukah, and even something like 'Happy Wiccan Solstice' or words to that effect. In the 1970s and 1980s, you were more likely to see that standard newspaper feature story around Halloween, which took the angle of 'Did you know that there are actually Witches here in our city? And they claim to be practicing an ancient religion. And they let us take pictures!' Now we have gained the status of pesky minority."

Clifton's views on Wicca as a religion that has survived since pre-Christian times are equally interesting.

"The idea that we had an unbroken ancient pre-Christian religion began to dissipate in the 1980s, I would estimate. That does not mean that some people still hold to it, but I think that today Wiccans are more likely to say, 'Ours is a new religious tradition inspired by ancient Pagan practices.' If you count simply from the 'Gardnerian revival,' Wicca is sixty years old, which means that even Gardner and Doreen Valiente are way back there to many contemporary practitioners."

Because Clifton is himself a practitioner, I asked him what he thought of the challenges college Witches face on campuses today.

"Any student Witch who feels restricted by university rules should either change schools, stop being such a weenie, or both," he asserted. "Can't have candles in the dorm room? Well, what are you doing indoors, anyway? Why not make contact with some of the Pagans in the surrounding community, which in these days with the Web is much easier than it used to be. Find or create your own ritual site. If you want to be more open, form a student Pagan association. That should be possible unless you're at a church-sponsored university. Deal with your student government, get the use of a meeting room. Just do it.

"I'm still impressed by the essay that Judy Harrow, author of *Wiccan Covens,* wrote about underage seekers in my *Witchcraft Today 2: Modern Rites of Passage.* It discussed how someone under the age of eighteen who did not have parental consent to associate with adult Witches could, nevertheless, still study, meditate, and learn on their own. Persons who are over eighteen don't have that problem, but they still need to understand that Wicca is 'mystery tradition.' That means it is not like a church! High priestesses and priests are not necessarily pastoral counselors. Some are, and some are not, but their main function should be to teach magick and to create the settings for your own magickal journey to continue. In fact—without naming names—sometimes it's true that a person can be an effective magickal teacher and yet still be untrustworthy in other areas of life. What people must understand is that the model of religious organization is different. So far, we have not gone to the congregation/clergy model."

In recent years, Paganism and Wicca have moved onto college and university campuses as well as into their classrooms.

"The academic study of Paganism is on the upswing," Clifton said. "British scholars seem to be in the lead, but there is the Nature Religions Scholars Network, which is an informal network within a larger organization: the American Academy of Religion. Members are from several other countries besides the United States and Canada. We have an active list-serv and include scholars working both in the humanities and the social sciences, as well as graduate and undergraduate students majoring in religion."

John Simmons, professor of religious studies at Western Illinois University, attributes the popularity of Wicca on college campuses to "culture ambience."

"We have almost thirty years of the environmental movement and about the same of the feminist movement," Simmons said. "Thus, a religion that is Earth-centered and acknowledges the feminine element in life, even highlights it as a goddess, is bound to be attractive and appealing for young adults. They picked up these ideas from their sixties' and seventies' parents. Free from the restrictions of home, whether they might take the form of religion, political ideology, mores, or customs, offers the college student a rare opportunity to experiment with new and exotic world views."

Simmons is also of the opinion that the Wicca of today is not necessarily linked to the Paganism of pre-Christian Europe.

"Here we have the complex relationship between myth and history, very much like what the indigenous peoples—the Native Americans or American Indians—are dealing with. Who really knows what Pagans actually practiced? Yet the myths, meaning the paradigm-laden narratives drawn from the past, certainly have power today and, no doubt, are being shaped and shaded by New Age ideologies. I think that is inevitable. It's also like African Americans 'reconstructing' their heritage in order to find self-esteem and empowerment."

Over the years, Simmons has granted interviews with various newspapers, including the *New York Times,* and feels that the media—with the exception of Christian-based sources—has been supportive of Wicca. Within academe, however, the non-dogmatic principles of Wicca are subject to criticism.

"I guess it all depends on the scholars and what their respective interests might be," he said. "I hang out in the American Academy of Religion with the New Religious Movements group, which, naturally, is intrigued by and supportive of Wicca. However, I can imagine more traditional scholars—those who promote strict definitions of religion, which might include having clear doctrines, established rituals, some sort of leadership hierarchy, sacred texts—being quite critical of Wicca. But because Wicca is non-dogmatic, it is more likely to respond to cultural changes. I see it as growing, yet always . . . what's the trendy word . . . *'morphing.'* If, indeed, Wicca is an earth-based world view, I expect it to respond to the challenges Mother Earth faces. If it is a religion that appreciates the feminine element—or the balance between masculine and feminine elements in life—it will respond to the challenges in those areas. But I don't expect to see Wiccan cathedrals dotting the cultural landscape of America."

At Western Illinois University, Simmons has come in contact with many Witches and Pagans.

"At WIU, I believe I know more openly Wiccan students than Methodists or Presbyterians. We have a lively coven in Macomb. It's out in the open, holds regular rituals, and I teach about it in my classes with absolutely no criticism from colleagues or the general public. I won't say it's mainstream yet, but if it works in Macomb, Illinois, it's on its way."

John Forrest, professor of anthropology at SUNY Purchase College, has studied folklore for years. He earned his B.A. at Oxford University, his M.A. in Folklore, and Ph.D. in Anthropology from the University of North Carolina at Chapel Hill. Among his steadfast academic interests are folklore dance and the exploration of the esoteric religious traditions of the nineteenth century. An ordained Presbyterian minister, he is the author of *The History of Morris Dancing,* a concise study of the "Morris Dancers" of England, who date back to 1458.

Pagan lore is threaded through the history of England, but, as Forrest explained, the past does not always mirror the present. His scholarly perspective does not support the theory that Wicca is derived from a religious tradition that was practiced in pre-Christian Europe.

"One of the aphorisms of anthropology, as I put it, is that all things always change," he explained. "The biggest problem with the theory that Wicca or any other facet of Paganism has survived through the ages is that it makes an assumption that the way things are being done today are the way they have always been done. The point of *The History of Morris Dancing* is to demonstrate that this is completely false. Rituals and practices become unrecognizable from one century to the next. The same would be true if you looked at Christianity. If you looked at the Presbyterian in 1550 and what his beliefs were versus those of a Presbyterian in 1950, they are almost unrelated. So my first reaction to any claim that Wicca today is a religion of whenever—fifteen centuries ago or during the Roman occupation—is that I just don't know anything that is the same as it was that long ago. The other problem that I think is devastating to those claims is that there simply isn't any documentary evidence to fully support them. There is oral documentation, but at some point in history, someone always writes it down. The Egyptian temples and the goddess Isis—that happened, but it isn't necessarily the same Goddess worship of today. We have no clue as to what ancient Egyptians did when it comes to their ritual practices. I don't doubt that the Greeks and the Romans also had goddesses to worship, but all kinds of people have had eminent spirituality."

In Wicca, spirituality begins with the female principle of divinity. Forrest also believes this is one of the main reasons people of all ages have come to view the Goddess as a potent force.

"Feminine spirituality can incorporate holistic views as opposed to male, analytic patriarchal views," he explained. "The feminine principle is more holistic, synthetic, more aimed at generative qualities, qualities of becoming, of integration, of community as opposed to power. The development of Wicca as a religion in the twentieth century was and is a very conscious and laudable attempt to introduce those female principles into spirituality where they have in many mainstream religions been denied."

Is Wicca also a political movement?

"It is, but not necessarily in the conventional sense. We won't see a Wiccan political party running for office! But the Wiccan perspective incorporates environmental issues, which have become a very big part of politics these days."

The relationship between academe and spirituality, according to Forrest, is an intriguing and sometimes dichotomous one.

"The main issue that is interesting to me as an academic is that the academic world, ever since the Enlightenment, has divorced itself from spirituality. Anthropologists of religion, for example, will analyze religion but it's considered a big no-no for that anthropologist to become religious. That's considered as 'going native.' If you actually start believing in the rituals of the people you are studying, if you actually start absorbing it, problems can arise."

Forrest then offered the example of the late Carlos Castenada, a prolific author of New Age and metaphysical books. "Castenada fell into that pattern when studying religion. He was a fraud, and I think most people understand that. But I think people were so upset with him because he was trying to become a shaman and he was taking hallucinogens in a way that blurred the boundaries of academic analysis and involvement. The boundaries weren't clear. What he was beginning to understand, and what I think is important to understand, is the meaning of objective observation and subjective understanding. But as academics we become very clinical and we take our lead from the natural sciences. We say that we have to observe from an objective way and that we have to remain divorced from it and we have to eliminate value, judgments, and even ethical concerns. This is a curious distinction. Scientists perfectly well know that the observer and the observed are part of the whole, and that the observer changes the nature of the observed and that every observation to one degree or another is subjective.

"From the Enlightenment point of view the goal was to become as objective and as analytic as possible, setting the stage for how to view things without invoking the metaphysical, and so we ended up with what the sociologist Weber called the 'disenchantment of the West.' The perception of the intellectual is now one of clinical distance, and that's what we teach in the classroom. Of course, that has transcended the university and become part of our culture as a whole. And people now realize that something is missing, that the spiritual element is gone. By and large, the adolescents and the post-adolescents growing up in this culture see that the spiritual is absent from the places of power. It's a void. It doesn't satisfy them. They search for something real, and that's wonderful. What troubles me is having to validate it historically. Why bother with that? Why not just say, 'This is brand new, and it's good.' The historical validation of religions like Wicca makes it difficult to take seriously. I understand that part of it is a feminist perspective that ties Witches to their oppressed sisters over time, going back to the Burning Times. It creates a historical unity with women in the past. That's fine, but when you do it by using bad historical methods, it turns people against you, and it ends up creating this strange dichotomy between the academy and the Witches themselves."

With regard to the widespread practice of Wicca on college and university campuses, Forrest believes it is a class phenomenon as well as an age phenomenon.

"Wicca on campus has some analogies with the hippie movement of the 1960s," he said. "But what really is found more among university students than anyone else is that they are privileged to have a full four years to look for themselves while other people in different economic classes are already out working. There's time for the college student to experiment with something other than what he or she is accustomed to. I think it's very much a phenomenon of the bourgeois. Even Gerald Gardner was a part of the British elite searching for an alternative to the mainstream. Going to college itself is a rite of passage. You're spending four years searching for identity, and it all fits very well with what Wicca has to offer and it provides a verboten alternative. College students experiment, and they do things most parents don't want to think about."

In Forrest's opinion, the future of Wicca depends on many factors.

How Do You *Rock the Goddess?*
Raelynn, sophomore
Juilliard School of Music, New York City

"Music is my lifeline and—next to being a Witch—it's the most spiritual experience I know. I play the flute and piano, and I love composing new melodies and songs that honor our Pagan ancestors. I rock the Goddess through song and sound and symphony. I get the essence of Nature and magick when I'm using the gifts bestowed upon me by the Goddess. It's a way of giving my knowledge back to Earth."

"If Wicca becomes completely acceptable in society, it will reach a crossroads. It will lose the vitality of mystery. If it takes that path it will become just another mainstream religion and it will suffer the fate of all mainstream religions—it will become tedious, doctrinaire, rigid. There will be books of discipline that will have multiple paragraphs explaining how to do this and that. It will become something, eventually, that other people will want to rebel against. So in a sense, complete acceptance will be the demise of Wicca. If it continues on something of an underground existence, it can roll along much like it does now. Undoubtedly, however, it will have to undergo periods of revitalization. It will move and change with the times. But no one can really predict in which direction Wicca is headed."

The academic view of Wicca and its collegiate adherents is diverse, with no single, defining point of view. Like all of the professors who offered their thoughts and opinions, John Forrest put it best when he said, "Ultimately, it's all good."

· 2 ·

Claiming Identity
The Collegiate Witch

Friday night, early spring. Students are milling around the campus in droves.

Kerry can see them from her window: walking toward any one of a dozen parties, reclining on the grass, lighting up cigarettes in front of the dining hall. Laughter echoes across the lawn and floats up to her second-story dorm room. The sound calms her. After a long week of exams and assignments, she is ready to embrace some much-needed freedom. Forget the professor who asked her to re-write a meticulous term paper. Ignore the e-mail from Financial Aid awaiting a reply. Tonight, she will live only for herself.

She stands before the mirror and takes in her own reflection. Brown hair falls in waves to her shoulders. Her complexion is pale. She is nondescript in her jogging suit, but it's nothing she can't fix. From the bureau she chooses black pants and a matching shirt. Scuffed combat boots complete the outfit. She dresses quickly and carefully.

Next, her makeup. She applies black eyeliner, a dark shade of lipstick, smooth foundation that lightens the pallor of her skin. The contrast is striking. She pulls her hair back into a ponytail and then goes about adding a fresh shade of black to her nails.

On the corner of her desk sits a jewelry box. Opening it, she studies the various trinkets before pulling out the silver chain and pentacle. She loops it around her neck, making certain the five-pointed star hangs on the outside of her shirt. She slips a moonstone ring over her index finger, a tiny ankh along her thumb. The outside chill calls for long sleeves, so she takes the black velvet shawl from the closet and drapes it over her shoulders. Standing before the mirror once more, she smiles.

They will look at her and know.

Their eyes will absorb the Goth attire and the glittering specks of silver. The pentacle, dazzling against the black shirt, will confirm any unspoken suspicions. The responses can be negative or positive, charged with awe or laced with fear. None of it matters. She has been here before—at the shadowy crossroad where public scrutiny meets private truth. There is no turning back.

She is a Witch. She is proud of the word and all the mystery it commands. When people ask, she tells them about the Goddess, the God, the casting of spells, and the lure of the Moon. Her identity is strong: it lives inside her and around her, a being all of its own. Her senses are alerted to the knowledge of Earth and her sacred place within it. Inspired by who she is, she longs to share herself with the outside world. Hence the clothing and the jewelry and the makeup. Mere decoration, but it enhances the magickal presence she seeks to impart.

In minutes she is out the door and strolling along the crowded lawn . . .

Across campus, Phil is taking a seat in the university lecture hall, where one of his professors will be giving a talk about modern-day Witchcraft. Students are filling the narrow rows and standing in the aisles. The buzz of conversation fills the air. He is content to simply wait, so he flips open his notepad and begins filling in assignments due the coming week. Soon he is distracted by a flyer that has been placed in the empty chair beside him. It lists the evening's program, along with a plethora of facts about Wicca and Paganism. He skims it, then smiles. He doesn't need to be educated on the ways of the religion that he claimed five years ago. He knows how to cast a magick circle in his dorm room and what phase the Moon is in just by looking up at the sky.

Scanning the hall, Phil spots a few other students from the campus Pagan group. He waves, eyeing them from a distance. Even in a thickening crowd, they stand out with their dramatic clothes and jewelry. He has never understood the point of such a public display: it seems to invite unwanted curiosity. He is content to simply blend in with the crowd, a nameless face indistinguishable from the next.

But it isn't shame or fear that keeps him hidden.

There is power in silence, in the nondescript, in walking between the worlds as a shadow rather than a spark. There is mystery in autonomy. And so his pentacle rests beneath his shirt. His various charms and amulets sit in a shoebox beneath his bed, within easy reach on the nights reserved for worship. Later, when he joins the other students from the Pagan group for an evening chat, he will feel completely at home in his plain jeans and sneakers. For him, being a Witch isn't about projecting an image. It is about preserving a history.

Identity and the Witch: *The Basics*

Leaving home. Walking away from your family and friends and the old neighborhood. You step onto a college campus that doesn't look quite as colorful as it did in that glossy brochure. Then there's the difficulty of dorm room life: an unfamiliar bed, a cranky roommate, the peculiar odor in the corridors that won't let up. Add to this a daunting schedule of classes you don't remember registering for but are required to pass . . .

In the beginning, it might suck. But soon the days begin to take on a common rhythm and you find yourself smiling with a group of complete strangers. You get used to the cafeteria food. You realize—sometimes quite shockingly—that you are alone and *on your own.* Emotional insecurity is normal given the enormous changes every college student must face. Nervous tensions mount. Stress levels pique. Hovering in that state between excitement and fear are the questions that just might take a decade to answer: *Who am I? What do I stand for? Who do I want to be?* Identity is a complex and risky issue. It involves the personal, the political, and certainly the spiritual. Some freshmen know at eighteen that they want to major in biology, go on to medical school, and have a traditional home and family. Some seniors are three credits away from earning that degree in liberal studies but don't know whether they want to join the Peace Corps or take up exotic dancing. This is the surface of identity. The depth goes much deeper.

Individuality is a process that requires equal amounts of serious soul-searching and reckless caring. One has to exercise caution when smoothing out the edges of his personality, yet he must also be open to new experiences and possibilities. Exploration is the key; it unlocks the door to a room that is anything but square. Your academic interests are being challenged and tested, but you are also discovering how well you adapt to new surroundings and diversity. You will make friends with people who would have been called freaks back home. You will leave behind the shell of your high school days and see the world through a different lens. Dating. Parties. Intellectual stimulation. Certain subjects might strike a chord within. Others will pass you by. What you believed when you were a teenager might have less validity now. It's all part of molding who you are and who you will become.

The college years comprise a series of events, experiences, and emotions unparalleled by any other time of life. We spend our adolescence dreaming about being adults—going out into the "real world," fending for ourselves, living by our own rules. Now young adulthood has arrived. The choices we make as college students—from our friends and our education to that first job—will inevitably impact the future. Eighteen is a special number: it augurs adjustments, variations, and transformations. Our parents will always see us as kids, but greater society will expect more than youthful exuberance. Professors, coworkers, and peers are apt to study you with that serious, expectant stare. Room for excuses is limited and living responsibly becomes an utmost priority.

For the college Witch, identity is doubly intricate. You are grappling with all of the above in addition to your spiritual goals and passions. We have all witnessed the burgeoning of Wicca in the United States and around the world, but the outer realm doesn't necessarily reflect the inner realm. In other words, living publicly and proudly as a Witch might look appealing from a distance and for other people, but broadcasting your own private business may spark a little fear. Understandable. There is a lot to consider and think about. Before taking that step out of the broom closet, however, you have to decide and ultimately know for yourself who you are as a Witch. And before publicizing or even feeling comfortable with your identity, you have to *claim* it.

More often than not, the media has portrayed Wicca inadequately. Feature films like *The Craft* and *Practical Magic* associated the Witch with negative connotations, and countless articles have linked her to dark rites and rituals. Thus, every young Witch has to consider where identity stands in relation to the public. This means being informed about Wicca completely—it tenets, beliefs, rituals, and historical origins. We have seen the positive ramifications of strong Wiccan identities since the 1950s, all of which helped steer Wicca into the mainstream.

Gerald Gardner, an English Witch, is often hailed as the "father" of the Witchcraft revival. In 1954 he published *Witchcraft Today*, and the instant success of the book spawned a resurgence of interest in Pagan-rooted spirituality. A diverse and accomplished man, Gardner ran his own coven, initiated other Witches, and was even honored at Buckingham Palace for his civil service work.

Another English Witch, Sybil Leek, gained popularity in America in the 1960s. She wrote *Diary of a Witch* and took to the media circuit, dismissing negative connotations and misrepresentation. In 1979, journalist and Wiccan priestess Margot Adler published *Drawing Down the Moon.*

Around the same time, Starhawk, activist and Witch, published *The Spiral Dance*, another powerful exploration of Goddess spirituality. Dr. Leo Louis Martello, an Italian American Witch, established one of the first tax-exempt Wiccan churches and spearheaded other Wiccan civil rights. He lived in New York City, where, in 1970, he organized a Samhain celebration in Manhattan's Central Park. It is because of these pioneering women and men that so much of modern-day Witchcraft evolved.

More recently, Witches like Silver Ravenwolf and Laurie Cabot—the "Official Witch" of Salem, Massachusetts—have garnered national attention. Cabot formed her own tradition of Witchcraft and today runs a popular occult shop. She is best known for her rather brazen identity. Black capes, ritual attire, and heavy makeup about the eyes are her trademarks. She has been featured on *Unsolved Mysteries* and a Lifetime Television special on Witches, among others. On several occasions, Cabot described the word *witch* as "delicious," brimming with mystery and powerful magickal undertones. Ravenwolf, a prolific author of Wiccan books, has also inspired a generation of Witches with her words, spells, and instructional advice. Numerous other Witches—Raven Grimassi, Sirona Knight, Sister Moon, Gerina Dunwich—live openly and are fully confident in their identities as practitioners, teachers, and role models.

Did any of them face discrimination, difficulties, or fear? Surely, many of them did. Many continue to face hardships. But what distinguishes the would-be Witch from the self-assured practitioner is knowledge. Learning how to cast spells and perform magick are only two aspects of Wicca (albeit the most popular). Learning how to feel comfortable with your identity as a Witch is far more significant because it will only strengthen practice. This means knowing the Goddess and God, the use of the elements, the phases of the Moon, the basic laws of magick. It also means considering the pros and cons of Wicca. The pros far outweigh the cons, but practicing Wicca is akin to living as a Witch. In certain communities, stereotypes will prevail. Are you capable of defending your identity from historical, spiritual, and practical perspectives? Do you know your legal rights as deemed by the First Amendment? It may all seem trivial now, but adopting a new religious tradition is demanding.

People interested in Wicca are seduced by its non-dogmatic principles. Too often, however, they equate the practice of Witchcraft with fantastical sorcery and power. They think lighting a candle will bring love, fortune, and fame. They believe that simply mentioning the Goddess will take them closer to deep universal wisdom. It isn't so. Teenagers and college students—eager to explore, impress, or rebel—are not excluded from this wandering group. The underlying themes that swim beneath the word *witch* act as easy doorways to hip and trendy labels. Witches are frequently perceived as mysterious individuals who live between the magical and the esoteric, but if building these empty descriptions is your ultimate goal, you will find nothing but frustration in Wicca. False intentions lead nowhere. Serious adherents, on the other hand, will know limitless possibilities. And so it is imperative that every student—indeed, every potential practitioner—claim his or her identity.

Wicca is abundant with spiritual, psychological, and personal gifts. Reaching the pinnacle of Wiccan wisdom is no easy feat, and only hard work can illuminate the path to enlightenment.

But be forewarned: once the Goddess and God have touched your life, they will remain forever a part of you. Once unleashed, the essence of the Witch will not let you go.

The College Witch Quiz

If you have been practicing Wicca since high school and have made the transition to college life easily enough, the following exercise will only solidify your knowledge. If, however, you are still flirting with the idea of biting the magick, take a few minutes to consider the questions listed below. Roll them around in your mind. Let them sit and settle into your psyche before providing answers. Write down what you feel are appropriate—and truly honest—responses. Nothing is correct or incorrect. (Later, this will make a great addition to your Book of Shadows.)

1. How did I become interested in Wicca?
2. Why do I feel an affinity with the Goddess?
3. What is my perception of a Witch?
4. What do I know about magick?
5. Has college life influenced or impeded my spiritual interests?
6. Will I be capable of handling the demands of practice with those of coursework, assignment deadlines, and social life?
7. What do I hope to gain from the practice of rituals and spells?
8. What is the Wiccan Redt?
9. What are my spiritual goals and aspirations?
10. Who are my role models?

Your reply to question number one may be quite long, and it should be. As the old saying goes: everyone has a story. Was it a dream that led you to Wicca? Did you always have an innate calling to the occult? Did a friend or family member introduce you to it? Did you just happen upon a book that sparked your interests? This is a highly significant question because it will allow you to explore the roots of your interest—or, in some cases, your "calling." If *you* motivated the initial curiosity, it is obvious that the spark was within you, waiting to be noticed. But if your answer points a finger at something less tangible—a movie, a television series, Harry Potter—you may want to dig a little deeper to make certain your intentions are sincere.

The second question should, even on a minimal level, tie into the first. The Goddess embodies the heart and soul of Wicca, and she is the divine in nature. Perhaps it hit you early on—a little jolt of excitement at the mention of the "G" word. The answer might be linked to your belief that a Supreme Being cannot only be male in thought and form. Again, there are no right or wrong replies. Important here is the realization that the Goddess—even from a purely mythological perspective—had an impact on you.

Question three is very personal. To some, the Witch is enigmatic. To others she is practical. Your answer reflects the identity you will most likely live by and impart to the rest of the world. If, by any chance, your perception of the Witch leans toward anything negative or inherently dark, you have misunderstood the tenets of Wiccan practice. A difficult cram session is on the horizon.

Question four cannot be answered definitively. Your knowledge of magick will grow with time and concentration. It is best, however, that you be aware from early on that "magick" is not the same as "magic." In Witchcraft, *magick* refers to the practice of spells, rituals, and certain rites. It is not the sorcery of fantasy or science fiction novels. In brief: don't go looking for a carpet ride in the sky. You won't find it here.

Questions five and six go hand in hand. You want to make certain that the stresses of college life are not the sole reason for your interest in Wicca. Joining the student-run Pagan group is a positive start, but Witches do not recruit followers and the majority of campus Pagan groups welcome members of all religious denominations. On the flip side, don't barrel down in the face of discrimination or fear. In the event that your chosen school is less than welcoming of your beliefs, consider exactly where you are and whether or not it will be conducive to your identity as a Witch for the next four years. Weighing practice with your coursework and your social life cannot be underestimated either. If you answered with an honest "No" to question six, it means one of two possibilities: you will have to manage your time wisely or you are not yet ready to commit to the demands of meditation, Full Moon observance, the Sabbats. A slight hesitation about practice is normal. Reading books and talking to other students about Wicca for a while longer is a good way to become more comfortable with the idea.

Question seven is, again, very personal. What your answer should *not* include are inferences to any of the following: power over others, the ability to hex or curse, influence over particular situations or events. Selfish intentions fail or, in the worst possible scenario, backfire.

There is only one answer to question eight: Harm none, do what you will.

Question nine is a way for you to explore the near future as a

Witch. Spiritually, you may want to educate yourself further on the Goddess and God or attune yourself with the lunar cycles. The next step in your journey might be to begin practicing regularly, which means using magick in your everyday life. Organizing your various tools, books and spells could be on this list. Perhaps you are practicing as a solitary and would like to one day join a coven or start your own on campus. Try to add to this question once a month, deciphering ways that will enhance your goals and aspirations.

Question ten asks you to look beyond yourself and into the outside world. Role models are important in every aspect of life, from education and career to family and relationships. Who is the person that inspires you and why? What virtues does this person live by and impart? How will you work to build on those examples? Your role model may be a friend or relative, a professor, or even a celebrity. He or she need not be a Witch. Maybe your role model is someone who carries a deep love and respect for nature and the human spirit. Explore your answer. You may come to realize that you are already a lot like this person.

Going back over these questions will enhance your thoughts and ideas about Wicca, spiritualism, and yourself. The answers are probably not definitive at this point in your life because there is much more to learn both during and after the college years. But concentrate on where you are right now. The magick is in the moment.

Exploring the Divine: *Pathways of Light*

It has been said that one's religious identity is like a mansion of many rooms: every doorway leads to a new place. This is true of Wicca. The Goddess and God, who are also referred to as the "All," comprise a system of polytheistic beliefs and different deities that serve different purposes. A Witch might summon Athena, goddess of wisdom, when casting a spell for advice or guidance. Apollo is the god of healing. Aphrodite rules sexuality and love. These three deities are Greek, but there are also Gods and Goddesses from the Hindu, Celtic, Roman, Egyptian, and Asian cultures. Just as Christianity and Judaism have their sects, so too does Wicca. A Christian might be Baptist or Pentecostal or Lutheran. There is reformed Judaism, Orthodox, Hasidism. In Wicca, there are varying traditions as well. Calling yourself a Witch is only half of the identity equation. What specific path will you choose to call your own?

The following pages describe the variety of traditions currently being practiced by Wiccans both in the United States and around the world.

ALEXANDRIAN

Alexander Sanders founded this tradition of Wicca in the 1960s. Born in England in 1926, biographical accounts of his life are brimming with minor scandals and bizarre stories, the first of which took place when he was seven years old. According to Sanders, he happened upon his grandmother standing in the center of a floor-drawn circle in her home; allegedly a hereditary Witch, she initiated him, and it was a short while later that he got in touch with his own psychic gifts.

The ways of Witchcraft were explored widely by Sanders. By the 1960s, he had begun accruing national attention, and he claimed more than one thousand followers in England. He was the self-proclaimed "King of Witches," often bragging about phenomenal magickal feats and healing abilities. But it was a dubious distinction, given the fact that Sanders admitted to using his "powers" for financial gain and influence. Nonetheless, he attracted major media attention and was at least partly responsible for publicizing the Wiccan revival.

The Alexandrian Tradition is still practiced today. Sanders favored "skyclad" (nude) worship, and many adherents continue to carry out rituals without the use of garments or customary attire. Here, the human body is a vehicle for transcendence and transformation. Inhibition is key to the ceremonial magick that Alexandrian Wicca holds in high regard. It is no secret that Sanders employed sexual acts within his coven's rituals, and although this particular aspect of practice has dwindled within American covens, it remains a fairly active custom.

Janus, a twenty-two-year-old senior at the University of Chicago who prefers to be called by his Wiccan name (an ode to the Roman god), chose the Alexandrian Tradition after exploring Wicca for two years. Despite a Methodist upbringing, Janus knew he was a Witch early on and began experimenting with the occult at age thirteen. First there was the Tarot. Next came the necromancer stage. By freshman year of college he was in contact with several Witches, all of whom practiced in different traditions. Today he is part of a coven comprised of five other students, but they have not sought recognition by their school.

"I experimented with many forms of Wicca early on," he explained. "With regard to identity, I found my own in the Alexandrian Tradition because to me it is more gray than white. It mirrors Nature as full of light and darkness. To say that a Witch can only practice 'for the good of all' is an unfair statement because Nature in itself is not completely good or pure. There is the hunt and the instinct for survival. I'm not saying that I hex people, but I do believe strongly in binding spells—magick that obstructs someone's will, such as an enemy or a criminal. If you really read into Alexandrian Wicca, you realize that it's about Witchcraft as a whole—the darkness and the light."

It should be noted that Janus's opinion is not the norm among those who practice the Alexandrian Tradition. In fact, it was Alexander Sanders who introduced Janet Farrar and her late husband, Stewart—authors of several books and long a freedom-fighting pair—to Wicca.

Another aspect of the Alexandrian Tradition that compounded Janus's identity is its connection to sexuality. Here, sex is not merely a celebration of the life force; it is part of the ritual. Openly bisexual, Janus asserted that he and his fellow coven members regularly engaged in sexual acts within the magick circle. This is "religious ecstasy" from a physical perspective.

"If the human body is a temple, why not worship it in every way possible?" Janus said. "Sexuality is one of the strongest components of Nature, not only in its capacity for procreation but also for enlightenment of the senses. Sex creates heightened states of energy, which is what the magic circle is all about. It's like using the body to transcend the body. As for bisexuality—I believe that everything is dual in nature. My views fit in to the Wiccan Tradition I practice."

GARDNERIAN

This is often deemed the most common Wiccan tradition. Shortly after the repeal of Witchcraft laws in the 1950s in England, Gardnerian Wicca came to fruition under the auspices of Gerald Gardner. He had been practicing Witchcraft privately with a coven when the laws were abolished, and decided to go public. Again, there was much media attention and Gardner found himself the object of widespread interest. Those who knew Gardner claimed that he edited and rewrote the Book of Shadows from his first coven to form the principles of the Gardnerian Tradition. Here, a Witch must be initiated by a coven, high priestess, or high priest. Years of study are required. Different degrees hold specific ranks of knowledge, and "graduating" to the ultimate rank means earning the title of a priestess or priest. The notion of a coven is important because Gardner believed that collective energy produced greater magickal results. Nonetheless, there are many solitary Witches who practice in the Gardnerian Tradition. Skyclad worship is common but not essential.

Sydney K., a student at Princeton University, started out as a "studious" Witch with no direct affiliations to a tradition. In time, she felt there was a lack of structure to her practice. She wanted her rituals and spells to have more focus, so she read up on Wicca and chose Gardnerian.

"For some people the non-dogmatic angle works out nicely," she said. "But I knew I'd be practicing as a solitary and I wanted a lot more structure. I wanted to know a definitive way to do a spell. Gardner had certain rules—but I hesitate to call them that. They're more like *strong suggestions.*"

Knowing she had to be initiated by another Witch, Sydney began searching the Internet for a Gardnerian coven or Web ring. "I found four or five good sites and wrote to them. One was in Montclair, New Jersey, and I liked that because it felt kind of local. The high priestess of that coven kept e-mailing me and we developed a cyber friendship. She was reserved and careful. I guess she wanted to make sure that I was serious. It was almost a year later that she and I finally met. After that I joined her coven for an esbat ritual, just to see what it would be like. A while later I was initiated. There are other Wiccans on campus here but what I've seen is a lot of self-dedication, a lot of going out when the Moon is full and saying, 'Hey, I'm a Witch!' That's okay if it works for you, but I prefer the structure of Gardnerian Wicca."

It should be noted that when I began seeking out college Witches who preferred the Gardnerian Tradition, I had little trouble finding them. Other students are attending the University of California at Davis, Pepperdine University, Reed College, Carleton College, University of Mississippi at Oxford, and Drew University.

DIANIC

Rooted in the feminist movement of the 1960s, the Dianic Tradition is Wicca from a purely feminine perspective. The Goddess, in all of her aspects as maiden, mother, and crone, is second to no God. Oftentimes, she is not even worshipped in conjunction with the masculine essence of the divine. Practitioners of the Dianic Tradition see the Supreme Being as female because Earth itself is born and reborn of woman—menstruation, conception, childbirth. Only the female body can give life. So too does it exist on a cycle, like the Moon. There are sects of Dianic Wicca that give praise to the God, but his is a minimal presence within the magick circle. Most Dianic covens are comprised of all women. Those that permit men are few and far between, but there have been exceptions. One of the most noted champions of this tradition is Z. Budapest. A high priestess of Romanian descent, she often refers to Dianic Wicca as a "wimmin's" religion, the intentional misspelling of the word employed to differentiate it from the gender terminology. In her now-classic book *The Spiral Dance,* activist and Witch Starhawk also addresses the issues concerning Dianic practice. Undoubtedly, it is a Wiccan Tradition filled with spirituality, but there is also a political slant to everything Dianic.

Teran, a student at Mount Holyoke College in Massachusetts— one of a handful of educational institutions with an all-female enrollment—is not a practicing Witch, but admits to a keen interest in Wicca, especially the Dianic Tradition. Her family hails from the Middle East, and she was raised with Zorastrianism. Wicca, she explained, intrigues her because it embraces theology from a female perspective. The Dianic Tradition complements her feminist political beliefs.

"Right now I'm sort of on spiritual overdrive," she said. "I know I don't feel connected to the Zorastrian faith, but I truly believe in the concept of a higher power. I'm a feminist, and the Goddess comes naturally to me. I've been reading tons of books on Wicca. I'm even speaking to students about it. I believe the modern-day Witch is much more feminine than masculine because historically, the goddesses were more powerful than the gods in polytheism. In those small European villages, the Inquisitors went for the women first because women were a threat. Their power in relation to the divine was staggering."

Teran first learned of the Dianic Tradition from reading Margot Adler's *Drawing Down the Moon.* In her freshman year, while visiting California, she attended a Pagan gathering in San Francisco, where she met many Dianic Witches. "I saw women binding together, getting to know one another. I remember one woman in particular, a breast cancer survivor, who said her body felt balanced in a magick circle where the energy was raised by a totally feminine essence. That makes perfect sense to me. I'm sure I'll delve deeper into it as I continue with college. And I'm lucky because I can explore and learn more while on campus. Being a college student gives you that extra room—you can explore Wicca intellectually or immerse yourself in it spiritually. That's what we're all here to do."

For Teran, the Dianic Tradition of Wicca is representative of a religion "for the new generation." Political awareness and spirituality are the two issues that interest college students most, and combining them, she believes, creates intellectual and numinous growth.

STREGA

The latter half of the twentieth century saw a flourishing of interest in Witchcraft because of Charles Godfrey Leland, an American folklorist who wrote *Aradia: Gospel of the Witches*. The book was a success both academically and commercially, though its authenticity has been disputed widely. Alive in its pages is the story of a woman known only as "Maddalena"; an Italian Witch with hereditary ties to Etruscan history, she told Leland of the "Old Ways" that had survived in her family throughout the ages. As the story goes, Aradia, daughter of Diana, came as a prophet to teach Witchcraft and various forms of nature worship. Both Leland and Maddalena claimed that the Italian Tradition of Witchcraft escaped the Christian conversion that eventually overtook Europe. The book was an original concept because it shed light on magickal spells and incantations.

The Strega Tradition is especially popular within the United States. One need not be of Italian descent to adopt the ways of Italian Witchcraft, but many Italian American families practice its tenets and beliefs behind the safe veil of Roman Catholicism.

Among the promises Aradia made to her devotees were success in love, luck, and the ability to communicate with the spirit realm. Spells and rituals are performed within the magick circle, and self-dedication is a common way to pledge oneself to the Strega Tradition. In Italy, curious customs closely related to Aradia have survived the influence of the Catholic Church. The *befana*—an Italian translation for the word *witch*—is a Witch who brings children bearing gifts in the New Year. In the small town of Benevento, a historical haven for Italian Witches, many still hail religion with the words "Ave Diana" instead of the more common "Ave Maria."

At Boston College, Donna is a senior completing her degree in English. She grew up in the Italian American community and has vacationed in Rome every summer since early childhood. Her parents, born and raised in Sicily, immigrated to the United States after marrying. Donna was raised a Roman Catholic but remembers her paternal grandmother performing "small rituals" all the time.

"My grandmother was a great woman, very traditional but also very liberal," Donna explained. "She had a way of doing things with olive oil and salt and bay leaves to remove negative vibes from the home. If I complained of not feeling well, she told me someone had given the evil eye, and she would look at my hands and make me flex them for minutes in a certain pattern. It always worked. There were lots of other customs like that, and it wasn't until I was a teenager that I understood them as Pagan rituals."

It was in college that Donna began reading up on Italian Witchcraft. Books served as her introduction to Wicca, and the day she turned twenty, she consecrated herself to the goddess Aradia. "My grandmother served as proof that the Old Ways have survived. I asked her about it once, and she told me that being a Strega was powerful and important. She had stories about her village in Sicily. The local priest there used to visit the Strega when all else failed. I feel a deep connection to it because of my familial roots, but also because I've always believed in the power of Nature. Now I look back on my four years of college and realize that they comprise a shaping of my identity as an Italian Witch. I grew up. I became an adult on campus, and it gave me the freedom to play around with rituals and spells. I knew a lot of other Witches—at Boston University and MIT—and I think we all have the same philosophy: live, learn, follow the Goddess. We'll all leave campus ready for the world. And when all else fails, there's always magick!"

CELTIC

A long and colorful history has given the Celts a lot in the way of enlightenment. The Celtic Tradition is the home of ancient myths, gnomes, and fairies. It also has its roots in Druid customs. Some of the most popular Goddesses and Gods are rooted in Celtic origins. Brigid, for example, rules healing. Morrigan is goddess of the Underworld and even has a warring aspect that will right any injustice. The god Cernunnos is the proverbial Horned Man and king of the woodland.

The Celtic Tradition is redolent with the sweet lore of fairies that dwell in gardens and sunlit groves, over lakes and through the mists. Elemental magick is especially significant to practitioners. Earth, Air, Fire, and Water are invited into practice in various forms: undines, crows, lions, wolves. Those who take to the Celtic Tradition go to great lengths in terms of creativity; they often draw inspiration from the folklore, legends, chronicles, music, and poetry of Irish culture. The rites of practice are akin to those of the Gardnerian Tradition, but there are countless Celtic Witches who pen their own rituals and disagree with skyclad worship.

Perhaps the best known of Celtic practitioners is the late Gwydion Pendderwen, a bard who wrote music, poetry, and many rituals. He was an environmentalist, politically active in the antinuclear movement, and favored a solitary existence. The Green Man, a Pagan deity of the woodlands and forests, was Pendderwen's greatest archetype. Pendderwen also cofounded the Faery Tradition of Wicca.

FAERY

Victor Anderson and Gwydion Pendderwen, who knew each other as children, are the founders of this tradition. As a child, Anderson was initiated by Witches. Early on, he experienced profound and moving visions of the Goddess and God. Described by many as "ecstatic," this tradition often encourages devotees to add their own personal touches to the rituals Anderson and Pendderwen wrote. Their most famous initiate is the Witch, author, and activist Starhawk. There are different spellings of the word "Faery." It sometimes appears as *faerie* or *fairy,* although these distinctions do not differentiate in meaning.

The Faery Tradition favors intense worship of nature and environmental activism. Most adherents are solitary.

*   *   *

Of course, there are many other Wiccan Traditions. Included here are some of the most popular. It is important to remember that Wicca has no "bible" or direct authority, so practitioners are free to either incorporate or create their own magickal systems. After careful study and evaluation, decide which tradition suits you best. If none strike you as adequate, you might want to consider starting your own. The only requirement or law is that it abide by the Wiccan Rede.

The Eclectic Witch

Confusion is a common reaction when one begins exploring Wicca. The amalgam of traditions, while all centered around the Goddess and God, partake of different views and practices. When one in particular doesn't satisfy the magickal need, there is eclectic Wicca. This is the combining of many traditions and, in some cases, other sects of Paganism, Native American rituals, and shamanism.

One of the most interesting eclectic Witches I came in contact with was Astara, a student at Montana State University. She takes her Witch name from Astarte, goddess of love and war, often connected to Middle Eastern cultures. Astara was raised in a strict Christian Baptist home. She rejected the male-dominated religious authority in her teenage years and discovered Wicca in high school. It was not an easy time.

"I lived in a small town full of Jesus-fearing folks," she told me. "There were very few kids who understood Witchcraft as being benevolent. I did a lot of reading and soul-searching in private, and gave myself to the Goddess when I was fifteen. It was hard because I had to pretend to live in two different worlds. A lot of people still don't know that I'm a Witch. My parents would probably disown me if they knew I owned a pentacle and prayed to the Moon."

Though she envisioned more freedom in her college years, Astara has remained cautious about her identity. "Montana is a great place. It's my home. But conservative opinions are still the norm here and it's just easier to keep my religious beliefs private. I told only one person about practicing Wicca. This girl who lived in my dorm . . . I thought she was cool and open-minded, but within days of my telling her, she distanced herself from me completely. I'm not a freedom fighter, so I just keep to myself. I think about the Pagans and Witches in the Europe of earlier times, the ones who had to live the way I do now. They survived. Staying in the broom closet is tough, but it's made me a stronger person and a stronger Witch."

In her freshman year, Astara read Gerald Gardner's *Witchcraft Today* and thought she would adopt the Gardnerian Tradition. She liked its notions about the coven as a collective power. Forming a coven of her own, however, seemed an impossibility, and she began widening her experiments with Wicca. The following summer she traveled to Italy. It was while visiting the American University in Rome that she discovered the Strega Tradition.

"In Italy I read a lot about hereditary Witchcraft," she explained. "I came across the Charge of Aradia and just fell into a trance while reading it. It spoke to me. I loved the Strega notion about the Tuscan Witches being taught by Aradia. I also loved the authentic Italian customs that were enmeshed within it. By the time I got home to Montana, I was practicing Gardnerian Wicca but praying only to Aradia—the queen of Witches."

Astara's spiritual pursuits didn't end there. She continued her travels well into her sophomore year, delving into her passion for Native American cultures. While visiting Sedona in Arizona, she attended an open Wiccan circle on an eve of the Full Moon. There she met a young man—"a total hottie"—who was a member of the Cherokee Nation. They became acquainted, and eventually formed a long-distance friendship. Astara was eager to learn about shamanism from a Native American perspective.

"My friend was reluctant to tell me about it at first because he felt it was a personal thing, but eventually he agreed to show me a couple of meditative techniques," she said. "I learned all about the harnessing of elemental forces and how to practice my breathing techniques. We explored Choctaw shamanism together. I got to know the medicinal uses of herbs and plants, and before I knew it, I was incorporating even that into my practice of Wicca."

In a single dorm room without roommates, Astara went about combining her eclectic tastes. "I started out every ritual by breathing with very specific techniques I learned from Native American shamanism. Then I cast a magick circle the way Gardner suggests. Next I read the Charge of Aradia. You're not allowed to burn candles or incense in your dorm room here, but I pretty much violated every rule and I did it safely. My results have always been incredible."

It didn't end there. In her junior year at Montana State, Astara began studying Hinduism. She developed a love for its traditions and customs, and formed a strong bond with Kali, goddess of nature and ruler of its destructive forces. Kali is often depicted in a very vivid light, her most shocking trademark a necklace strung with human skulls. For Astara, the goddess Kali is synonymous with the uncontrollable energies Mother Nature can unleash—storms, floods, earthquakes. The Hindu religion is also alive with its own myths and legends.

"Kali serves as a reminder to me of one simple fact: that all humans are governed by Earth," Astara said. "We can't challenge Mother Nature. We can't stop hurricanes or blizzards. In the Hindu faith, Kali is a creator and a destroyer, which is a true depiction of nature. I like that realization. So now, I include a chant to Kali with every ritual I perform. I ask her to guard me against those potentially destructive forces."

Future goals for Astara include visits to Egypt and Hawaii, where she hopes to further her knowledge and identity as an eclectic Witch. Hers may seem a multifaceted story, but it is truly no different from that of any other eclectic practitioner. Walking the diversified paths of a religion as autonomous and non-dogmatic as Wicca is part of its immense appeal. The marrying of different traditions can herald a time of deeper understanding about your beliefs, your goals, your very self.

The Male Mysteries: *Wicca and the Masculine*

The God. Images of him are etched into the subconscious of every Witch. There is the male figure partially clothed in leaves, the fabric of the forest his eternal cloak. He is also half beast, the horns of a stag rising like a crown from his head. Mars, the Roman god of war, bears armor and shield. The two faces of the god Janus have simultaneous insight—one sees the past, the other the future. Pan, the Greek god, shares his human form with that of a goat. Hermes is a young man, chiseled with strength and youth; his winged helmet implies flight. No matter the description, the God serves a highly significant purpose: he creates balance and harmony with the Goddess.

In Wicca, the God plays many roles. He is the mate. He is the protector and caretaker. He is both giver and destroyer. A hunter, he roams the wild with predatory instinct and fair precision. A lover, he exudes sexual stamina and potency. Man and woman together bring forth life, and the Goddess and God are symbolic of this universal union. One cannot exist without the other. The God is summoned through invocation, and his vigor enhances every ritual.

Symbolically, the Goddess is associated with the Moon. The God, however, is synonymous with the solar cycles. The eight Sabbats that comprise the Wiccan calendar are all about darkness and light and how each affects the change of seasons. At Samhain, the tradition Celtic New Year, autumn is in full swing and the days are growing colder and shorter. Here, the God is preparing to enter the Underworld. The Sun's power lessens. By Yule, or the Winter Solstice, the God has already begun his long journey into Earth's unending rhythm. He emerges again with the Spring Equinox, just as daylight strengthens. The Goddess gives birth to the Sun once again, and into summer goes his reign. Thus, the God is a reminder of the cycle of death and rebirth.

Like plants, flowers, and crops, the God diminishes in nature but blooms again without fail. The Wiccan calendar, or Wheel of the Year, is a circle. It is the core of existence. It is the womb of the

Goddess. The God's light throbs in the sky, stroking the seas and the air, penetrating the soft silky soil, letting go the seed of bounty that ends in creation. His is the mystery of polarity between the sexes. What is male is also female, and vice versa. The God, in all his masculinity, does not shy away from the possible blending of his own essence with that of the Goddess. They are separate but still conjoined. They stand apart but are linked at the core—much like all of humanity.

Traditionally, monotheistic religions have a single, conclusive representation of God. In Christianity, the life of Jesus Christ is set forth clearly in the Bible. His image remains consistent in nearly every artistic portrayal seen throughout history. So too is it for Allah of the Islamic faith and the Buddha. The God of Wicca, however, has no definitive image. He is human and animalistic. He can be a young, virile man or an elderly bearded soul. What is perhaps most intriguing about the God in Wicca is his sometimes-androgynous nature. Because the God is never to be feared, he is himself fearless. When invoked, the God can be masculine and feminine within the same breath, but this willingness to coexist on all levels of human consciousness is not a threat to his divine place within the universal wisdom. The God is confident. He transcends the boundaries of religiosity.

Men who come to Wicca often feel that there is much emphasis on the Goddess but not enough on the God. If one does not educate himself correctly, this will seem quite true. That is precisely why constant reading and researching—of both the current and the historical kind—are necessary. Several male college students with whom I spoke were of this opinion. They went to great lengths to discover the God within themselves and within ritual.

Greg, a freshman at Penn State in Pennsylvania, actually questioned whether or not to call himself a Witch because he felt that the God was absent from practice. "A lot of guys fear admitting their interest in Wicca because it is still considered a religion geared toward teenage girls," he said. "When I got to campus I met a lot of other Wiccans and Pagans, and they all talked a lot about the

Goddess. I'm fine with that, but as a man, I definitely want to connect with the masculine side of divinity. It was a while before I truly understood who the God was. And once you find him, you find balance."

At the University of Oklahoma at Tulsa, twenty-two-year-old Syrian Dragonwyld, who prefers to be called by his Witch name, is the youngest member of the outside coven to which he belongs. On campus, he lives a very quiet and academic life. It was his exploration of the God that brought him full circle to Wicca. "I started researching Greek and Roman mythology when I was fifteen," he explained. "It was my hobby. I came across all of these incredible images and deities, and they spoke to me. I'm a Witch, a soon-to-be high priest, but I identify more with the God than with the Goddess. I invoke him in every spell and ritual I do. He's taught me that men and women are equally the same in everything. We all have qualities of the opposite sex inside us, and that's nothing to be ashamed of. Power comes from duality, and from knowing both sides of the human condition. That's the God to me."

When a coven convenes for a ritual, the members recite the "Charge of the God" just as they do the "Charge of the Goddess." He is called by various names: Hermes, Zeus, Hades, and Janus, among others.

Wicca and the Feminine: *The Female Mysteries*

The Goddess is alive and well today. We know that much. But how deeply she is embedded in the annals of history remains an enigma. Ancient art depicts her as young and beautiful: statues carved as shapely figures with curvaceous hips and breasts, long hair, large eyes. She has also been portrayed as full-bodied and plump, as though heavy with pregnancy. And still other images illustrate her as an old woman, her face lined, her mouth thin and pursed. These all lead to one question: Who is the Goddess? On the surface, all practicing Witches know the answer. She is queen. She is life and death and ultimate rebirth. She exists in the subconscious, the conscious, Earth and the Moon.

The feminine mysteries teach us that the Goddess is the divine force in three aspects: maiden, mother, and crone. In her maiden aspect, the Goddess is a young woman, brimming with confidence and power and imminent knowledge. She is virginal, but not necessarily in the traditional sense. Here, the concept of "purity" is akin to strength and solidarity—one who stands alone in her identity and does not require a partner to complete the circle of self-growth and accomplishment. Young women—most often teen- and college-aged girls—associate with this image. The maiden is fresh and brave and eager. There is a sense of calm to her, but also an inevitable and heightened excitement to all that she does. The future is building to a summit. Much experience is yet to come. Thus, the maiden is linked to the time of the New and Waxing Moon.

The mother is the second aspect of the Goddess. Here, she is a mature woman in her prime, full of love and insight. She is caring. She is nurturing. She lifts her children up and cradles them against the womb of Earth. She also knows sexuality and carries within her the sensation of a man, of true womanhood as gleaned through encounters of the mind, soul, and body. She is a symbol of wholeness. Behind her is the tumultuous nature of youth, but gone too is the restless fervor of that time, the giddy and sometimes reckless passion that accompanies exploration and inquisitiveness. The mother is symbolized by the Full Moon. Glowing and bright, ever-present and abundant, she is at the pinnacle of her existence.

The crone is the third and final aspect of the Goddess. Here, she has achieved that which lies at the core of the human condition: wisdom. Through imagery, the crone is portrayed as an old woman, replete with wrinkles and a heavy face. She does not hide her appearance because old age is synonymous with the beauty of antiquity, of a life lived in accordance to one's own rules and goals. There is compassion within the crone. There is knowledge of laughter and love and light. But it has begun to pass away now, and the illumination she knew with the Full Moon is growing weaker by degrees. The circle is near completion. Darkness, cool and fluid and bucolic, approaches. The crone is preparing herself for the ending that can only lead to one place: rebirth. The Waning Moon and its dark phases are correlated to the crone.

The feminine mysteries in Wicca are complex and layered, but they show us that balance and polarity between genders promotes harmony. And harmony is what all religious traditions seek to live by and impart.

The Pentacle: *Mark of the Witch*

The pentacle is the Witch's symbol: a five-pointed star held within a circle. Together, the points represent the Spirit or "All" as well as the elements of Earth, Air, Fire, and Water. No matter how it is used—worn on the body or placed upon an altar—the pentacle serves as an emblem of protection. Catholics have the cross or crucifix. The star of David represents the Judaic faith. Wicca uses the pentacle for the same purpose.

The pentacle (referred to as a *pentagram* when the star is not within a circle) has a long and colorful and misunderstood history. This mysterious symbol has appeared in ancient Greek and Roman cultures, within Egyptian hieroglyphs, and on various artifacts unearthed in the ruins of Mesopotamia. A knight's shield was often emblazoned with a pentacle because it was thought to aid in defense. Interestingly enough, Christianity has several connections to the pentacle as well. Hildegard of Bingen, a Benedictine nun and the celebrated author, composer, healer, and mystic whose writings and music continue to inspire people today, is believed to have associated the pentagram with the human form. Her theory poses that the five points are synonymous with the head, arms, and legs. It was during the Inquisition that the pentagram was branded evil. Today, many continue to associate it with satanic rituals and dark rites, but the true meaning of the pentagram has nothing to do with corrupt practices.

Wearing a pentacle as a symbol of your faith is yet another important decision. Once spotted, it will undoubtedly arouse suspicion or curiosity among your friends, family members, and peers. People

SPOTLIGHT
Nemeton, Pagan Student Alliance at Boston University
www.people.bu.edu/nemeton

In September 2000, Seamus McKeon, a sophomore at Boston University, set out to establish the first on-campus Pagan group. He got the signatures of five prospective members in one day and, by the end of that first week, had no less than ten interested students. At the student activities expo later that year, he signed up more than fifty names. A professor, Anthony Barrand, enthusiastically agreed to be the group's advisor. And so Nemeton was born.

Today, it is a group comprised of twenty-five students at Boston University and others from Northeastern University and Emmanuel College. Its popularity has increased over the course of a year, and the Web site is well trafficked and artfully conceived.

In his own words, McKeon described for me the mission and purpose of Nemeton. "We have a meeting once a week in which we discuss future plans, and then we have a workshop of some sort," he explained. "Either we'll have a guest speaker from a local coven or a practitioner from another Pagan path, such as Asatru, Strega, or Druidry. Usually we have workshops on things like the Tarot, runes, palmistry, energy work, healing, and reiki, among other things. We also have discussions about various aspects of Paganism and Wicca, such as magick, celestial influences upon magick, astrology, timing magick, herbalism, and stones. We've held one official ritual at Boston University, and a few more at my own off-campus apartment. Usually we travel to different places in Boston where open rituals are held, like psychic salons, tea rooms, and churches that lend space to various Pagan and Wiccan groups."

Seamus's advice to college Wiccans and Pagans, as well as students interested in exploring their spirituality further, is simple. "Just go for it," he said. "The people in college are amazingly open-minded, and don't let anyone put you down for it. You're doing your community a favor."

have been subjected to discrimination for wearing pentacles, and many court cases to this effect have attracted media attention. Again, it is important to weigh the pros and cons on a very personal scale.

Richard, a freshman at the Cooper Union in Manhattan, grew up in Brooklyn and began practicing Wicca in high school. It was the pentacle that sparked his initial interest. "I knew it was something magickal the first time I saw it," he said. "When I was a kid watching horror movies, I always saw those devil-worshipping scenes that included an inverted pentagram drawn on the floor or on someone's body, and as I matured, those negative images bothered me. If you really look at a pentacle, if you study it closely, you see a human body with arms and legs outstretched. You're also reminded of the five human senses."

When in class or commuting on the subways, Rich wears a gold pentacle—which symbolizes the God—around his neck. He even has one taped to the visor in his car. "I never experienced problems as a result of having a big pentacle dangling in front of my shirt. I get looks from people sometimes, but it's nothing major. Here at school, everybody is cool about it. But that's probably because I live in New York City, and here nothing is a big deal."

Once, while registering for classes, Rich was approached by a fellow student who questioned him with fear. "This girl came up to me and just pointed to my pentacle," he explained. "She was like totally freaked out. She asked if I worshipped Satan, if it was a Baphomet and why I would wear something so 'scandalous.' I told her about Wicca and all the history behind the pentacle, but she wasn't hearing it. The whole thing bothered me, but what could I do? I just let it go. At this point in my life I don't feel like I need to offer explanations."

A young woman who introduced herself to me as Merla had a different story to tell. She was a junior at St. John's University in Queens, New York, and grew up in a home with Wiccan and Pagan influences. Her father hailed from Salem, Massachusetts, and had many old friends who were practicing Witches. Merla attended a number of rituals as a child, where she saw pentagrams inscribed on stones and flat rocks. She was formally initiated into Wicca at sixteen and has worn a silver pentacle—symbolizing the Goddess—ever since.

"I never thought it would be a problem," she told me. "But last year I had a couple of bad experiences with students. A few of them made comments when I walked by—the usual crap about being evil and drinking blood and praying to the devil. One guy in particular—a born-again Christian—told me after class that I was setting a bad example and should have more respect for a school where Jesuits taught. And I was like, 'Are you kidding me?' He was convinced that I was into dark things, and he probably still believes that. It was a bad feeling. I hate having to constantly defend myself about it."

Later, Merla spoke to one of her professors—a Catholic priest—about the whole scenario. "He was actually very cool about it," she said. "He told me that I shouldn't let it bother me and that it was my right to wear a religious symbol. If a priest can understand, why can't everyone else?"

Wearing a pentacle has proved to be something of a challenge for Merla. Having second thoughts, she said, was inevitable. "I'll still wear it (the pentacle) in public, but I don't think I'll be displaying it as openly as before. Lately I'm more cognizant of my surroundings, and if I feel like I'll run into any trouble, I just slip it under my shirt."

Pentacle-inspired jewelry has become more popular in the last few years. In addition to online stores, rings, amulets, and other charms can be purchased in any occult or New Age shop. They come in all shapes and sizes, in various colors and adorned with certain stones or crystals. Many Witches design their own pentacle symbols as well. Whatever your preference, just know the facts and understand the realities. To wear or not to wear? The choice, like the power, is yours.

The Psychic Realm: *Science or Stigma?*

As we have seen, what the ordinary person considers "supernatural" is commonplace to the Witch. Psychic phenomenon falls into this category. It is rare that one will ever come across a Witch who does not claim some measure of heightened mental ability. This may be in the form of Tarot cards, palmistry, or the reading of tea leaves. The psychic realm also encompasses remote viewing, channeling, precognition, and automatic writing. And, of course, there is always that favorite of spooky encounters: communication with the "Other Side." We are all familiar with the scene in the feature film *The Sixth Sense*, in which a child utters four chilling words to a psychiatrist: *"I see dead people."* By some accounts, such otherworldly conversations are indeed an impossibility. The international resurgence of interest in metaphysics, however, has led to a number of intriguing studies and experiments that have garnered attention from the scientific community. Do brain waves act like receptors to the universe? Is extrasensory perception (ESP) truly a "sixth sense"? Can deep meditation and concentration tap into energy fields once thought non-existent? It all depends on whom you ask. Just as there will always be a population of supportive believers, so too will there be crowds of skeptics.

Unequivocal is the significant place psychic phenomena plays in Wicca. One of the basic tenets of the Witch is a belief in a parallel world: that of spirit. When casting a spell, one's mental power must transcend mere thought to harness the forces that will serve as agents of change. Energy fields raised during rituals are drawn psychically as well. In fact, many Witches find their way to Wicca because of their own psychic experiences. No other religion embraces the unexplained with such fervor. As you claim your identity as a Witch, you will inevitably begin to develop a penchant for psychic phenomena. By way of Wiccan philosophy, this is a good thing. But it is important to impart your knowledge accordingly, and with equal amounts of responsibility and prudence. Wearing your psychic individuality like a tattoo does not always foster the best results. The more you know, the better your experiences will be.

Austin, a senior at SUNY Purchase College in Westchester County, New York, came to Wicca because of his interest in parapsychology. He had numerous encounters with psychic phenomena as a child and, when I first met him, claimed to possess the rare ability to converse with the dead. It was a shocking assertion. I had seen Austin on campus many times, but his unassuming disposition didn't offer the slightest hint that he studied parapsychology or even practiced Wicca. He wore no pentacle. Jeans and sneakers were his trademark. On the evening of our appointed meeting, I found him sitting in an empty classroom in the Humanities building quietly flipping through the pages of a book.

"I'm more open about being a Witch than I am about my psychic abilities," he told me. "Wicca is becoming more recognized and accepted, but the whole psychic thing tends to steer people away from you. There are some who believe and want to know more, and that's mostly here on campus. But in other places it isn't so easy."

He then mentioned a part-time job from which he had recently been fired. It was a small office, and Austin's supervisor allegedly overheard him talking to a coworker about channeling. The supervisor made her dislike of the subject known. Austin alluded to his own personal experiences and beliefs, and discord soon reigned. The "downsizing" in the company, he believed, was really an excuse to get him out of the way.

"That's a prime example of ignorance," he said. "But it does happen. I've told many people that I'm a Witch and explained all about Wicca. Generally they seem less concerned with worshipping the Moon and casting spells than with psychic ability. But here at school it's been a little different. Some of my friends and I have actually held séances in our dorm rooms, and the results have been spectacular. So can it be something of a stigma for young Witches? Yes, it can. Skeptics will call you crazy and the fearful will do everything short of dousing you in holy water. Caution is the key."

I asked him to provide me with an example of his abilities. We walked to his dorm room, a single decorated with crystals and lava lamps. Faint traces of incense lingered on the air. From under his bed, Austin pulled a small box and shook it. The noise was like a rattling of coins. Inside were a handful of different colored stones.

Closing my eyes, I plunged a hand inside and picked one out. It was bright green and smooth.

"Aventurine," Austin said. "That means good luck and protection." He held the stone and cocked his head to the side. Then he mentioned a name—that of a deceased friend of mine. He went on to describe her personality quite accurately, and even alluded to her intense religious devotion. "She's near you, kind of watching over you. She says you worry too much and need to calm down."

It all rang true.

I had told him nothing of myself and admitted, later, to being impressed.

"The more one studies Wicca, the more accurate his psychic abilities become," Austin said. "It's something to be proud of, but I still would never flaunt it. I think it makes Wicca look a little too flimsy if you're going around telling people you can read their minds and summon up ghosts."

But there are others who disagree.

Mona, a student at the University of Hawaii, said her psychic abilities were a blessing that complemented everything she did as a Witch. "It isn't a stigma. I know sometimes people think I'm strange when I tell them that I am a psychic, but denying it makes me feel like I'm in some way ashamed of Wicca, which is far from true. I'm a Witch because I have these abilities and because I want to develop them further. It's easy to be open on a college campus, but I've come across some bad experiences. You can't let it bother you. Would a Catholic deny believing in apparitions of the Virgin Mary, a supernatural phenomenon if ever there was one? No, of course not. It's a part of that faith. Psychic ability is a part of mine. If you're practicing Wicca, you're becoming more psychically inclined every day."

Dennis is a graduate of Harvard University and a current student at Cornell University's graduate school. He is not a practicing Witch but has studied the relationship between physics and the supernatural. "I knew many Witches and Pagans in college," he said. "What's interesting is the way they portray psychic ability. Witches really don't go about claiming to have ESP. They relate psychic phenomena to nature and some even refer to a number of scientific methods—the Hermetic Principles, the REM, and non-REM states of mind. There are aspects of the physical world that science has not yet explored. Magnetic fields are energy. So are solar-powered tools and machines. Energy is everywhere. Truthfully, no one can say definitively whether or not the human brain is capable of psychic feats, but it helps to keep an open mind."

Science or stigma? Only you can decide how you will choose to wear this aspect of your Witch identity. For further study, students

---

HOW DO YOU *ROCK THE GODDESS?*

Ryan Starblade, senior
Princeton University, Princeton, New Jersey

"Living on campus can be really hectic. Your life becomes nothing but papers and studying and the occasional party. I don't always have the time or the availability to observe the nights of the Full Moon, and being in a dorm room makes it really difficult. But when I do call on the Goddess and God, I find a quiet place—either the library or somewhere private on campus—and I write in my Book of Shadows. I use it as a journal that details my ideas for spells and magick but it has also become like a diary to me. I write letters to the deities I feel closest to. I get out everything in my head, all the worry clogging my soul. It's a very personal thing but I know that I'm being heard and guided in the right direction. I know the Goddess listens."

---

should check out The American Society for Psychical Research, located in Manhattan. The ASPR, a non-profit organization, has an impressive list of members and has sponsored scientific experiments in the psychic realm and other areas of the supernatural. The Rhine Research Center does the same and even hosts a summer semester for would-be parapsychologists or anyone interested in expanding his or her knowledge about the occult.

Within the university setting, psychic phenomena and many other aspects of the supernatural realm are alive and well. At SUNY Purchase College, for example, the anthropology department offers a course titled Magic & Witchcraft. In the Humanities division there is Gods, Goddesses & Demons. The New School University in Manhattan offers a course on parapsychology, and Nazareth College in upstate New York includes several writings about Wicca on their Web site for the Religious Studies Department. Colby College in Waterville, Maine educates students on the way of the Witch via a course titled Contemporary Wicca: Formalists, Feminists and Free Spirits. Bates College, also in Maine, features Wiccan holy days on its list of holidays for students.

3

Psyche's Fire
Stories in the Dark

In dreams, the spirit finds me.

A woman stands at a distance. Light pulses behind her and a shadow obscures her face. She emerges from a spinning vortex, taking slow steps through fog, wind, and rain. There are familiar sounds: of dogs baying at the Moon, of blackbirds cawing at the sky. A chilled hum pervades the narrow space between us. Gradually, she reveals herself to me.

First, I see the flames that are her hair. Next, the smooth pallor of her neck and breasts. My eyes take in her crimson lips, the swift glisten of her tongue. A serpent, coiling in motion, wraps itself around her shoulders. She is beautiful in her exotic way, compelling and strangely seductive.

I stand still, waiting. Words escape me.

The flames dancing around her face grow brighter, and suddenly her full form is illuminated. Where there once was unblemished skin, I now see faint traces of blood. Scars riddle her hands. A deep gash mars her chin. It is as though she is wounded and healed in the same moment.

She stares, unflinching.

Finally I find my voice. "Who are you?" I whisper.

"You know who I am," she replies. Her voice is soft but firm. She

spreads her arms out wide, showing me her breasts and the perfect contours of her body. In the shifting glare, her physique hardens, the muscles of her torso deepening, her chest widening. The serpent slithers down her side and stands erect, like a phallic symbol.

A man's form? Yes. The spirit is both feminine and masculine. The spirit is without gender.

"Are you . . . the Goddess?" I ask.

"No," comes the reply. "I am the Psyche of the Goddess and God, the heart and soul of the Witch both past and present. Look at my eyes: they are the color of the ocean and the soil. My hair is the heat of the Sun and the fire that once ravaged so many. My body, chiseled and strong, is without shape, a sculpture of the All. Behold the serpent: it moves in a circle around me, like the knowledge of Earth. My scars are the pain of those who died, but my beauty is the resurrection of an old way reclaimed."

"You're everyone," I say.

"I'm everyone and no one. The Witch has been persecuted, shunned, and killed. But she has also been revered and celebrated. Above all, the Witch has never been forgotten. She is a staple of consciousness, a part of every culture. Today, the Witch is both male and female. She is scarred and untouched, public and private, enthusiastic and somber, fearless and frightened, exalted and oppressed. I am the Witch's mind in all its incarnations."

It has been said that the mind is a labyrinth, an intricate web of thoughts, memories, sorrows, and triumphs. Each of us is a weaver. The threads may be thin or thick, studded with diamonds or torn by rage. But from them come the seeds of stories. It is in the words that true magic dwells—the timeless power to move and mark and mystify. When all else dies or disintegrates, only the tales survive. Thus, the human psyche and the Goddess are inexorably linked: each acts as a vessel for spiritual fulfillment and change.

The spirit hovers close to me. There are flashes of light, images at once disturbing and bold.

I say, "Tell me your story . . ."

The Witches Speak: *A Generation in Voices*

It was time for my nightly ritual. All was quiet beyond the window of my bedroom, but my computer was singing the log-on song. I waited, then heard the familiar voice telling me that I had mail in my in-box. Before I could click the letter icon, however, I was assailed by nearly a dozen Instant Messages.

"Hello!"

"Greetings!"

"Merry meet, Anthony!"

"Hey, remember me?"

My fingers went into typing mode and I began the several hours of cyber-conversation. My online buddies were all college Witches from various corners of the United States. I had met them in chatrooms, via message boards, and through Yahoo clubs. I knew them only as their screen names: a plethora of similar words verging on the magickal and the esoteric. A few had e-mailed me their opinions on the college Wicca scene, and others had answered questions and offered me personal experiences. There were rituals being held on campuses and dorm parties for Pagans. There were links to Web pages and search engines that might be of help to me. But there were also heartfelt, moving, and sometimes disturbing stories about being in college and being a Witch. Most of these had nothing to do with dorm room spells or nasty roommates. Quite the contrary. A number of stories transcended the campus mind-set and went deeper into the psyche.

"My parents kicked me out of the house when they found out I was a Witch," once appeared on my computer screen as an Instant Message.

"My understanding of Wicca is different from that of other people because I discovered true magick through personal trials," was another.

A particularly memorable experience occurred two days before Samhain, when I cruised into a chatroom for Wicca and became acquainted with a young woman who told me she was on leave from college for a semester. I asked her what she was doing in the meantime. Several minutes passed before I got a reply.

"It's kind of personal," she wrote back.

"That's cool," I replied. "How long have you been practicing Wicca?"

Another stream of hesitant silence. I began wondering if she had logged off and forgotten all about me.

Then the response came: "I'm in a psychiatric hospital in Florida. I'm not crazy, but my parents just didn't know what else to do with me."

"What happened?" I asked.

"I got into crazy stuff my first semester. A lot of partying and drugs and trouble. They took me out of school and made me stay home. They thought the Church was the best remedy for my problems."

"But it wasn't?"

"No. I ran away, got into more trouble. Then I figured I might as well end it all and I tried to commit suicide. So my folks locked me up."

My fingers froze on the keyboard. I didn't know what to say next. Would I offend her by getting too personal? A minute ticked by. What do I say to that?

She answered by changing the subject. "My past isn't all that important. I just wanted you to know that I'm doing really well now, and I've made progress because I found my calling. I've been reading a lot about Wicca and I know that I'm a Witch. The Goddess is the best 'treatment' I ever could have gotten. I didn't mean to bother you, but you're the only college student in this chatroom and I figured maybe you'd understand better than most where I'm coming from."

I knew I wanted to hear her story. And as I began back-tracking through my mental notes, I remembered that I had come across a number of equally visceral experiences. Sure, I thought: thousands of college students find Wicca because they want to explore their spiritual sides, but there are other, deep-rooted reasons for claiming the way of the Witch, too. This story was one of them.

I wrote: "What's your name?"

She hesitated. "Why?"

I quickly typed out my answer, explaining that I was writing a book on college Wicca.

"Well," she wrote back, "in that case, my name is 'Neeve.'"

I noted the use of quotations. She had offered me a pseudonym. "Would you be willing to answer a few questions for me, Neeve? I'll give you my e-mail address."

"No."

"Why not?"

"Because I'm a private person and I don't want to leave a paper trail."

"I'm just curious about how Wicca has helped you and why you found yourself attracted to it."

"It's different for everyone. I didn't get into Wicca because my friends back at school started a Pagan association. It's much more personal than that. I don't think I'm ready to share my story with anyone yet."

Fair enough, I thought. Disappointing, but fair. In fact, the unwillingness to "get personal" in print or on tape was becoming a pattern. Students were eager to tell me about the spells they had cast or how the latest meeting of Campus Pagans went, but piercing the surface of reality was different. Piercing the surface, many told me, was "scary." Being open in college was one thing. But being open *all the way* was another thing entirely. Parents wouldn't understand. Some had future jobs and careers to think about. It was risky business.

I went back to my computer screen. Neeve was waiting, but she'd made herself clear, right? Never one to give up, I decided to drop the journalistic approach and try my hand at groveling.

"It's for a good cause," I wrote. "And you'd be helping out a fellow college student."

I waited. Nothing.

"Come on, Neeve. Be a good Witch, will ya?"

"I'll think about it," she replied. "Maybe when I get out of here I'll chat with you again."

That was it. She had logged off and was gone. But my interest in her story—and in other intensely personal stories—only increased. I had a few, but as I read over my notes from previous conversations and chats, I realized that I wanted more.

I began writing e-mails and perusing message boards. I took to the phone and started calling colleges and universities all over the country. I even hit the streets, dropping in on the local area campuses where I knew I'd be welcomed.

Eventually I found what I was looking for. The Witches spoke.

Into the Light: *The Goddess Calls Me*

Dante was Italian American. His story, he told me, started *there*. Born and raised on Mulberry Street in the Little Italy section of Manhattan, he knew early on the importance of family and a close-knit community. He attended a local Roman Catholic school and described his childhood as "happy." His favorite memories revolved around the dinner table. There, his parents often entertained him with tales of small mountain villages in Rome and the long-gone ancestors who had "the power." He remembered the story about a great-great-aunt who knew how to give people the "evil eye." Another familial fable told of a distant cousin who possessed the rare ability to unleash rainstorms with a sacred chant.

Today, Dante is a twenty-three-year-old senior at Hunter College, City University of New York, in Manhattan. He has been practicing the Strega Tradition of Wicca for three years.

"I didn't know anything about Wicca as a kid," he told me. "In Catholic school, you're taught to believe that Witchcraft is evil and Satanic. The nuns are very clear about that. At home, my parents told me stories that had a lot to do with magic, curses, and people who were healers. They grew up in villages in Italy where Paganism is still very much alive, but their concept of the Witch—or

Strega—is different from the modern American concept. Italian Witchcraft is still very steeped in Catholic lore."

During his teenage years, Dante found a passion for all things academic. He loved history and psychology, especially the writings of Carl Jung. "I started thinking a lot about human consciousness in relation to the self," he said. "And then I started exploring the whole religious side of myself. Catholicism had been ingrained in me since I was a baby, and that was okay because it gave me a glimpse into ritual and the idea of a higher power. But when I was sixteen, things started to change."

The "change" came with his budding sexuality. Dante discovered that he was equally attracted to women and men, but his desires had no place in his religion or his home.

"I was going through all of these emotions and feelings," he explained. "I was a good-looking kid, I took care of myself and was really athletic. Girls used to come up to me all the time, and I dated a lot. I tried my best to suppress my feelings for men. I even convinced myself that I was just trying to be different, to rebel against very conservative parents. Deep down, I knew it wasn't that simple. It took me a long time to accept my bisexuality, but even when I did, I was miserable. I was confused about everything."

By this time, religion had taken a backseat in Dante's life. "Well, there I was: a bisexual guy living a double life. I was the perfect Italian son at home, but then I'd go out and fuck anything that moved—I had a girlfriend and a boyfriend. I went from incredible physical pleasure to complete emotional guilt all in the same night. But that's who I was. I couldn't help it. I loved men as much as I did women. Because of everything I'd been taught, I viewed myself as evil and screwed up. I knew that religion didn't want me. How could I rationalize being bisexual and a good Catholic? It didn't make sense to me. The Church stones people like me, tells me that I have to ignore 'that part' of myself. Sex is sinful. I wasn't paying mind to any of the commandments or laws. I knew that if I went to confession, a priest would just tell me to stop and forget and repent. So I left religion altogether. But I did it through anger. I really believed there was nothing in the sky except clouds and rain. No God whatsoever."

At eighteen, Dante left Manhattan for a private, liberal arts college in New Hampshire. He continued his study of psychology and history. Then he came across Charles Leland's *Aradia: Gospel of the Witches*, an account of the folklorist's experiences with Italian Witches.

"That was my first glimpse into the Old Religion," Dante said. "I remembered all the stories my parents told me, and the customs Leland wrote about were strangely familiar to me. I called my mother and asked her if she knew anything about a woman named 'Aradia' and she basically recapped everything in the book. I was amazed. My mother told me that her own aunt dabbled in being a *Strega*. There were whispers of it all throughout my lineage."

Eventually, Dante met up with students who called themselves Witches. He became educated in the phases of the Moon, the various astrological symbols, and the historical aspects of Paganism. But it still wasn't enough to quell the storm raging inside him.

"It was a very dark time in my life," he said. "I was completely removed from anything religious or spiritual. I was a full-blown atheist and I didn't give a damn about what was happening in the 'New Age.' I knew I had been born a certain way, predisposed to an attraction toward both sexes, but I couldn't understand how to incorporate my sexuality into any kind of religion honestly. I was of the existentialist school at that point. I was doing what my body felt was good, but mentally I was bankrupt. I didn't go home for the holidays or make many friends. I just stayed to myself, ashamed, pathetic, and angry at a God I didn't believe existed."

At the end of his sophomore year, Dante returned to New York and entered Hunter College as a transfer student. Thoughts of *le streghe*—the Witches—stayed with him, as did his moderate knowledge of Wicca. Back home after two years, he had a difficult time adjusting to life with his parents and spent most of his free time locked in his bedroom, reading. He also surfed the Internet. To counteract the loneliness, he escaped into the underbelly of Manhattan nightlife. Bars, clubs, and pubs became his places of worship. He binged on alcohol and sex.

"I would literally wake up in people's bedrooms and wonder what I had done. I wasn't going to class or paying attention to my grades. Everything took a dive. For a while I just told myself that this was part of my age group. I figured all college students were finding themselves but losing themselves in the same instant. And then, one day, I got a phone call that totally jarred me. A guy I had dated briefly told me that he was HIV positive and that I should go and get tested. And of course, I freaked out. The next day I went to the doctor and took the test. It was a wake-up call. I sat in that waiting room and everything I had done in the last two years came back to me, a bunch of images and pictures, and I knew that I had to change. But before making a change in my life, I had to figure out why I was allowing myself to crash.

"I realized that the answer was staring me in the face all the time. It's really the same story for any young adult who has sexual identity issues. The gay and bisexual lifestyles tend to be destructive because it starts out as an underground exploration. We're all ashamed of it because society has told us to be ashamed. Religion tells us constantly that it's wrong and evil. I wanted to believe in something. I'm a spiritual person, but my self-afflicted problems were clouding out all reason. I knew I would never make peace with my spiritual side until I made peace with who I was as a bisexual man. When my test came back negative, I felt like I'd been given another chance."

The very next day, Dante received a postcard from a young woman he had known back in New Hampshire. She included in her note the address of a Wicca open circle she was planning to attend the coming week in Manhattan. She suggested he join her, if only to catch up on old times.

"She was one of the only cool people I knew in New Hampshire, so I decided to go," Dante said. The decision would prove to be an epiphany. "It was an open circle not too far from where I lived. This girl and I met up. She asked me how I was doing with Wicca, and I confessed that I really wasn't practicing and hadn't read up on it in a couple of weeks. She was shocked. She told me that I was a natural Witch and she had just assumed that I'd been practicing for years. When I got to the open circle, I spoke with a lot of Witches and Pagans, and something came over me. I was amazed by how serious everyone was. They were *religious* about their beliefs, and yet there was no preachy crap to what they were saying. I met lawyers and accountants and cops and parents. I met a bunch of different people. It was the first time I admitted openly that I was bisexual. I said the word, and then I waited. I thought people were going to respond strangely, but everyone was like, 'Hey, that's cool.' And then we got into the ritual, which was a Full Moon esbat. I got into the circle and just let myself go. I felt the Goddess and God and all the energy. I felt the magic of unity among free-thinking people. That was the biggest awakening—the notion that spirituality can embrace free thought and action."

Dante's transformation would evolve over the course of the following year. He began attending open circles all over New York City and Long Island, and even met up with a few student Witches from Hunter College. Here, the journey from atheism to Goddess spirituality emerged not by way of spell-casting or Moon lore or media representations, but from purely fundamental soul-searching. In his quest to understand himself, Dante found a connection to the divine.

"Wicca, to me, is about balance. The Goddess resuscitated the self-respect that had died in my subconscious. The one thing about myself that I hated most is now the core of who I am. It's what I'm most proud of. Bisexuality is a gift—it's the ability to appreciate humanity from both angles and both sexes. I'm not ashamed of myself any more. I know there's a Supreme Being who views me as an individual regardless of something as trivial as the person I'm attracted to. I'm a Witch because I'm completely in touch with my psyche and my soul. I found myself in Wicca, but the Goddess called me."

Witch: *A Nun's Tale*

The Catholic University of America in Washington, D.C., is the only pontifical college in the United States. Theology is among the most popular majors, and CUA often serves as the foundation for those who choose the religious life. By the time Evelyn arrived on campus as a freshman, she already had her entire future mapped out. She was seventeen years old, intelligent, confident, and idealistic. She never made a decision without consulting her foremost peer: Jesus Christ. Back home in St. Louis, Missouri, she had attended an all-girls parochial school, where she led extracurricular activities like the Bible study group and the Sunday afternoon Holy Rosary Club. For as long as she could remember, her days passed in a steady, pleasant rhythm: homework, chores, and dinner with her parents and two younger siblings. Happiness was rooted in family, and Roman Catholicism dominated even her free time.

"There was a crucifix on every wall in my house," Evelyn told me when I met with her in Georgetown, a comfortable distance from the Catholic University of America campus. "My mother liked to tell people that she collected religious art, but it was her devotion to the Church that made her decorate every corner with crosses and statues of the Virgin Mary. She and I would go hunting for little Catholic treasures on Saturday afternoons."

Now a junior at CUA, Evelyn lived off campus. She was small, introverted, relatively unassuming. But then again, she liked to keep a low profile. She enjoyed living in the nation's capital, which she described as "the complete antithesis" of the small suburb where she had been raised.

"I never thought I'd get comfortable in a city with a pulse," she remarked. "But being in a fairly diversified atmosphere kind of complements who I am these days."

Evelyn was a Witch. She was not public about her identity on campus and had confided in only a handful of friends about her spiritual beliefs. She had come to CUA with a mission: after earning a B.A. in theology, she planned on entering the convent and had even hand-picked the religious order she wished to join.

"I felt the calling when I was a kid," she explained. "I loved going to Catholic school, and the sisters that educated me really were role models. They were strong women and most of them were always happy. I used to love sitting in the chapel watching them pray. Everything about it touched me, especially the peace I saw on their faces. At first, I kept the desire to emulate them to myself. As a teenager, my friends were interested in the normal things, and I tried my best to play along with slumber parties and chasing boys and all of that, but deep down, all I wanted to do was go to church."

It was in her teenage years that Evelyn developed an affinity with the Virgin Mary. She was inspired and intrigued by the stories of Fatima, Portugal, and Lourdes, France, where apparitions of the Virgin Mary are believed to have occurred. In Lourdes, Saint Bernadette found the gushing spring of water that has healed the ill and comforted the afflicted for decades. Catholics all over the world interpret these "meetings with Mary" as both miracles and warnings. The Virgin Mary comes to Earth bearing messages or secrets about the unfolding future of the world. The most dire predictions are viewed as potential chastisements. The phenomenon has continued right up to the present day. The most recent example is Medjugorje in the former Yugoslavia, where six "visionaries" have experienced ongoing conversations with the Virgin Mary since the early 1980s.

"I remember being enthralled by the apparitions," Evelyn said. "My parents bought me books and videos about Fatima, Guadalupe, and Knock, Ireland. Looking back, I think that was my first initiation into the concept of feminine divinity. The nuns told me all the time that the Virgin Mary was human and not necessarily divine, but that didn't matter to me. I prayed to the Virgin Mary, and my rosary was the most powerful thing in the world. I pictured her as a beautiful woman 'clothed with the sun,' just as she's described by those who witnessed the apparitions. I felt connected to her because she was a woman, a mother, and a powerful essence. When the nuns described

Armageddon, they used to say that the Virgin Mary would come to Earth and 'crush the serpent's head.' How powerful is that?"

It was powerful enough to shadow most of Evelyn's teenage years. She spent her weekends volunteering at homeless shelters and teaching Sunday school. In her quest to be like the saints she so admired, Evelyn began fasting three times a week and attending Mass daily. She stayed in school most afternoons in the happy company of the nuns, helping out in the kitchen and rearranging books in the library. Evenings were reserved for prayer.

"I spent hours concentrating on the rosary," she explained. "I would lock my door and go through all the Mysteries. There are still passages I can recite verbatim from *The Story of a Soul,* Saint Thérèse of Lisieux's autobiography. Again, I now see this as an initiation into feminine spirituality. I really identified with the female saints, the nuns, and the Virgin Mary. My adoration of Saint Teresa of Avila became really intense at that time. I mean . . . *really intense.*"

When I asked Evelyn to clarify the extent of her "intensity," she stretched out her arms and splayed her hands. Looking closely, I saw small scars in the very center of both palms; one resembled an S, the other a T. What did it mean?

"I started bleeding in spurts from my palms," she told me flatly. "People don't believe me when I tell them, but I know it's true because it happened before my eyes. My parents witnessed it. No joke."

Evelyn relates her experiences to the life of Saint Teresa of Avila, who in her own autobiography claimed to have suffered from *transverberatio*—the literal piercing of the human heart by God's love. Saint Teresa is also believed to have levitated while in prayer, and she suffered numerous physical and mental afflictions throughout her "ecstasies." In fact, according to Roman Catholic lore, Saint Teresa died in ecstasy in 1582.

"I don't believe that I suffered from what is commonly referred to as stigmata," Evelyn said. "I actually don't think I was touched by God when I bled from my hands. It took me a while to realize that I was in my own state of religious ecstasy, not only wishing for something so grand but *making* it happen with my own mind. I was sixteen years old and I thought the archangel Michael was trying to send me messages. But now that I'm a bit older, I understand what happened to me. I was thirsty for a true divine experience, and because of my religion I believed it could only come through suffering. I was a die-hard Catholic, and my only point of reference was the crucifix, which I thought was beautiful because it symbolized giving up your will to God. I could never have imagined how much I would change in college."

The Catholic University of America seemed like an obvious choice to Evelyn in her senior year of high school. She remained devout in her longing to enter a convent through her freshman year, but she did encounter difficulties.

"I was away and on my own for the first time. I sort of grew up and started seeing things in a different light, and what I saw was a very male-dominated community. I loved learning about theology and being close to religious men and women, but as my intellect expanded so did my desire for liberal thought. I mean, why couldn't women be anything more than just nuns? I started seeing my own self apart from the image of the Catholic school girl and the imminent nun. For the first time, I accepted my femininity, but it took a while before that image transformed into something attractive and sacred and worthy of a divine experience on the same level as the masculine."

The following summer, Evelyn spent two weeks at a convent, exploring the structured life of a nun. She slept in a small room, awoke before dawn to pray, dedicated herself to various chores. It was a contemplative time. But what she found was more than she had anticipated.

"Even then, nuns represented an amazing community of women to me," she said. "But I came away from my stay at the convent confused. I struggled a lot, spent hours in church crying because I didn't know what God wanted of me. I still felt the burning desire to serve humanity through God, but I didn't know whether the convent was the right place for me. I didn't understand why the role of women hadn't changed in the two-thousand-year history of the Church. There was a certain confinement to it, a limiting of abilities and actions. I was really shattered. I realized that my religious beliefs as they were could only go so far before hitting a wall spray-painted with a sign that read 'sin: go no farther.'

"And then I had an amazing experience. I went through my old journals and diaries and read over my entries from years before. All along, I had been praying and worshipping the Virgin Mary *alongside* Jesus Christ—not as an intercessor to him, but as his equal in divinity and spirituality. I truly never saw the concept of God as wholly masculine. I never accepted it. As a teenager I was unwilling to admit that to myself, but I wrote about it. My soul was completely wrapped up in the notion of a Goddess, not a God. Or, at the very least, a Goddess and a God. I even found an entry about Joan of Arc, and I wrote that I didn't understand why she was burned as a Witch. I was using Catholicism as a safety net to something deeper. I came to understand that the answer to my spiritual quest was *here* all along—on Earth, in the present moment, and not above me in the afterlife. That summer, I became a woman who defined her own spirituality. I was no longer a woman defined *by* religion."

At the beginning of her sophomore year at CUA, Evelyn began reading books on Wicca and Witchcraft. Fearing that other students would discover her new-found quest, she kept it a secret.

"There is, obviously, a very strong Catholic and Christian vein here at CUA," Evelyn said. "There are lots of student clubs and organizations, but I've just never felt right about going public on campus. I know plenty of professors who would probably be interested in hearing what I have to say about Wicca, but it's still very personal to me. I know I'm not the norm—a girl who wants to become a nun but ends up a Wiccan priestess. Now I plan on continuing with my degree and teaching at the university level. Maybe then I'll be in a place where I can share my knowledge of spiritual transformation openly, but now it's just too soon."

It wasn't until she moved off campus that Evelyn began exploring the fruits of magick and ritual. That first exposure came from attending a Pagan festival in Maryland. She met other college Witches and started networking, albeit cautiously. Among a few early difficulties was rejection by a close friend who spotted a copy of Scott Cunningham's *Living Wicca* in Evelyn's apartment. Another was the negative reaction she received from a family member back in St. Louis.

"I told a cousin of mine about it," she explained. "He and I had always been close, but he didn't like any of it. He told me I needed a psychiatrist and asked me not to call him again until I got my head screwed on straight. But I tell you, my head has never been stronger or clearer."

Today, Evelyn is a full-time college student and a part-time waitress. She is not completely "out of the broom closet," and keeps a low profile on campus. She meets once a month with a small coven, but she also reserves time for solitary practice. Interestingly enough, Evelyn often combines elements of Roman Catholicism with Wicca. Before we parted ways, she provided me with an example.

"I believe in the angelic counterparts of Catholicism, and I revere certain saints because they truly were extraordinary people," she said. "When I cast a spell, it's not uncommon for me to call on the archangel Michael, and I use a great spell that praises Saint Anthony of Padua. As a Witch, I view myself as a walker between the worlds, and that means being able to tap into all levels of energy and divinity. The Goddess is the true source of power, but all spiritual paths ultimately converge toward one goal: a direct union with peace and harmony."

Going Goth: *Freakish or Fashionable?*

In late November 2001, I was contacted by a young woman who called herself Priestess Sepho—a shortened version, I later learned, of the name for the Greek goddess Persephone. Sepho called me and said she had gotten my number from "someone" at a Manhattan university who knew that I was writing a book about Wicca and college students. It didn't surprise me. Since July, I had passed around my number and e-mail address like beer cans at a frat party. I was grateful for yet another willing interviewee.

Sepho was a twenty-two-year-old junior at Columbia University, majoring in sociology. From the very first, she was witty and snide. "Are you interested in talking to me and hearing some of my viewpoints on the Wiccan college scene?" she asked me flatly.

"Sure," I replied. "Just tell me where and when."

Before making a date, she laid down some ground rules. She was not ashamed of her identity, she assured me, but she worked as a part-time administrative assistant for a conservative law firm and made it clear that she didn't want her dirty laundry hung out to dry. The people who signed her paycheck would be incensed if they knew "what she was doing" in her private life.

I agreed to meet her alone, with nothing in hand but a notebook and a pen.

"Good," she replied. "Now take down this info, and get it right."

On a balmy November night, I made my way to Madame X, a trendy hot spot in Greenwich Village. Sepho assured me that she'd be waiting in the shadows. As I bypassed a waitress dressed in leather and fringe, I spotted her: she was thin and pale, her black hair pulled away from her face, her hands adorned in lace gloves. Sepho stood up as I approached the table. It was only then that I saw the rest of her. A black velvet gown trailed over her boots, which looked scuffed at the toes. An intricate piece of silver jewelry glowed like pewter from around her neck. Her lips were pierced. A diamond stud glittered from her left nostril. Above and around her eyelids were dark penciled circles that trailed over her temples. When we shook hands, my fingers brushed against an assortment of rings, one of which—a large skull—shadowed her entire thumb. Pentacle earrings dangled from her lobes.

"You're surprised that I'm Goth," she said with a smile.

"Actually, I'm not," I replied, sweeping my eyes across the dark and decadent atmosphere of the club. And in truth, I wasn't. I had already met a number of Witches who preferred the Goth look—or, as one pointed out to me, the Goth lifestyle, which was comprised of an entire culture and psychological mindset. I knew from the start that Sepho would agree.

I sat down and flipped open my notebook. "How long have you been a practicing Witch?" I asked.

"I've been a Witch my whole life," she told me. "I was born on a Full Moon, and my mother is very sensitive psychically. I first found out about Wicca when I was thirteen. I picked up a few books and that was it. When the next Full Moon came around, I went out to my backyard and consecrated myself to the Goddess."

She had been raised in rural Connecticut, and with no organized religion. Her mother had been politically active in the feminist movement of the 1960s and, while admittedly unconcerned with religion, had exposed Sepho early on to the concepts of Eastern philosophy and spirituality.

"There's a vein of Paganism that I think runs through Eastern thought," Sepho said. "All those concepts are one way or another grounded in nature, and they're all about the self. Wicca is the same way. A Witch has to know herself before embarking on the magickal journey."

I asked her to tell me about her penchant for the "Goth look."

"Goth is really a lifestyle," she answered, as if reading my mind. "On the outside it's all about dark hair and white makeup and clothing like the dress I'm wearing. Inside, though, it has to do with recognizing the darkness that exists in all of us. Not 'darkness' in a bad way, but the darkness of life—the stuff that brings about emotions and eventually counteracts pain and sadness."

"That sounds like a hyperbolic description of the Goth *look,*" I remarked. "How is Goth a lifestyle?"

She rolled her eyes and smirked, mumbling something unkind about writers. "The lifestyle is a lonesome one," she then said. "It's existing in solitude but choosing of your own free will to do so. I can tell you my own personal experiences. I'm a child of the night. I'm only comfortable after the sun goes down, under the moonlight. There's a quiet pace to the night, a fluid rhythm. Goth people are naturally in tune with it, just as we're innately drawn to dark things—horror movies, scary stories, mythology. One Goth person looks at another. They could be complete strangers but there's a total understanding between the two of them, an instant link. So I mostly live by night and hang out in the Goth scene."

It was all very interesting, but how did it tie into her identity as a Witch?

"There's a chronology to that question," Sepho began. "Think back to what history tells us about pre-Christian times. Pagans lived by the Moon and the Sun, the Stars and the Wind. Paganism was also the religion of the oppressed and peasants. Eventually, they were forced to hide their religion, or were killed for it. So they all sort of took it underground, creating a secret society where the Goddesses and Gods were worshipped and where knowledge was handed down from one person to the next. Pagans fled into the forests and the woods, to any place hidden. Look at the Egyptians. They decked themselves out before entering the temples of Isis. Cleopatra was known for her use of makeup, and the pharaohs wore headdresses gilded in gold. Today that would be considered Goth!

"Witchcraft is a religion of the night, whereas I view Christianity as centered around the day," she went on. "The Witch does her magick by the Moon and astrological elements and by candlelight. Covens go out into the woods at night. Doesn't the Witch, in all those tall tales, fly through the sky on her broom at night? I guess what I'm trying to say is that being Goth—both outwardly and inwardly—brings me closer to what it means to be a Witch. I think of it as honoring the Old Ways but also as a vehicle against oppression. I'm drawing attention to myself and telling the people who gawk at me to fuck off. I feel like I'm fighting off all those people who called Witches freaks. So for me, the Goth girl and the Witch go hand in hand."

I proposed an interesting—and by some measures, controversial—viewpoint. Didn't all that attention contribute to the negative public-relations campaign waged against Witches in the past and today? What about the Witches who were fighting to present a very "normal" image of themselves to society, wearing jeans and T-shirts and no pentacle?

Sepho shook her head. She said simply, "That's false. In part it's because of the subcultures of the world—the Goths and the Punks—that Witches were able to make such great strides. We all laid down the ground for other 'esoteric' and even 'unacceptable' ideas to come through. Wicca is still considered freaky to many folks out there. They see a modern-day Witch and clump us together in one big group—Goths, Pagans, Punks, even vampires. This kind of 'publicity' has nothing to do with wanting attention because I'm starved for it, or because I'm just narcissistic. But it has *everything* to do with refusing to live in the shadows, railing against a puritanical culture that wishes I would just go away. Goth is how I look, but it's also how I feel. Why should I hide it? It's given me strength, and that's made me a stronger Witch."

I then asked Sepho why she hid her Goth side from her co-workers.

"At work is the only place I hide it," she assured me. "I don't like being confined to an office, but I get paid good money and I don't want to jeopardize that. I know it sounds hypocritical, but everyone has to think of making a living. The people I work with are conservatives who freak out when a woman wears a tight skirt at the office. A bunch of Republicans. One of the bosses once made a comment about my hair being so black, and he asked me whether I dyed it this color on purpose. He's a prick, and there are dozens like him. If you're not Christian, you're Jewish. It's one or the other, but mentioning something like Wicca would cause an uproar. And sitting at my desk dressed like this would get me fired. When I'm there, in slacks and a shirt, I feel totally out of sorts, but I deal with it because I have to. I don't have any other choice."

Studying her, I wondered if she combined her Goth tastes with her practice of Wicca. Did it make her magick . . . darker?

"Like all Witches, I worship the Goddess as the source of all life," she explained. "But I have a definite relationship with the goddess Hecate, who rules magic and sorcery and is sometimes associated with dark images."

In fact, the goddess Hecate is often depicted with three heads and three sets of arms, in which she holds daggers and torches. She is the ruler of the Underworld. Hecate is said to walk with ghosts and spirits, and she was venerated in pre-Christian Europe at the crossroads, the proverbial sign of her presence. Some legends claim that when a dog howls in the night, it is because Hecate is nearby, roaming with her pack of wolves. In Wicca, she is often invoked during the dark phase of the Moon.

"I think my strongest point as a Witch is in banishing and neutralizing negativity," Sepho continued. "I probably get darker and deeper with my magick because I'm Goth, but I never break the Wiccan law. That's the biggest misconception Goth Witches face—that we dabble on both sides of the fence. We don't. I guess we're kind of a subculture within a subculture, and that can be a lot to handle. But there are a lot of Witches—in college and much older—who are Goth. We probably all find our way to Wicca for the same reasons, which have to do with not being accepted in society, with being viewed as freaks and outcasts. We all tend to be free thinkers, and Wicca embraces identity in all forms. In both Goth and Wiccan communities, I know I'm accepted and respected."

Pagan Parental: *A Mother Speaks*

I met Doris by chance. On a mild Saturday night in October, I was browsing through one of the small and funky shops that line Mac-Dougal and Bleecker Streets in Greenwich Village when an attractive, middle-aged woman approached me. She looked me straight in the eye but didn't speak.

"I don't work here," I told her, and went back to perusing the shelves of silver jewelry and candles.

"I know," she replied nervously. "But you look young and I thought you might be able to help me. I'm trying to buy . . . something for my daughter. Her birthday is next week and I'm not really sure what to get her in a place like this."

The woman was nervous and obviously uncomfortable. She was dressed in a tailored business suit and, given the less than fashionable surroundings, looked completely out of place. "What do you want to buy for your daughter?"

She glanced around the narrow aisle, as if to make certain no one was listening to our conversation. The guy at the cash register eyed us curiously. "My daughter is turning nineteen. She's away at school now," the woman explained in a shaky voice. "She asked me to buy her a—"

I waited. "A what, lady? The clock is ticking."

"A *pentagram,*" she finally whispered. She nearly shut her eyes in shame.

Inwardly, I laughed. The gods were working in my favor. Promptly I asked her, "Is your daughter a Witch?"

"Oh . . . a . . . I . . . well . . . I guess she is."

"It's nothing to be ashamed of," I pointed out.

She cracked a ghost of a smile. "It isn't?"

I led her to the front counter, where the silver jewelry was lined beneath a glass top. After a few minutes, I helped her choose a beautiful silver pentacle studded with chunks of moonstone. "Your daughter will like that a lot," I assured the woman.

She thanked me, introducing herself. Her name was Doris and she lived on the Upper East Side. She was a corporate attorney, she explained quickly, and she really didn't have much experience with "this kind of thing." She said, "You've really helped me. How do you know so much about this stuff, by the way?"

When I told Doris that I was writing a book, and that she had just earned a rightful place within its pages, she grew pale.

"I don't think so," she said. "I don't know anything about it. My daughter has tried her best to assure me that the whole Witch thing isn't bad, but I really don't know what to think. My husband and I never even mentioned this sort of thing, so it came totally out of the blue."

After some coaxing, Doris and I exchanged phone numbers. I assured her that I would be calling because I wanted to hear the viewpoints and opinions of a spooked mother. Like so many before her, Doris was afraid of the potential backlash she would get if people knew her daughter was a practicing Witch.

I phoned her two days later and left a message on her answering machine. When three days passed without a response, I tried again. Doris picked up on the first ring. She didn't sound thrilled to hear from me, but agreed to settle in for a chat.

I asked her how she found out her daughter was practicing Wicca.

"Last year, when she was a senior in high school, I found a bunch of Tarot cards and crystals beneath her bed," Doris began. "I thought it was just teenage interests and a little bit of rebellion. My husband and I are Protestant, and our home was anything but esoteric. I just always assumed my daughter would grow up and adopt the same values and beliefs."

A short while later, Doris confronted her daughter about the Tarot cards and crystals.

"It began and ended as a fight," she said. "My daughter was reluctant to get into why she was interested in this stuff, but I was concerned and wanted to make sure she wasn't getting into anything dangerous. Then she just flat-out told me that she wasn't a Protestant and didn't believe in organized religion. I was shocked and asked her what the Tarot cards had to do with it. And that's when she told me she was practicing Witchcraft."

I asked Doris to explain what her initial reaction was.

"I freaked out," she said with a chuckle. "I saw a bunch of horrible images and thought back to the movie *Rosemary's Baby*. I figured it was all Satanic, and that scared me. I asked my daughter if she was casting spells, worshipping the devil. I didn't know anything about Witchcraft as a benevolent religion. That wasn't a part of my growing up. I mean, I remembered the feminist movement and some talk about a goddess, but I never took it seriously. It was all new to me, completely foreign."

Doris was reluctant to hear anything about Wicca, and for several weeks she and her daughter didn't broach the subject. But more revelations would emerge. Doris spotted a pentacle on her daughter's neck and found in her room a number of books on the Goddess.

"We went at it all over again," Doris said. "And then finally my daughter sat me down and gave me a crash course on Wicca and what it really is. She showed me the symbols for the elements and named the various deities. She even showed me her Book of Shadows, and I was amazed because she had apparently been lighting candles and worshipping the Moon in her bedroom, and I had no idea whatsoever. She told me she felt a connection to the image of the Witch because of her interests in astrology and the occult. My daughter is also an environmentalist. Little by little, I started to read up on Wicca, just to see if everything she'd told me was true. My daughter is a good kid, and I've always been able to trust her in the past, but I was having a hard time with this. I still am."

Doris said her daughter chose to attend a college in New England that had a large population of practicing Witches. It was cause for yet more disagreement.

"I didn't like that idea," Doris admitted. "My daughter was going to be away from home doing God knows what, and at first I told her I wouldn't pay a cent if she was going to be running into the woods every time there was a Full Moon in the sky. But eventually I had to accept it because I realized just how serious my daughter is about it. I met a couple of her friends, and she told me that they've formed a coven, or a group, and now they meet regularly and do things together. She seems happy."

But Doris, on the other hand, was not.

"I feel like all those mothers who have to come to terms with having gay children," she explained. "It's the whole coming out process, and the attempt to understand a lifestyle that doesn't fit into the mainstream. Like all mothers, I just want what's best for my kid, and I still don't think Wicca is it. I have to be honest with you: I don't understand the whole Witchcraft philosophy, and in my mind it's still a lot of fluff. I think a lot of it has to do with being cool and different. I still have my suspicions, too. Maybe that's just a mother's nature, but I've had to resign myself to accepting it because my daughter is headstrong and determined. I raised her to be that way, so maybe it's partially my fault. I don't know. But whenever I visit her at school, I see how much of a movement Wicca is on campus, and that helps me because I know there are other parents out there who are going through the same thing. It's hard, to say the least."

Doris said she was slowly coming to terms with her daughter's Witch identity but did not foresee a day when Wicca would be welcomed in her home.

"I don't tell people that my daughter is a Witch. None of my coworkers know, and neither do my relatives. That angers my daughter, and I'm sure it'll anger all the other people who will be reading this, but that's how I honestly feel. Parents have a right to know what their kids are doing on college campuses. I always worried about drugs and too many parties, but never in a million years would I have thought that my daughter was going to end up incorporating Witchcraft into her academic goals. It still bothers me. On the flip side, parents going through the same thing should be open and hear their kids out. When kids are away at college, they're going to do what they want to do anyway. It's better to try and make amends rather than risk losing them. I'm not happy about it, but there are worse things. The bottom line is that I love my daughter and I'll have to do what mothers have done since the dawn of time: grin and bear it."

Witch, Interrupted: *Maiden and the Mind*

Two weeks to the day that I had first chatted with her online, Neeve and I were back in touch. I logged on for my nightly ritual and she quickly greeted me with a "Hey, what's up?" She told me she was back home. The psychiatric facility had released her three days earlier. Neeve and I started conversing and over the course of a few evenings became acquainted with each other. Her story, she warned me, was dark.

It began with her freshman year at the University of Florida at

Tallahassee. Leaving home was a "necessity" because Neeve had been "a problem" for her parents since high school. When she was thirteen, they rediscovered religion and joined a Christian Baptist church, often urging their daughter to attend weekly services. Neeve refused, much to their disappointment, and secretly explored her interests in New Age spirituality. In college, she quickly met up with students eager to explore different paths. Many of them were Witches.

"There were about seven of us who got together, usually once a week, just to talk about different spiritual things," she told me. "We all had dreams of experimenting with the occult and magick, and maybe one day traveling to Egypt and Europe where so much of Paganism began. It was nice to talk freely about it because I could never have done that at home. My parents and my little sisters were into being Baptists, and anything like Wicca was to them just plain evil."

But Neeve lost her spiritual niche a few months later when she met a young man at an off-campus bar. They began dating, and their relationship progressed. She described the former boyfriend as a "Goth kid" who had explored many different things. He used drugs recreationally and was a heavy drinker. It wasn't long before Neeve fell into step beside him.

"I had never even smoked cigarettes," she confessed. "And all of a sudden I was drinking a lot and doing a lot of ecstasy and smoking blunts. I really loved the guy, so I guess I was afraid to lose him if I didn't join his crowd. When I think about it now I realize how stupid I was. It was all about peer pressure. I lost everything because of dumb choices, including my life as a student. I missed nearly all my classes that spring semester, and all I did was go to the dorms to sleep."

The university put Neeve on academic probation and sent a letter to her parents.

"They freaked out, of course," she said. "They came to get me before the semester ended and brought me back home. I was still in love, but they forbade me to speak to my boyfriend. They thought I was just slacking and had gotten mixed up with the wrong crowd. They had no idea I was using drugs. I stayed in my house that whole summer, locked up like an animal. My parents told me the only way I'd be able to go out and see my old friends was if I agreed to speak to their minister. I had no other choice, so I agreed. But it was wrong. Once when I was talking to him, I mentioned that I didn't believe in Christianity and he blew his top. He told my parents not to let me go back to school in the fall, which I really wanted to do. Everyone was convinced that I didn't have 'the fear of Jesus' in me. But in reality I didn't have the fear of anything in me because I was pretty much an atheist. All my dreams and expectations about Wicca and other New Age things evaporated."

But that fall, Neeve did return to college. She threw herself into her studies and did well those first few weeks, but couldn't help hooking up with her old flame once again. What followed was an identical pattern of drug abuse and drinking. While partying at a friend's house, Neeve nearly overdosed. When it all became too much, she sought help from a counselor who in turn contacted Neeve's parents.

"It all came out into the open," Neeve said. "They knew I was using drugs and that I didn't care for being a Baptist. When they brought me home at the end of that semester, they swore it was for good. My mom spent her days reading to me from the Bible and would only let me out of the house to go to church services. They didn't trust me enough to even let me get a part-time job. No friends, no school. Just the church and a hope that the Holy Spirit would save my soul."

I asked Neeve whether her parents had ever questioned her actions while away at school, whether they ever sought to understand the troubles festering beneath the drug abuse.

"No, never," she replied. "You don't go looking for the reasons behind a sin if you're a Baptist. You only care about repenting for it and correcting it."

Next, I asked her if she knew why she had let herself stray down that dark path.

"I had lived a sheltered life," she explained. "Throughout my teenage years all I knew was my parents' religious fanaticism. I wasn't allowed to go to school dances or have boyfriends. None of that normal stuff. So I guess when I got to college and was finally on my own, I just busted out with it. The freedom was too much for me to handle. I wanted to try everything and know everything. And I guess I was also a little depressed because I knew that if I followed my true dreams, I would lose my family anyway. I was never going to be the good Baptist daughter they wanted. I wasn't going to get married and have kids or anything like that. They were never going to understand me. They still don't."

The confinement began to weigh on Neeve's emotions. The religious purging her parents hoped for had also manifested itself in the wrong way. The more Neeve railed against the teachings and the Scripture she did not believe in, the deeper her depression got. In February, just after her twentieth birthday, Neeve walked into her bathroom and attempted suicide by slitting her wrists with a razor. Her father found her unconscious on the floor. She was rushed to the local emergency room and saved. What transpired in the hazy zone between life and death would ultimately alter Neeve's perceptions about herself, her past, and her future.

"I had a near-death experience," she explained. "I remember all of it. There was sharp light and the sensation of floating. There was no pain or hardship, and I remember thinking to myself even as it was happening that I had made the right choice, that it was beautiful and calming. The colors were incredible, all these flashes of reds, purples, and blues. It was like watching a thousand sunsets backlit by fireworks. It lasted for a few minutes, and then I just remember waking up in the hospital."

Neeve also mentioned seeing a "woman" within the exploding kaleidoscope of light. She said she could not explain that part of the near-death experience because to do so would be injustice—it was simply too moving. But she believed the woman to be the Goddess in her maiden aspect: young, hopeful, and filled with promise.

"The first thing I thought about when I woke up was my first semester of college," she said. "I flashed back to those discussions I used to have with my group of friends, and I remembered how comforting it was to talk about the Goddess and Wicca and how in that philosophy, life was sacred because you *learned* from your mistakes and didn't suffer because of them. It was the only thing that comforted me."

After receiving medical treatment, Neeve was sent to a private psychiatric facility. Much to her surprise, it had no religious affiliations and the frequent therapy sessions allowed her to explore her thoughts about Wicca. In fact, she was cruising a Wiccan chatroom the night she met me online.

"I haven't read many of the books that explain how to do spells and rituals," she told me. "But I read *Witchcraft Today* by Gerald Gardner and *The Spiral Dance* by Starhawk. It's the Wiccan philosophy that really heals me. I look at it like a metaphor. I was in this terrible darkness and then I saw light, and now that light is brought to me by the Moon. I don't feel guilty about my past anymore, but I know I've made mistakes. And I really do believe that all humans are connected to Nature, and that death is only a beginning and a doorway to a cycle of life, a rebirth. I pray a lot to the maiden aspect of the Goddess."

A few days after her release from the psychiatric facility, Neeve was sitting in her bedroom at home preparing for a special occasion. It was the night of the Full Moon.

"I walked into my backyard and I lit a candle and I just sat there, watching the sky," she explained. "I recited *The Charge of the Goddess*. I cast a spell for healing and for strength, and I felt the Goddess comforting me. There's no question about it now. I call myself a Witch. My parents don't understand and never will, but they see the change in me and I think they're grateful for that."

Next year, Neeve will resume her academic career at another university not far from her home in south Florida. She plans on joining or starting a Wicca/Pagan campus group and continuing her studies in near-death experiences. She is currently designing an "in-depth" spell that will combine luck, healing, and cleansing, to be performed at the time of the New Moon and dedicated to the Goddess in her maiden aspect.

Daughter of the Moon: A Path Defined

I had seen her walking along the campus of SUNY Purchase College several times. She was thin and striking, with dark hair and regal features. She seemed to have a preference for black clothing, dramatic scarves, and silver jewelry. Stylish and confident, she also exuded an air of mystery. Only later did I learn she was a Witch.

Her name was Diana Bayard. She was majoring in anthropology and had a minor in women's studies. A few days before Samhain 2001, we met through a professor and Diana agreed to an interview. She was public about her identity and highly knowledgeable about Wicca. In fact, Diana's insight had even attracted the attention of a local news channel that had profiled her earlier in the year.

I began our conversation with the most daunting of questions. How, I inquired, did she come to call herself a Witch?

"Traditionally, I was raised with religion," she began. "It was pretty much of the born-again Christian variety. My parents were Christian at one time, but interestingly enough, they've both moved into different spiritual phases in their lives. Now their beliefs are essentially focused around Paganism. My dad is very much into nature, but he doesn't like to put a label on his beliefs. My mother has moved into alternative spirituality, and she has explored Wicca, but neither of them are Witches, per se. They're both very accepting of me and I come home and tell them about the Goddess and magick and they're always very interested. They listen."

Diana credits her father with planting the "Wiccan seed" in her mind. When she was fourteen, he took her to a Samhain ritual, and the community and mysticism Diana witnessed there had a grand impression on her.

"I had always been interested in the lure of the Witch," she explained. "But I remember watching that Samhain ceremony and thinking it was very cool. It was always in the background, but then it moved into the forefront. The woman who ran the ritual day was a friend of my father's, and she's actually been an incredible teacher for me. It turns out that years later I'd end up working for this wonderful woman, who owns an eclectic shop in Poughkeepsie, New York, called The Dreaming Goddess. That was the ultimate experience for me—first seeing a Wiccan ritual and then working in this great store. It expanded my spirituality. I mean, I was still a teenager but I felt a definite connection to Wicca from then on."

In high school, Diana did not have many friends who practiced Wicca. Although a number of her classmates called themselves Witches, they did so through imagery rather than serious devotion.

"You had the few people that everybody knew were Witches. They were open about it, but not in a positive way," she explained. "They were more like, 'I wear black and here's my pentacle, so don't bother me or I'll cast a spell on you.' That was never my view of Wicca, so I really disassociated myself from that group. For many years I wore a pentacle, but I kept it under my shirt because I wasn't interested in making some sort of impression on people. Sometimes that's what it's about for teenagers who get into Wicca. They're interested in it because they think it can bring popularity and power. I've found it to be different in college. I think college students get more serious about it."

Before attending SUNY Purchase College, Diana studied at the Fashion Institute of Technology in Manhattan. She met several students who practiced Wicca, but the urban campus, she believed, hindered them from forming any sort of group or coven. Many of the college Witches she knew at FIT belonged to outside covens or were solitaries. She transferred to Purchase after deciding to explore her interests in anthropology, psychology, and women's studies. But still holding tight to the connections she had made back in Poughkeepsie, Diana did not seek out other like-minded students on the Purchase campus. For her, college was a place to expand her intellectual passions. Education and diversity enhanced her perceptions about spirituality, but she was content to remain a solitary Witch.

"College students are drawn to Wicca for a number of reasons," she said. "I minor in women's studies, and so I think Wicca is em-powering women because it embraces the feminine principles of the divine, which is something that many people aren't used to. Through Wicca women can speak their true voices. Students see it as making sense. Organized religion has less appeal to us today. They don't have all the answers and all of the dogma is spoon-fed to us. It doesn't allow us to be ourselves. So I feel that Wicca is big among college students because it's a very accepting religion. No one cares what you look like or where you came from. Wicca not only lets students and young adults *be* who they are, it lets them *find* who they are. There's no belief in destiny. You really can find your own path."

Diana did not dorm on campus, but she was outspoken about the rights of college Witches everywhere.

"I dormed when I was at FIT," she said. "There was the usual policy about no candles or incense, but I knew a lot of students who did rituals in their rooms anyway. I think that's a basic right. The university administrations all over the country should give us more credit 'cause those Witches who are serious about practice are going to do it anyway. An argument is absolutely relevant. How are students who live on campus supposed to observe Samhain or any other Wiccan holy day? Personally, I don't have that problem because I live at home now, but I still take off October 31st. I don't come to class. That's my New Year. It's a religious holiday for me. Every-body else gets to celebrate *their* New Year, so why shouldn't I. Why shouldn't all the other college Witches?"

In fact, Diana often made it a point to tell her professors that during Samhain, her courses and assignments take second place.

"I've never had a problem with any of my professors here at Purchase," she told me. "I just explain it in a very educated way. Wicca is recognized by the Constitution, and I have my rights. Col-leges and universities should be doing more to help the Witches and Pagans on campuses, but I do think we have to take it into our own hands. We can't just expect our schools to say, 'So you're a Witch? Well come on in and do whatever you want!' We need to make our voices heard as Witches before the administration lays down laws and prohibits certain things. Activism is part of the Wiccan philosophy."

Like many college Witches, Diana believed she was "called" to the Goddess.

"I think the experience is different for everyone," she said. "Some people are called to be Witches because they truly feel a connection to the divine. Other people explore Wicca and realize that there's nothing else like it. I was called because I felt comforted, and I also felt linked to the feminine psyche. It can be the same for men. When we talk about the divine, I think of a pure, radiant white light, and from that come the Goddess and God. It's a universal source of energy."

Today, Diana juggles her time between courses, work, and Wiccan practice. She told me that she considers herself a solitary but sometimes joins in on rituals with a women's group. She is an eclectic Witch. A few years of solid study—and very cool parents—have shaped her spiritual knowledge positively.

"I see myself as a Witch," she said. "But I also see myself exploring spirituality in deeper ways, through myself and through the divine. Wicca is the beginning of a journey. I'm very glad that I found this path because it's defined and yet very open to new possibilities. I know that Wicca will help me in every area of my life—from the rest of my college and graduate school years to my career."

Letters for the Goddess: *The Witches Write*

In addition to meetings, telephone conversations, attendance at campus rituals, and online chats, a number of students from all over the country e-mailed me their views, opinions, and personal stories. They told me about magick and ritual, transformations and transgressions. Many contacted me and offered to answer questions about college Wicca as well. In turn, I asked what I thought were the most probing questions. In many instances, I encouraged students to simply write what they felt about Wicca, the Goddess and God, and magick. What follows is a sampling of the most absorbing letters.

ARADIUS, MIDDLE TENNESSEE STATE UNIVERSITY

Dear Anthony,

Well, I was brought up in a Church of Christ household. During high school, I met a girl who soon became my best friend, and who was involved with Wicca. My immediate reaction was that Witchcraft and anything to do with it was Satanic, so we left the issue of religion untouched. Though my views on Witchcraft remained the same for a while, I became increasingly curious about psychic phenomena. I would occupy my afternoons going to a local bookstore and flipping through the books on that very subject. Of course, such books are found in the New Age section alongside those about Wicca and Paganism. Well, my curiosity got the better of me and I eventually caved in and bought my first book on Witchcraft. I started learning as much as I could about the subject and finally realized that it had nothing to do with Satanism. That was the latter part of my sophomore year in high school.

During my junior year, I began reading books about the Strega Tradition of Wicca. And though I probably do not have a drop of Italian blood in me, Strega called to me. Ever since, I have followed an eclectic version of Strega. I prefer making my own rituals, from the heart, to better connect with Deity. Now I am a sophomore at Middle Tennessee State and I am still very strong in my Wiccan beliefs. However, I attended Lipscomb University my freshman year, a Church of Christ school in Nashville, because of my parents' wishes. And no, my parents do not know I am Pagan. My mother once found books about Witchcraft and my Tarot decks in a drawer at home and when she confronted me, I just told her that it was a phase and I no longer dealt with it. That was a few years ago. Because my mother still supports me, I do not want to cross her any more than I already have—she knows that I'm gay and abhors even that. Knowing that I have totally abandoned Christianity would probably kill her. My father died when I was twelve, and his only

SPOTLIGHT

Kallisti, University of North Carolina, Chapel Hill
www.unc.edu/student/orgs/Kallisti

Kallisti prides itself on being the first student-run Pagan organization in the United States. According to their Web site, the organization began several years ago and has existed under many names. Today, it is comprised of a fair number of students who meet on a weekly basis—undergraduates, those in medical and law school, even those curious about alternative spirituality. Their site lists the group's officers, as well as the mythological meaning behind their name.

Tamastry, a student who identified herself by her Witch name, attended a number of the Kallisti meetings but decided against becoming an active member because of her solitary preferences. She described the group as "enlightening and very focused."

"There is a lot of meaningful and intellectual discussion about the Wiccan and Pagan path," she said. "Students really come together and blend their beliefs. The group is open to just about anyone. At some of the meetings I attended, I met students who weren't Wiccan at all but who were just curious about what it meant. There was a lot of support. The other great aspect is that the Student Pagan Association here at Chapel Hill really has a history. It has been around for a long time. It has changed hands and gone through different names, but the mission has always remained the same—to act as a gathering place for college Witches and Pagans, to enrich its members intellectually, and to offer the public the correct information about what Wicca is."

wishes for me and my brother were that we grow up to be good Christian men.

Putting my family aside, I am very open about my beliefs, but only to those who ask me. Yes, I do wear a pentacle occasionally in public, but it is not for the attention. It's for the same reason Christians wear their crosses, because of what it represents to them on a personal, spiritual level. I do not make proud boasts to the masses about how Christianity is wrong and preach about my Pagan beliefs, because none of that is needed. I believe that everyone has a path to follow, and if someone chooses Christianity as their path and they can spiritually evolve because of it, I'm all for it. Likewise to any other religious path (but I do not support religious paths that hinder spiritual growth, like Satanism). It's sad because many Witches and Pagans develop a sort of hatred for Christians because of the ancient past—the Burning Times, the Inquisition. This hatred is pointless and really goes against many traditions of Wicca that accept all paths that lead to the divine. Those people I really don't consider Pagan. As for my campus, Middle Tennessee is a very accepting atmosphere. Being both gay and Pagan, this is a very comfortable place for me because the school has organizations for both. I have yet to meet anyone who dares to just start preaching at me, which happened a lot at Lipscomb University.

Practicing Wicca in a dorm room . . . quite terrible actually. One of the rules is no burning candles or incense. However, if the residential advisor lets smoking marijuana and cigarettes pass on our floor, I do not feel at all bad about burning a candle or some incense (which actually helps the smell of sloppy boys!). Also, there is a rule about no weapons, but every other guy has a pocket knife he waves around to look butch or macho. And so again, I don't feel bad about having a small athame, which I only take out on the nights of the Full Moon. It's hard, though, because a lot of people probably aren't as daring as I am, but then again, I don't openly display my rituals. I also don't practice large stylized rituals. The rituals usually come about from my heart as I connect with Deity and become more like a meaningful prayer. That much I can do in silence. I'll be thrilled when I have my own place, where my rituals will be more elaborate. But living in a dorm teaches one very important lesson: that religion must come from the heart first. Only then will a path be truly fulfilling.

Bright Blessings,
Aradius

In subsequent letters, Aradius expressed his desire to one day write for a living. He currently pens poems and short stories and maintains his own Web page at www.geocities.com/aradius13.

MINDY, WASHINGTON COLLEGE, ST. LOUIS, MISSOURI

Dear Anthony,

To answer your questions, the Pagan/Wiccan scene at Washington College was always a fairly strong underground family, but it didn't really knit together and become more public until my junior year. I was approached by a fellow student after a Writers Union meeting at the Graveyard who asked if I wanted to join the newly formed Pagan club. I have to say that I was rather surprised. Up until that point I thought there were only a few people on campus who knew I practiced magick, but as it turned out, my reputation preceded me in a lot of my classes. The group met regularly and had discussions, banded together, and had a good time. Since then they have done a few ritual gatherings. I wasn't a real member of the group because of my fears, I guess.

If I have experienced any discrimination, I would say thus far it has been self-inflicted. What I mean by that is quite simple—back at Washington College I wasn't a member of the Student Pagan Organization because by the time it had formed I was a resident assistant and in charge of a whole floor of students. I was suddenly very careful about my religious beliefs, and it was a rare day when I would wear my pentacle in public. I was afraid if a student had a problem with me, my religious practices would be used against me and that students would tell their parents to complain to the school. Washington College was a liberal place, but I was afraid it wouldn't be liberal enough.

Here at Miami University I am immersed in a VERY strong Christian population. I'm not even sure if there's a Pagan club here, and I certainly don't know anyone who is Pagan. Because of that, I'm even more self-conscious, especially because now I am a teacher. Over the course of my first semester as a teacher, I've learned through students' reactions, papers, and class discussions that there are quite a few die-hard Christians in my class, and just like I felt when I was a resident assistant in college, I fear now that if a student was to take an issue with a grade I handed down, he or she would use my religious beliefs as an opportunity to cause a scene, which I can't afford.

I think the up and coming generation—our generation—has seen more love in the world than previous generations ever have experienced. I think this allows them, especially college students, to feel safe about turning inward and examining themselves instead of worrying about the world. And through self-exploration, I think people are finding that the traditional religious paths aren't satisfying the current needs. And so many turn to Wicca.

Finding my own way to Wicca is kind of an interesting story. The first spirit I ever saw was when I was five years old. I was chanting my own simple spells when I was eight, and when I was just twelve I began dreaming of the future. By the time I was fifteen I had read up on all sorts of magickal paths, and I knew it was my path. So in a way, I was raised magickally—but not by my parents. I was led by my will and the spirits who guided me . . .

Cheers,

Mindy

SEAMUS, BOSTON UNIVERSITY

Dear Anthony,

I became interested in Paganism and Wicca when I researched the religion at the public library one day. I found information on Hinduism and thought that it was amazing and that Christianity was really lacking. Then I found Wicca, and all of a sudden I had a name for most of the things I had believed on my own without having learned them from someone else (a.k.a. Catholic school). I felt as if I found home. I also read Mists of Avalon *by Marion Zimmer Bradley, and I found exactly what I had always hoped for and believed a religion should be.*

Initially, my parents were not pleased. I was informed a number of times that I was still and would always be a Catholic. My father threatened to desecrate my altar by throwing it out the window. I was asked repeatedly if I was Jewish, was even told I was practicing Judaism because I was lighting candles in my room. It was rather tough. But they got over it eventually. They don't discuss it now. I was informed the other week by my aunt that I am still Catholic, which unsettled me, but I know it was because she simply couldn't conceive of the possibility of my being anything else. Most of my relatives don't know, though I don't hide it.

I practice solitary, as well as with a group. I am not in a coven. I live in an apartment so I have no dorm regulations whatsoever to

---

HOW DO YOU *ROCK THE GODDESS?*

Kitt, freshman
SUNY Purchase College, Purchase, New York

"After I completed my first semester of college, I went home for January break and decided to do something meaningful for Yule. Throughout that holiday season, I volunteered at a soup kitchen and at an inner city children's center. It was an amazing experience. I saw nature in a totally new light and it had nothing to do with the elements or the landscape. This was nature from a human perspective—the desperation, the fear, and even the incredible hope. It was another reminder that we're all linked by the same things, and that the Goddess is alive in anyone who chooses to recognize her. Practicing Wicca is, for me, all about giving back to the world to make it a better place. Not just environmentally, but with human interaction. I don't get to know people; I get to know *souls.* That's magick."

---

worry about. Though when I was in a dorm, I blatantly violated the rules to practice my faith. I lit candles and burned incense at my rites without worrying about anything. As far as Wicca goes, my friend Donna is a role model to me. She lives her faith. She owns a psychic studio, where I work on weekends, and she's amazingly psychic. That is also something I'd love to have as a part of my life, though it's proven difficult.

As for who I am as a Witch . . .

I am a Witch in that I practice Witchcraft when I do magick. I am Wiccan in that I embrace the theology of Wicca and incorporate it into my practice of Witchcraft. I am Pagan because I am Wiccan and because I honor divinity as imminent within Earth. I believe in Deity as manifest through a Goddess and a God, who each reveal themselves to us under thousands of names and faces, in a myriad of ways and forms. I am reverent toward other forms of spirituality and faiths and seek only tolerance for my own. My spiritual aspirations are to become an instrument of Deity to help others find their own spirituality, and to help them express it in a positive and benevolent manner. I aspire to be a resource for others who are searching for their own spiritual path, as well as those who tread a path similar to my own. I aspire to embody the loving and nurturing aspects of the gods in my own life and in the relationships I have with others. I also wish to bring knowledge of Wicca, Paganism, and Witchcraft to the forefront of our society so that others may be comfortable with those who practice our ways.

In Love, Light, and Laughter,
Seamus M. McKeon

· 4 ·

Magick and Ritual
Where It Begins

In darkness, the drums beat like a wild heart, and the steady pummel gives way to chanting. Bare feet dig into the sandy ground. Candlelight flickers in the corner of the room, a wave of yellow that drowns out the shadows and ebbs the altar. It sits in the center of the consecrated space. Flower petals cover one end; a jug filled with water sits on the other. Those who have gathered are young and old, black and white, male and female. They are Witches, priests, and priestesses of Voodoo, shamans from various Native American tribes. Religion is secondary to the intended goal. The worship of Earth has no specific affiliation, and ritual belongs to every creed and culture.

On this, the eve of the Summer Solstice, the group has joined forces to honor the birth of the God. For the moment, daytime and nighttime are equal, but soon the Sun will reign supreme in the heavens. Blessed light. It is the season of fruit and bounty. It is the time that augurs a renewed sense of life and passion. Earth, having slept through the long winter months, is now ready for a rebirth.

A woman dressed in white moves to the center of the circle. Following the rhythm of the drums, her body jerks and bounces beside the altar. She wraps her hands around the jug of water and, praising it as a symbol of the ocean, lifts it above her head. "Hail to Macomba," she cries out. "Goddess of sea! We give honor!" She

115

dances clockwise, pausing before a young man holding a ritual dagger in his fingers. Together they drift back toward the altar. The cadence of the drums is furious. The young man freezes, looks up, and with his dagger carves a pentegram on the air. "We honor the elements of Earth and the Spirit of the divine!" he shouts. He turns to glance at the woman. She is trembling in the immediacy of the moment, a soul possessed.

Others come forward. They scoop the flower petals from the altar and sprinkle them across the ground. An elderly man utters a prayer before dropping a handful of seeds at his feet. "We honor the God," someone says. "He who is known as Apollo, Pan, Hermes, Zeus, and by many other names . . . come into our circle now! Grant us health. Grant us union with the universal forces that are your guides! Come!"

The drummer—his face covered by a red mask, his head adorned with deer antlers—stands and walks forward. He pauses. There is silence. A collective breath pierces the air. They listen as the candle flames crackle and a soft wind stirs.

"Now!"

The drum is struck—a single, deafening boom. Something moves but everyone remains still.

The woman in white holds out the jug of water, uncaps it. "May our knowledge flow like the boundless oceans of the earth," she says, pouring the water over the sandy ground and the scattered seeds. "May the power of our minds grow like the sweet bounty of the earth."

The drums resume their chilling beat. Arms outstretched, the men and women dance and pull at the sky, summoning the forces of a new dawn.

Magick: The Source of Power

All religions hinge on the supernatural. In Buddhism, the Bodhisattva is a being who holds the power to alter or postpone nirvana for those that remain in the wheel of rebirth. The once-banned Huna tradition of Hawaii partakes greatly of the psychic realm. Roman Catholicism is overflowing with the supernatural as well. Mary, the mother of Jesus Christ, conceived of the Holy Spirit after being visited by the archangel Gabriel. Apparitions of the Virgin Mary and countless saints continue into the present day. Is not prayer and deep meditation a facet of supernatural? If an occurrence cannot be explained through "rational" or wholly scientific methods, it is subject to a supernatural label.

In Wicca, all that the ordinary person would quickly deem supernatural is, in fact, perceived as natural. This means that what cannot be explained is simply attributed to the vast and powerful universal forces that govern existence. Herein lies the Witch's power. Magick is the practice of Witchcraft—the physical and mental doing of one's action or will. Casting a spell is akin to saying a prayer or novena. It begins in the inner sanctum of the mind and heart, a kernel of desire to take a certain situation and make it better. Maybe you want to improve your health. Maybe your love life needs some serious resuscitation. Your finances might be balancing the bankruptcy line. A common need for college Witches is the improvement of grades or study habits. Whatever the case, magick is there to help. But it is not as easy as chanting a few words and lighting a candle. Quite the contrary, magick requires great skill and concentration and frequently takes several years of study to master.

It is very likely that the notion of magick sparked your initial interests in Wicca. This means that your mind is open to new possibilities. It also means that you must make yourself aware of what magick is in Wicca, and of what it can and cannot do. Jumping headfirst into a spell or ritual can be disappointing and very dangerous. At the very least, ask yourself what you think a concise definition of magick truly is. Start your interrogation on the surface and slowly work your way down.

First, peruse the obvious. Witches practice magick—spells, Moon and solar rituals, herbalism, the making of amulets, talismans, and "poppets" (small dolls or figures), and varying forms of alchemy. The Goddess and God and other deities are invoked for specific purposes. Special tools are also employed in the casting of a spell: an *athame* or ritual dagger, and pouches of felt and velvet that contain charms, oils, and scented water. When a Witch does magick, he or she invokes the gods. This means to call forth from within. The energy that will ultimately propel your magick is already inside you, flowing like the blood in your veins. Once you harness this energy, it is subservient to your will.

Delve a little deeper. Think of the mind—it is limitless and uncharted and your greatest tool. We have all experienced the power of psychology. Remember that class you thought you were going to flunk? The very mention of the words "summer session" frightened you into submission, so you crammed and made yourself understand the foreign material in your notes and textbooks. And then you aced the final and passed with flying colors. You joined the debate club because you were attracted to a certain someone, then realized a bit too late that it was your turn to speak in front of fifty people. You were spooked, but buckled down and presented your argument like a professional orator. These aren't examples of "magick" by most standards, but they offer a glimpse of the mind's power and its place in the magick of Wicca. The mind builds the bridge to the land of great results. When preparing for a spell or ritual, you must be in the proper frame of mind. Meditation is the key, but so is confidence. A Witch does not begin a spell thinking that the deities will do all the work. As a Witch, you have to raise the energy that will attract the deities. Think of it this way: if the party is loud and funky enough, the whole campus will show up at your dorm begging entrance. Focusing your mind means attuning yourself to the task at hand. Relax. Concentrate. Don't be afraid to scale new heights. You are, after all, working within the realm of your own body.

Science actually plays a significant role in magick. The Moon is the symbol of the Goddess, but it is also a potent universal force. The tides are determined by the Moon's phases. A woman's body mirrors those same phases via the process of menstruation. Ask a farmer about the Moon and he'll educate you on the growth of crops and topsoil. Police officers and emergency room employees know that when the Moon is full, their workloads increase. Lunar influence is a fact all over the world. The Moon is an authority not to be underestimated or shunned. It has a current, a pull, an intense verve. It affects the mind. Witches know this firsthand. When the Moon is waxing or on the increase, energy is building to a summit. This tends to attract good fortune and positive strengths. When the Moon is waning, or decreasing, magick is used for banishing or the expulsion of negativity. The bottom line is simple: the Moon is more than just a rock in the sky; it controls the oceans and countless other "earthly" functions. It is nothing short of preposterous to perceive ourselves as somehow beyond its grasp. Smart people—that means Witches—use this to their advantage.

Now put it all together. You have the mystical. You have the mental. You have the scientific. Blend these into a hot little threesome and you have the basics of magick.

Magick: A Warning

Early in my college career, I met a young woman who seemed to know all about Wicca. She and I would embark on long and stimulating conversations that began with pre-Christian Europe and would culminate with which covens were holding open circles the following Friday. She proudly proclaimed herself a Witch. She wore a pentacle and scrawled the names of various goddesses inside the covers of her notebooks. I thought she was well informed about magick, too. One day, however, we were standing outside the Tenth Avenue building where John Jay College of Criminal Justice is located when she pointed to a guy sitting on the steps nearby. He was a blond jock, and the object of her affection. My Witch-friend had tried to get his attention via the normal route, but had yet to experience any success. She told me that at the next Full Moon she was going to cast a love spell over him. It struck me as an injustice. I warned her of the possible negative side effects, then left her alone to her intentions. When I ran into her a few weeks later, she had quite a story to tell. After casting the spell, she waited for the blond jock to jump her bones in between classes. When he finally did approach her, he was anything but polite. He told her to stop following him, to quit making cute comments when he walked by, and to stop eyeing him in the chemistry lab. The guy explained that he had a girlfriend and wasn't interested in someone else's coy little winks. I listened to the story and was not at all surprised.

One of the rules of magick is never to interfere with another person's will. You may be a Witch who has tapped into a font of churning energy, but using it unwisely will only get you burned. Love spells seem to attract this bit of advice quite frequently. There's nothing wrong or unnatural about wanting affection, companionship, or some good sex. Wicca can certainly open the doors to all of these, but one has to go about attainment with an informed hand. College Witches are often guilty of this abuse of power. At any point in the semester, we all come under stress and restlessness. We all want to speed up the process or lessen the daily grind. And sometimes we turn to magick as an easy outlet. *Oh, what the hell. Who's it gonna hurt? What's the big deal? I can do this without bringing myself any negative vibes.* When the impatient thoughts creep into your brain, think twice.

David, a sophomore at the University of Arizona, offered an interesting example of a spell gone awry when I contacted him just after Samhain 2001. "I was nearing that flat-out broke point and I really needed some money," he said. "I waited for the Waxing Moon and then went about collecting my tools. I was home that weekend, and I picked a green candle and used some scented oil to anoint it. I really concentrated on my objective, but I didn't get specific enough. I just said, 'I need money and let it come to me as soon as possible.' Well, about two weeks later, my car was stolen. It was insured for full blue-book value and I got more money than I needed, but it wasn't the way in which I had hoped it would come. I guess I was a little hasty, and I didn't project the right images into the spell. So you have to be careful. I learned my lesson about the power of magick then and there."

On the flip side, a Witch from Marymount College in Tarrytown,

New York, told me of her very positive experience when casting a healing spell. Jenna's brother, an athlete, had shattered his knee while playing football and was recovering at home. He was depressed and out of sorts. Jenna decided to send him some restorative energy when the Moon was waning. "I sketched a picture of him and identified his problem area, drawing a big X over his right knee," she explained. "I used a purple candle, and I transferred my own healing energy to him. Then I worked at banishing his depression and what I believed was some plain bad luck. He got better, and within a few days he was cheerful again." She went on to illustrate how the spell also worked in her favor. "I have a degenerative respiratory disorder that usually acts up at the end of summer and the beginning of fall, when ragweed is in season. My allergies go nuts. After casting that spell, though, nothing debilitating hit me. I breezed through the season without so much as a doctor's visit. I attribute that to my own energy and the spell's return effect."

It has been said that being a Witch can bring about wonderful spiritual gifts. This is absolutely true. But being a Witch also carries a price. Magick is beneficial, yet it also holds the potential for danger. Remember that you are cinching a vital, powerful, and very real source of energy. There is no room for error or selfish endeavor. When performing any magick or ritual, the Threefold Law must remain at the forefront of your intentions. Simply put, whatever energy a Witch sends into the universe returns with three times the initial intensity. That spell you cast to turn the folks in Financial Aid into squealing pigs may result in some unsightly weight gain. The burning candle meant to come between your boyfriend and his new best buddy will shatter a few of your own personal ties. By the same token, if you cast a healing spell for an ill relative, your own health is bound to improve. Focusing your energy on good fortune for another will bring mounds of luck into your own life. Magick is a two-way street. Follow the crosswalk and you'll be fine.

THE LAWS OF MAGICK

1. Responsibility: Before diving into the magickal realm, take a moment to ground yourself. Sit down and, alone, sketch out the details. What is your spell or ritual all about? Why are you utilizing your time and energy to do it? If your magick is meant for someone else, make certain that you are not interfering with that person's will. Be responsible about the whole process. Check the proper Moon phases and, if you wish, the proper astrological correspondences. Casting a spell or doing a ritual in the wrong Moon phase can produce no results or a result that completely opposes your intention. It is also important to ask yourself a few important questions. Are you prepared to work magick of this particular magnitude? Are you feeling well, both physically and mentally? Another issue, indigenous only to college students, is that of safety and regulation within a controlled setting. The overwhelming majority of colleges and universities require that students sign a contract with the Office of Residence of Life upon moving into a dormitory or campus apartment. Embedded within this contract is a little clause that prohibits you from burning candles or incense. While it is true that college Witches sometimes violate these rules, any and all should exercise caution when doing so. Do not leave candles burning unattended, and go easy on that incense. Exposure can carry a hefty price: fines, suspension, even expulsion. Here, responsibility and the practice of magick is a two-sided issue. Be responsible with your actions and within your setting.

2. Respect: The Goddess and God—or any other deity—demand true and utmost respect from those who invoke them. Once you have begun a spell or ritual, see it through to the very end, and maintain your levels of concentration and meditation. Do not take any deity for granted, and never try bargaining with the gods. Always ask the Goddess and God, as well as the elements, to guard your rite and neutralize any negativity. It is also important to offer your gratitude upon completion of the spell or ritual. The old adage certainly applies here: if you want respect, you have to give it.

3. Self-Assurance: Performing any new spell or ritual is a lot like facing a new experience. Remember how you felt the first day of classes? You didn't know anyone. You got lost in the Humanities building. You were afraid to ask your roommate to stop playing his or her music so loud. Eventually, you overcame these obstacles. You were confident and self-assured enough to speak your thoughts, admit your own sense of loss or confusion, and find the right alternative. With a self-assured mind is the only way to begin a spell or ritual. If you have even the slightest twinge of fear or doubt, hold off. If you are perplexed about a specific Moon phase or deity, research it accordingly. Self-assurance gives way to relaxation and stable concentration. Magick can be fatiguing, but raising energy will be easier and more beneficial if your conviction is grounded and secure. Take whatever action you deem necessary. If you generally feel better after a workout and a shower, get to it. If you need a cup of coffee and a walk, don't hesitate to do both. We all have different ways of solidifying our sense of confidence and self-worth, spiritually, physically, and intellectually. Take your steps and don't look back.

The Wheel of the Year: Rituals in Motion

Birth. Death. Rebirth. This is the cycle of Earth and of the seasons. It has been so since the dawn of time. The midsummer Sun blazes intensely before weakening in autumn's grip. Then the light wanes and leaves crackle underfoot. The air goes clean and cold, welcoming in the night. Silence. Darkness. There is a pall in the atmosphere. And then the buds sprout from the ground. The grass unfurls in waves of green and a soft, fragrant wind brings in the spring. Earth is reborn.

The seasons are a reminder of the natural magick that lives in the atmosphere at all times. The images beyond the window may change, but nothing is ever lost completely. Thus, Witches turn the "Wheel of the Year," mirroring the seasons as they spin on Earth's axis. A ritual is a celebration, a vibrant passage that connects the human psyche to the divine. At each of the Wheel's eight points, Witches honor the Goddess and God in their ever-changing aspects. Colleges and universities all over the country have held public and private rituals at these times. On large campuses, students utilize space and usher in the semester come September, the traditional Witches' harvest feast. In April, the holiday of Beltane is commemorated with the popular spring "maypole" dances. Like every other religion, Wicca has its reverent days. Some Witches party in covens, or at large festivals. Others are content with solitary praise. The turning of the Wheel of the Year is both humbling and exhilarating. With each new ritual, a Witch learns the importance of Earth and its relation to the human mind and body.

SAMHAIN: THE NEW YEAR

Of all the Witches' holidays, Samhain is by far the most significant—and the most misunderstood. It is celebrated on October 31. For Witches, this day has nothing to do with its more popular counterpart, Halloween. Samhain is the traditional Celtic New Year, a time for self-examination and goals of change. Here, a Witch seeks to better him- or herself physically, emotionally, and spiritually. Earth is also undergoing transformations: the darkness is strong, the last of the crops have died, the pleasant chill is replaced by the frigid cold. This is synonymous with the notion of death. As the God, old and wise but nonetheless done with his journey, descends into the Underworld, he takes with him all his knowledge. And so it is an ending.

Samhain is also a somber occasion for Witches because it is when they remember and honor their lost loved ones. As the day draws closer to the midnight hour, the veil between the spirit world and the world of form thins dramatically. The dead are nearby. The dead speak. Rituals are usually held at night, and psychic channeling is frequently employed as a means of honor and homage. A Witch recalls with vivid intensity how others have touched his or her own life. And so Samhain is as much a time for celebrating as it is for reflection, redirection, gratitude, and veneration. Death has reached the threshold, but in another room waits the promise of blessed rebirth.

YULE: THE WINTER SOLSTICE

On the longest night of the year (December 21), the God begins his rebirth into Earth's dark heart. Following this day, light starts to wax little by little. Much like the traditional Christian holiday of Christmas, Yule calls for holly and mistletoe, trees and wreaths. Witches bring the natural environment into their homes. Following ritual celebrations, they often exchange gifts as symbols of the good hope and fortune to come. The Goddess has also bequeathed gifts on Earth, most especially in the form of the Sun. At Yule, Witches make preparations for the coming season of light.

IMBOLC: THE SUN IS BORN

Celebrated on February 2, Imbolc honors the God as a young deity, a fresh and fair child whose light is maturing. The Goddess, his new mother, is preparing to welcome him to Earth, full of strength and warmth. The days are filled with a sort of restless longing during this time of year—winter is far from over but spring is within sight. We yearn for that comfortable breeze, that polished blue sky. Common rituals revolve around the cultivation of herbs, plants, and flowers. Seeds are consigned to the ground. Garden landscapes are prepared with great care. A Witch "germinates" his or her ideas and goals.

OSTARA: SPRING EQUINOX

The Goddess and God are still young within the Wheel, but they continue to grow in union with the Sun's light. March 21 marks the first official day of spring. It is the time of fertility and true renewal. Earth is reawakening, blooming, breathing in the sweet air of life. Wiccan rituals reflect the joyous nature of the day and time of year. There is a discernible shift in the patterns of light, and covens and solitaries alike often give praise at sunset, when the horizon is colorful and wide. Seeds, plants, and gardens are again brought to attention. With the newest buds beginning to form, Witches are reminded of their own heightened spirituality.

BELTANE: LAND OF PLENTY

Spring is in full swing on or about May 1. The weather is warm and inviting and the daylight hours are prolonged. The nights are soothing. The God is exploding into manhood at this time of year, flexing his muscles and his virility. The Goddess has joined him in partnership, in a sort of celestial marriage that produces a bounty of good things. Growth is everywhere. The most common Wiccan ritual is the dance of the Maypole—a fun, roaring, and sometimes riotous dance around a large pole. The circle is representative of the Goddess and her womb; the pole, of course, is the phallic symbol of the God.

SUMMER SOLSTICE: RAY OF LIGHT

June 21, the longest day of the year, sees Earth thriving with life. The grass is green. The oceans and the seas are blue. Flowers blossom in gardens, along roadsides, on rooftops. Just as the summer season begins to peak, so too do we see the Goddess and God at the pinnacle of their magical union. The Sun—the power of light—has triumphed. While many view this as the start of summer because of rising temperatures, it is in fact an ending: from this point on, daylight wanes minute by minute. Wiccan ritual generally calls for the worship of the element of Fire. Symbolizing the Sun's heat, the Fire also mirrors the most powerful moment in the journey shared by the Goddess and God.

LAMMAS: THE FIRST HARVEST

It may seem a bit early to think of cool temperatures and golden leaves (August 2), but this Wiccan holiday marks the start of the autumn harvest. The Wheel of the Year has almost completed its full turn. Here, the God is weakening along with the Sun. He is moving away from the Goddess and preparing for his journey back into the Underworld. He is fully aware, of course, that he will be reborn again come Yule, but this sees a letting go of the light. Earth once again spins toward a term of necessary darkness and death. While Witches keep that point in mind, they celebrate the enormous bounty of good that comes with this time of year: fruits, vegetables, and grains. In ritual, they begin to give thought to the imminent end and take note of their spiritual transformations.

MABON: THE FULL HARVEST

Come September 21, we begin to feel the first fingers of autumn pinching at the sky. The equinox sees day- and nighttime hours balancing out on equal scales. The God draws closer to death and the underworld as the Goddess reluctantly releases him. The cycle has slowed down, and though it will never stop spinning, there is a definite deliberation in the Wheel. The last of the great harvest is upon us, and Wiccan ritual calls for a celebration of the past and the present as well as the future. What have you learned? What do you hope to know? What will you impart? And so the Wheel of the Year spins on . . .

THE MAGICK BOX: INSIDE A WITCH'S TOOL DRAWER

One uses various tools when casting a spell or performing any kind of ritual. The following list has been tailored for the college Witch. Before beginning, however, it is important that you understand the meaning behind the much-used word "consecration." When a Witch consecrates tools or other magickal objects, he or she usually cleanses and mentally "charges" them. This means imbuing an athame or candle with your own personal essence. Every one of us holds a specific touch or feel or scent; directing the essence of your person onto a magickal tool will enhance any spell or ritual.

Once you have decided on your tools, sit in a quiet place, gather them in your hands one by one, and begin meditating. Simple visualization techniques work best. Mentally raise energy until you feel heat permeating your palms. What is the purpose of this object? Will it be used to adorn your altar or will you carry it with you as a charm or amulet? Your intention is important. After consecrating your tools, put them away in a clean, special place. You will only be using them for magick or ritual.

THE ALTAR

It is quite common to find a Witch's altar in a room of his or her home. It may be a small table occupying a corner, decorated with fresh flowers, a pentagram, and scented candles. Some are elaborate. Others are simple. There is no set way to build a Wiccan altar, and it all depends on your preferences. The altar is a sacred place. It is your focal point when performing magick or rituals. It is your sanctuary, a shelter for your spiritual hopes and dreams. In the privacy of your own home or bedroom, you might be able to arrange an altar as you see fit, but if you are living in a dorm room or campus apartment, free rein isn't always a possibility. Space can be an issue. Desks are small and cramped, and you will have to move objects around when settling in for a night of homework or studying. Your roommate might not be keen on the idea of an altar, either. Whatever the obstacle, don't be discouraged. There are always alternatives.

Many college students go to great lengths in constructing the perfect altar. A popular method is to build the altar only when you need it, simply but sincerely. To do this, take a regular shoe box or a small block of wood. Drape a sheet or cloth—even a pillow case—over it. The pentagram is an important symbol; you may have one, purchased from a store or occult shop. If not, draw one on a piece of cardboard and laminate it. Jewelry can work too. Instead of wearing it, place it on the altar. Arrange your other tools around the pentagram—dabs of salt, a cup of water, leaves or flowers that represent a season. Feathers or Native American dream-catchers are often used to symbolize the element of Air. Stones do the same for the element of Earth. The element of Fire is usually depicted by the burning of candles, but again, certain rules may restrict you from lighting them. The solution? Think metaphorically: a piece of charcoal, a lighter, or matchbook—even an unlit votive candle can work. A fellow classmate of mine at Purchase College lived in an apartment that permitted smoking; she lit cigarettes when performing rituals to symbolize the element of Fire.

If you have a spare bookshelf in your room, it too can act as a makeshift altar. In truth, any flat surface can be arranged and decorated accordingly. The altar is a reminder of your spirituality. When you sit, kneel, or stand before it, you are pledging allegiance to the Goddess and God.

THE ATHAME

Sometimes called a ritual blade, the athame is technically a double-edged knife. In ritual, it is used for the "cutting" of the air or the drawing of pentagrams; its phallic shape also acts as a symbol of the masculine. Oftentimes, the athame is inserted into the chalice of water or wine, which represents the female. While harmless, you may be up against yet another rule if you live in a dorm room or campus apartment. Many colleges and universities prohibit students from possessing any kind of "weapon," and the resident assistant may catch a glance of your athame and deem it illicit. The solution? Think metaphorically: a letter opener on your desk can be used instead of a traditional athame. Other options include a thick chunk of branch or bark, a hollowed pen, or sharpened sketch pencil. It may seem inadequate at first, but any consecrated object will work in conjunction with a focused spell or ritual.

THE BOWL

Small amounts of salt, soil, sand, water, or herbs can be deposited in a bowl and then set upon your altar. It can be ceramic or glass, copper or metal. In desperate times, Styrofoam bowls—from the four-star, Zagat-praised dining hall—can be used as well. The bowl is representative of the Goddess—the womb of the divine, the wellspring of the earth. What you put in the bowl will vary in meaning. Salt is always used to cleanse and purify. Water, soil, or sand can represent Earth. You may be employing herbs in your magick. Consecrate the bowl you have selected, and if you plan on reusing it, make certain to wash it out after the spell or ritual is completed.

CRYSTALS, STONES, AND GEMS

Clear quartz crystals have long been regarded as magickal; their beauty is ethereal, and people all over the world utilize them as good-luck charms, healing amulets, and for protection. The amethyst stone is linked with meditation and serenity. The shiny gray of the hematite fosters tranquillity and is reputed to cleanse the blood. Gems hold similar properties. It is always favorable to have at least one crystal, stone, or gem on your altar or in your pocket. When working magick or ritual, they are visually appealing and can be applied to aid you in a spell.

THE MIRROR

The practicing Witch knows that a mirror is not merely a tool for reflection. Once charged and consecrated, a mirror will help you see beyond the surface image. It is a tool for scrying and divination. It is also a gateway to the self: immersed in ritual, the gods will show you the inner workings of the psyche through the mirror. Size and shape do not matter so long as you use the mirror solely for magickal purposes.

THE NEEDLE AND THREAD

Pouches or small bags made of felt or velvet can be powerful tools. It is best to fashion one by hand, from scratch. Witches fill the pouches with herbs, stones, crystals, or other personal items—locks of hair, collected coins, trinkets of jewelry. Once you sew the bag together, decide its purpose. A love pouch, for example, may contain rose petals and a verse written to the goddess Aphrodite. Good fortune is summoned by way of clovers, an ankh, and aventurine. A protection pouch can be filled with salt, a lock of hair, a small pentacle. They are placed on altars or carried. The needle and thread are an important part of any Witch's magickal toolbox.

INITIATION: Of Different Degrees

In truth, it's a lot like being baptized. Initiation is the experience of rebirth, recognition, and revitalization. It is a rite of passage signifying one's place within a sacred realm. For a Witch, it marks a turning point as both a beginning and, in some ways, an ending. When you choose to be initiated into Wicca, you are telling the Goddess and God that you are eager and ready to accept the knowledge of Earth and the responsibilities of practicing Witchcraft. Undoubtedly, you have spent a great deal of time reading books, surfing the Internet, and speaking with others in your quest to learn as much as you can. The past was an exploration. You might have done so in private, and with initiation you are confirming to the world your desires, goals, and identity. One phase of your spiritual life is over. Another is poised to begin.

The most common way to be initiated is through another Witch, a peer who has been practicing for a number of years and who will act as your mentor. You do not necessarily have to join a coven. A high priestess can choose to bring you into the circle of knowledge and perform the rite. Oftentimes, initiation is rendered through an elaborate ritual. You may be asked to recite the Charge of the Goddess or a personal vow you wrote. It can also depend on the Tradition of Wicca you are pledging yourself to. Gardnerian Witches, for example, favor initiation via the high priestess, while the Strega Tradition allots room for self-created rituals.

Self-initiation is an increasingly popular choice among Witches, especially those in college. It is not supported by all adherents, but again, there is no law or dogma that prohibits or discredits the practice. If you feel more comfortable going at it alone, take ample time to prepare yourself for the experience. Design it as simply or as elaborately as you see fit. You may want to begin with a dedication rite, wherein you stand beneath a Full Moon and vow your devotion to the Goddess and God.

Generally, there are three degrees of initiation.

• The **first degree** is granted by a high priestess or priest about one year after the initiate begins his or her studies. Your time spent studying and learning has merited a promotion. This degree welcomes you into a coven. You are still a student of the magickal arts, but your education has been furthered and your knowledge has deepened.

• The **second degree** may come a year or more later. This marks significant achievements as a Witch. You are now experienced enough to teach and impart your lessons to others.

• With the **third degree** of initiation comes the title of high priestess or priest. Your knowledge is at its pinnacle, but never is it completed or closed off. At this point, many Witches begin forming their own covens. Solitaries run workshops or classes or volunteer their time at festivals.

While searching for college Witches who had undergone formal initiation, I traveled to Salem, Massachusetts. There, I met a young woman who called herself Ceres, a name derived from the Roman goddess of the harvest. Ceres was a senior at Salem State College completing a B.S. in biology. She was raised in Newport, Rhode Island, in reformed Judaism. She chose Salem State because she wanted to be "close to the action and history" of America's Witch-craft past. In fact, she had turned down acceptances from two Ivy League universities to live in Salem.

"When I started reading up about Wicca in high school, I always came across references to Salem," she said. "I took a trip up here when I was seventeen. I couldn't believe my eyes. Everything here is about Wicca and the Salem Witch Trials. I had a hard time meeting someone who *wasn't* a Witch! I knew from back then that this is where I wanted to be."

As a freshman at Salem State, Ceres immediately jumped in to her surroundings. She visited the many occult shops that line Essex Street and began networking. Her roommate was a Witch. So were many of her classmates, and, according to Ceres, one of her profes-sors. She apprenticed herself to an older woman who had been prac-ticing Wicca for twenty years and running her own coven for eight.

"My mentor is a woman who knows everything about Wicca," Ceres said. "She's a hereditary Witch, and her family has been in Salem for decades, even before the 'Wiccan boom.' I met her after attending a lecture about the Witch Trials in Boston, and we became friends. She was like a surrogate mother. I began studying with her and after a year I was initiated into her coven."

Ceres enthusiastically described the initiation ceremony, which took place on the night of the Full Moon. She stood in the center of the magick circle and recited a poem she had written in honor of the occasion. The High Priestess and Priest recited the Charge of the Goddess with her. Then Ceres was presented with a specially charged athame.

"In my initiation, the athame symbolized an extension to the universe and my own decision to become a Witch," she explained. "Figuratively, I was free at that moment to cut my ties and change my mind if I wanted to. When you're being initiated, the Goddess and God are becoming a part of you. They're linking you to the divine."

The athame was then passed around, from one coven member to the next. Each charged and blessed it. Upon its return, Ceres kneeled on the ground and drove it into the soil. Thus, her identity as a Witch was rooted in the earth, and so was her knowledge.

"Personally, I liked the whole ritual process of initiation because it felt very official, and it was witnessed by a few people who celebrated with me," she said. "I feel more confident because of it."

Ceres planned on continuing her studies at the graduate level in nearby Boston. Among her future plans is the goal of attaining the rank of high priestess within her coven.

Throughout the course of my research, I met several Witches who had initiated themselves without the aid or guidance of a high priestess, priest, or coven. One of the most inventive self-created ceremonies came from Tanya, a junior at Iona College in New Rochelle, New York. As a student at a Christian Brothers school, she found it difficult to make connections and decided against going public. She spent three years studying Wicca on her own, then began her own formal process by performing a rite of consecration.

"I was still living at home at that time, so I had to plan all of my rituals around my parents' schedules. They don't know I'm a Witch," she admitted. "One night in the summer of 1999, I was alone, and the Moon was waxing. It was a beautiful, clear night. I went into my backyard and settled down in the grass beneath the Moon. I wrapped myself in a white sheet, then lit a candle. I didn't chant or recite anything. I just sat there and let myself become entranced. I dedicated myself to the Goddess in mind and soul."

Two years later, after more study—which included trips to Glastonbury and Stonehenge in England—Tanya felt confident in her abilities as a solitary Witch and decided to perform a self-initiation ritual. She waited for the Full Moon, then began gathering the necessary tools. She chose two candles—gold for the Goddess, silver for the God—and a single bowl of water. She arranged the items on a makeshift altar along with pictures of her deceased relatives.

"I started by reflecting on the consecration rite from two years earlier," she said. "I thought about everything I had learned and gone through. There were wonderful experiences and sad ones, too. Everything was a lesson. Then I inscribed my name into the wax of both candles and meditated for a long time. I had written my own initiation charge, which I recited three times. I asked all the people I knew who had died to help me. I asked them to be my witnesses. As the candles burned down, I felt myself descending deeper into my meditative state. When there was nothing left, I gathered the remnants of the wax and mixed them in with a few strands of my own hair. The next morning, I drove down to the beach and threw the whole mixture into the water. That way, I was a part of Earth mentally and physically."

Initiation is an important step in the life of any Witch. If you are a member of a student Pagan association or group, propose the idea of an initiation ceremony or discuss the possibilities of branching out into the greater community for help. Alone, seek to make your experience as memorable as possible. You may also decide that you don't feel the need to validate yourself before the Goddess and God, or a coven. Bypassing initiation will not make you any less of a Witch. The decision, like the power, is entirely your own.

Book of Shadows: A Personal History

Did you keep a diary or journal as a child or teenager? If so, you will remember the feeling of empowerment that seized you every time you scrawled a new page, filling it with your secret desires, fears, hopes, and dreams. Every entry is a chronicle of your past. Looking back, you will recall the experiences that moved you and changed your perceptions about people and life in general. Those pages are a personal history. In them live the good and bad days that molded you into the person you are today.

A Book of Shadows, by way of Wiccan ideology, is an archive of your life as a Witch. Surely, what you learn spiritually will differ from other, everyday lessons. The Book of Shadows is a place for reflection and goal setting. It is also a private scripture of the countless spells and rituals you will create and perform, either as a solitary or as a member of a coven. A common practice for Witches is to write down all that happened immediately following a ritual, spell, workshop, or private meditation ceremony. Did you feel something physical? Did you plunge into a blissful trance? Was anything garnered or lost from the Full Moon rite? It all belongs in your Book of Shadows.

Established covens, or solitary Witches who have been practicing for several years, keep their Book of Shadows in beautifully decorated covers or on bond or parchment paper. They sometimes use rare inks to differentiate between an ordinary journal and what is in essence a very sacred text. Later on, you may want to adopt the same methods. But for now, a simple notebook will suffice. If you're more technological, head to the computer and create a file. This does not lessen the personal nature of your Book of Shadows. In fact, you can design it with special font or images and graphics.

In your Book of Shadows you will want to include a bit more than your spells and rituals. If you are in college, your bank of knowledge is constantly changing and growing. Undoubtedly, you will discover striking similarities between your life as a Witch and your life as a student. When did you first see your campus as filled with *nature* and not just teeming with bodies? When did you finally approach that intriguing classmate and find out he was a Witch? Every special moment counts. Keep a section for dreams too. Where is your mind traveling when your body is at rest? Work at keeping your entries neat and organized, and be careful whom you allow to view your words. What flows from your heart and soul is consecrated dialogue.

Your Book of Shadows will record your progress as a Witch

SPOTLIGHT
Student Pagan Organization, Middle Tennessee State University
www.mtsu.edu/upagan

The Student Pagan Organization at Middle Tennessee State University (S.P.O.) is comprised of several students from many different backgrounds and diverse interests, both spiritually and academically. Their Web site lists a number of important questions and answers. If you have ever wondered what a concise definition of "Pagan" is, search here for the answer. You will also find a wealth of helpful links and other information. The S.P.O. abides by a constitution, and students hold the offices of president, vice president, secretary, treasurer, and sergeant-at-arms. They meet weekly and include University staff members among their discussions.

Jeffrey, a member of the Student Pagan organization and the group's coordinator, holds the group in high regard. "We're a very diverse bunch. We're non-profit and we welcome students and faculty of any and all faiths. We absolutely do not discriminate on the basis of race, creed, sexual preference, or socioeconomic status. Our weekly meetings are lively and we get a lot done. It's an open discussion, and we've talked about magick, ritual, psychic phenomena, and the history of Paganism from an academic standpoint. We're definitely building community."

The number of students eager to join the S.P.O. has increased steadily. "I think we're going to keep growing," Jeffrey said. "Wicca and Paganism attracts so many people in college, and we all need an outlet for our spiritual pursuits. The S.P.O. offers just that."

---

throughout your college years. Farther down the road, when you are a high priest or priestess, it will serve as a historical handbook and a tool for teaching.

Poor Little Witch: Magick on a Budget

Life on a college bank account flat out sucks. With each new semester, there are books and supplies to buy, financial aid payments to make, new CDs to add to that growing collection. The purse strings can get even tighter for the college Witch. With its use of oils, herbs, and magickal tools, Wicca has a tendency to be expensive. Shopping for items isn't always easy either. You might be far away from the nearest occult supply store or confused about what, specifically, to purchase. Oils can be quite costly, and slick salespeople will do their best to convince you that the fifty-year-old piece of cloth from Egypt is an *absolute* necessity. By the same token, online retailers can charge a lot for shipping and handling costs. You need very little, however, to perform a spell or ritual. Take the following advice when building your magickal toolbox.

1. The pentacle is an important symbol for Witches. If you want to wear one as jewelry, chances are you are going spend a couple of bucks for sterling silver and a chain or strip of leather. But are you hanging it from your neck for the world to see because you want that bit of attention it will draw? If so, you are not accomplishing much. The pentacle is worn for protection, not publicity. If you cannot come across something reasonably affordable, bring out your creative side and make one. You can draw one or you can shape one from black string by gluing the strips onto a colored piece of paper or cardboard; cut around in circular motion and you have just what you need.

2. If scented oils pique your passion, think wisely about the money you will spend for just a small vial. Is it really worth it? A beautiful fragrance can enhance a ritual or spell, but there are simple, easy, and inexpensive ways to go about it. The purely natural approach never fails. Dilute rose petals or any other flowers in a sealed glass jar; let it set for a couple of days and then enjoy the redolence you created. A favorite perfume or cologne can also be a substitute for oil. Potpourri wrapped in tissue is another way to attain

a sacred scent. It's also a bargain compared with what some shops and retailers charge for specially made oils.

3. Assuming that you live at home or in an off-campus apartment, candles are surely a favorite item. For a spell or ritual, don't splurge on those that promise to enchant lovers or turn your battered car into a shiny new Lexus. Occult shops sell candles that are visually appealing and jam-packed with herbs and spices. These might motivate you for a moment, but ultimately, it's the energy you put into a spell that counts. Drug stores and supermarkets sell simple colored candles for as little as a single dollar and sometimes less. You can dab some of that self-made rose water on a candle and still produce awesome results.

4. Ritual attire is an issue that has been touted in countless books and articles about Wicca. Some suggest keeping a black robe at the back of the closet, away from everyday, ordinary clothes. A popular suggestion is dressing up for the occasion in the same way you would for a party or important social event. If you are a student at the University of Jupiter and have *that much* closet space—not to mention time—then go ahead and do it. Otherwise, forget the lessons you might have learned about ritual attire. Simply put, street clothes will suffice. Do not spend money needlessly on velvet shirts, dresses, and capes. These articles of clothing might enhance your ritual for the first few minutes, but they are not a necessity. In this instance, it's comfort before style.

5. Charms, amulets, and talismans are a booming business. Again, be judicious when dropping cash or swiping cards for anything that promises magickal results. While it is true that certain stones and crystals possess mystical properties, many are used as eye candy or for simple decoration. Charms can be made with your own hands and power. Protection might come from a ring or necklace or pin that belonged to a relative. Once you consecrate and charge it, the magick is all yours. If you need something for good luck, craft a symbol yourself or draw it on a stone, like a rune.

When incorporating magickal tools into your budget, do it wisely. Try to visit the occult shop or online retailer as infrequently as possible. If, however, you feel better about shopping in the traditional sense, remember not to buy several items at once. Purchase exactly what you will need for one spell or ritual. It is better to have a single candle than a box filled with materials that may go unused for another year.

Stoned: The Hallucinogenic Witch

The employment of drugs in ritual is far from an original concept. Native American "medicine men" and shamans of all cultures have been doing it for decades, and in the 1960s mind-altering substances were a religion altogether. Mescaline and LSD topped the list. Do certain drugs truly aid in achieving higher states of being, or is the notion of "religious ecstasy attained via psychedelics" merely an excuse to get stoned? Opinions vary. In Wicca, there is no definitive answer. Witches who favor the occasional hit while performing magick or rituals are not an overwhelming minority. They certainly are not a majority, either, but the absence of dogma in Wicca leaves room for exploration on every level.

The current generation of college students—indeed, of young adults—in America has witnessed an explosion of activity spawned by particular designer drugs. Ecstasy is by far the most popular, trailed closely by Special K. Both, according to the Drug Enforcement Agency, are Schedule I synthetics. The illegal importation and distribution of ecstasy has evolved into a war of its own. The crackdown imposed by local, state, and federal law-enforcement agencies has not stopped the drug's proliferation, and illegal manufacturing continues unabated in "clandestine" laboratories. Ecstasy is not considered a hallucinogen; users have described it as a "feel good" drug that induces pleasurable sensations and overt behavior. In the 1980s and early 1990s, the drug was a staple of the rave culture and urban area nightclubs. It has remained a favorite for recreational users and those curious about the relationship between consciousness-altering agents and spirituality.

Clay, a twenty-two-year-old student at a university in the south-eastern United States, grew up in a Pagan household. He was raised by his mother, a high priestess of the Faery Tradition. At age fourteen, Clay was initiated and has been practicing Wicca ever since. While a freshman in college, he became intrigued by the writings of Aldous Huxley, an advocate of mystical experience gained via drugs. Clay also delved into the study of transpersonal psychology. He was in high school when he first tried ecstasy. Then, it served to fuel his nocturnal partying binges. He was not a habitual user, and the urge for "Adam" (as ecstasy is sometimes called) tapered off until he reached college.

"When I first started using, I was a dumb kid who was just following the leader," he told me. "I would go to raves or parties at clubs and do it with my friends. I remember being able to go for hours without drinking anything, and I felt really giddy. I'm a pretty introverted person, and when I took ecstasy I was the friendliest person in the world. It helps you lose all of your inhibitions."

Living alone at school, Clay practiced Wicca as a solitary. The confinement of dorm life, however, led to stagnancy in his magick. To counteract a dry spiritual period, he sought refuge in experimentation with drugs. LSD was the first.

"I was back home for vacation and I decided to do a Yule ritual to honor the God," he explained. "I've always been devoted to the Greek god Dionysus because he represents a sort of wild animal instinct. I cast a circle and took a hit of the LSD, and I experienced what felt like a whole new world. It opened a doorway in my mind. I went into a trance and stayed there for hours. I know the experience was spiritual because I didn't have the effects others do when they take LSD. I didn't have vivid flashes, and nothing became animated. It was all mystical. I totally transcended my ego."

When I asked Clay to describe the experience, he would say only that it was like "being comfortably trapped in a realm that defied human thought." He elaborated vaguely by mentioning that the four elements surrounded him in their "literal phases." For example, he felt the cool waves of Water without being close to any ocean, river, or stream. Despite an absence of Fire, he experienced a sensation of immense heat in his hands and legs. The Yule ritual served to heighten his awareness about the physiological components of the human mind.

"I think meditation and concentration can take everyone to a mystical peak," he said. "But certain drugs can help to activate and elevate the senses. Sure, they're all chemically engineered, but drugs are botanical in their purest form. The brain reacts, and if you're able to bring in a strong psychological hold, the experience can just blow you away."

Clay said he only used LSD that one time but admitted to employing ecstasy on several other occasions.

"When I take ecstasy, it's usually for a ritual and not a spell," he said. "I don't need or want my consciousness to be altered for a spell. I use ritual as a way to connect with Deity, and taking ecstasy aids me in that goal. The effect is one of pure happiness. I'm not afraid to draw down the Moon or invoke the darker aspects of the Goddess. I forget my reservations and that leads to something very sacred. I don't worry about going too deep or not going deep enough. Ecstasy has that effect on me—it allows me to leave behind the more reserved parts of my personality. That alone is an important part of being a Witch. You can't reach the Goddess and God if you have inhibitions. A lot of other Witches I know always tell me that they sometimes can't connect to their energy. I never have that problem. Sure, I can do it without ecstasy if I want to, but I don't see anything wrong with taking something that's going to expand my horizons and my emotions."

Clay then made an interesting metaphoric reference to the drug ecstasy and the meaning behind the word.

"History is filled with people who went into ecstatic states because of their religious beliefs and experiences. It happened with so many of the Catholic saints. Look at the Salem Witch Trials. That wasn't ecstasy so much as it was hysteria, but who can say what really happened there? Was that ecstasy manifested the wrong way? It's spiritual, but it's also psychological. If you're fulfilled through religion and a concept of God, then you're happy. You don't question anything. That's how I think of the drug ecstasy. It got that name for a reason. When you take it, you don't question the mundane. Everything comes into focus. For me, it blends in with the meaning of ritual and the meaning of 'religious ecstasy.' It's transcendent and transpersonal at the same time."

As I listened to Clay's views and opinions, I couldn't help but question the validity of this sort of "mystical experience." I asked several other college Witches what they thought about drug use and ritual. Many waved it away and deemed it insignificant. Drugs, they said, had nothing to do with religious growth or knowledge. Others disagreed, and while many did not confess to using, they admitted a certain level of tolerance for the Witch who chooses to explore this side of the spiritual divide. Still, the majority of young Witches seemed turned off by the idea.

Selena, a sophomore at Manhattanville College in Purchase, New York, was blatant about her disagreement.

"It's nothing but a complete and utter lie when someone tells you they're doing drugs to get somewhere spiritual," she said. "It's just an excuse to get high. Wicca is about living a healthy lifestyle through the fruits of the earth. How and where do drugs play into that?"

When asked, Tiffany, a senior at Yale University, told me she did not favor the use of drugs in ritual but would not discriminate against anyone who chose that path.

"Wicca tends to attract very open-minded people to begin with. We're not prudes when it comes to sexuality and other issues that might be taboo. Drug use falls into this category. I could never imagine doing it, but I'm willing and open-minded enough to listen to someone else's experiences. There's no harm in that."

Wyn Kindragon, a high priest of the Blue Cove Coven in New York City, has been practicing for twenty-five years and remembers well the psychedelic drug craze of the 1960s. The use of drugs in ritual, he told me, is far different today from what it was three decades ago.

"People who used LSD to alter consciousness in the 1960s were part of a political movement," he said. "Wicca was still a very radical idea back then, and it was almost synonymous with feminism. The way of the shaman adopted a lot of psychedelic drugs, and what might have been a bad trip for someone was often interpreted as

---

HOW DO YOU *ROCK THE GODDESS?*

Ian, senior
University of California, Santa Barbara

"I remember one time where the phrase 'rocking the goddess' really applied. I was living off campus with a roommate and we decided to throw a party the first weekend after the fall semester started. I invited a lot of the students I knew who were open about practicing Wicca on campus and I even went to one of the spiritual centers that had publicized an open circle and invited them too. About forty people showed up. In the middle of the party we decided to mix a few different types of music, and we ended up with Enya set to a hard rock back-beat. Ten of us formed a circle in the living room and we lit a candle and just started chanting the Charge of the Goddess. We brought out our student ID cards and used them to perform a protection ritual. There was so much energy in the room that night. It was a beautiful experience. Now we do the same thing at the start of every new semester."

---

something emotionally reverent and even spiritual. But as the war on drugs evolved, people smartened up and came to understand the dangers of LSD and mescaline and psilocybin. The young adults of today aren't a very politically active bunch, in my opinion. Drug use is rampant on campuses all over the place, and I don't see any window for spiritual interpretation there. College students are using because they want to. Ecstasy and Special K are designer drugs, not psychedelics. I think they're more cool than esoteric. Witches who truly believe in the effects of mind-altering substances are few and far between these days."

Book Two

•

A WITCH'S POWER

•

Electives

· 5 ·

Coming Out of the Broom Closet

Hello Mother, Hello Father . . .

I know it's been a few days since I last called home but things have been hectic here. The semester is turning out very nicely. It's very busy. I have a lot of exams and term papers, but I'm getting it all done. The sweater Uncle John sent me is coming in handy. Of course, I have to wear it inside out because I'm not too fond of the furry polar bear print on the front, but at least I'm warm.

I know it's rare that I take pen in hand to write you guys. It's just easier this way and for some reason thoughts are clearer when I put them to the page. I've been thinking a lot about the past these days. Last night I went through my box of pictures and I found that cute little snapshot of me Dad took on Halloween. Remember? I came down the stairs dressed in a black robe, and you pointed to that funny FIVE-POINTED STAR around my neck and thought it was adorable that I'd decided to go trick-or-treating. I looked like a WITCH, yes I did. For some reason it never escaped you that I was almost seventeen at the time and not all that impressed with minia-ture chocolate bars. In the picture I'm holding the BROOMSTICK Dad took from the hall closet. The two of you laughed and laughed. I'm sure you remember. Well, I did end up going out that night, but I didn't go door to door asking for candy. Oh, I had fun with my friends. We kind of sort of had a party of our own. It was OUTSIDE. Under the MOON. We lit a little FIRE and then DANCED around. When I got home you asked me jokingly if I had CAST ANY SPELLS. Heh . . . heh . . . heh . . .

Am I making any sense?

Well, here's the thing. Let me start by saying that I really enjoyed all of the great things I did with you guys as a kid. Not only the nice private schools, but the Christmas celebrations with Grans and the Chanukah parties with Uncle Irv and Aunt Rachel. You might not have noticed, but I was paying close attention to all of the RITUALS and religious PRACTICES I was exposed to. Isn't it funny how people can get along despite the differences in their faiths? I mean, when you really think about it, who cares which God, or GODDESS, someone prays to? Like you said, Mom: what matters in this world is polite manners and good dental hygiene. Well, my teeth couldn't be whiter—

Oh, hell. Why am I wasting all this time and paper? I may as well just put it to you straight.

I'm a Witch. I practice Witchcraft. There's nothing evil about it and no, I don't wear the cape when I walk to class on campus. I figured this was the easiest way to let you guys know. It's all good, really. So when you send the next care package, nix the cookies and throw in a few bottled jars of herbs. Nothing fancy. Whatever's in the garden will work.

I love you both and we'll chat soon.
Your only child,
Chris
P.S. SEND CASH

The Broom Closet: In or Out?

The issue of going public as a Witch is multifaceted. Some people simply pick up wherever they are and shout it out on a crowded street corner. Others let a few select friends or relatives know. And then there's the silent population: the women and men who live alternate lives, playing it safe in class or at work and then assuming their true identities in the privacy of their own homes. The degrees of freedom vary. Oftentimes, freedom isn't even an option. The reasons for this are as numerous as the practitioners of Wicca themselves: fear, embarrassment, rejection, the threat of violence. As is implied by the above anecdote, Mom and Dad aren't immediately prone to understanding, and breaking the news to them can be a project in itself. By the same token, Wiccan and Pagan parents frequently remain closeted because they are afraid of what potential openness can bring to their children. The confusion affects every corner of life. Witches can lose and have lost their jobs, their friends, and the support of their academic colleagues and institutions. Nonetheless, the need for acceptance—even approval—remains an ardent desire. It is a part of the human condition, not only for Witches but for any person who chooses to digress from what society considers "the norm."

Aside from all of the other pressures the college years hand down, students who wear their Witch identities proudly must be prepared to deal with the consequences of public life. The overwhelming majority of universities and educational institutions are accepting of their Wiccan student bodies, but sometimes geography matters. Schools with a large Christian focus, for example, may harbor certain rules—unwritten or unspoken—that can make the coming out process difficult. Outright harassment from professors or administrators is rare because no one wants to risk the possibility of legal action, but fellow students might be a different story. They might casually disagree. They might voice their dislike of you or deem your beliefs "evil." A fundamentalist just might attempt to beat you down with a Bible. Whatever the case, remember to hold your ground and keep your temper cool. Chances are, those unwilling to see your point of view have not been properly educated about Wicca.

When Ruben, a student at St. Francis College in Brooklyn, New York, first voiced his Pagan beliefs in class, he was met with a multi-

tude of reactions. There was anger, shock, disagreement, and dis-
taste.

"It was a theology class, and I really didn't think anything of
speaking out loud about being a Witch," he said. "The professor
was really cool. He just nodded and started talking about history and
the Burning Times. But a couple of students turned around and were
like, 'Are you serious? You're some kind of nut.' I got a lot of
strange looks. After class, one guy approached me and asked
whether I worshipped Satan and why I felt I needed to talk about it.
I didn't pay him any mind, but I was looked at strangely from then
on. It's a very small Catholic college, and there's a sense of community here, but I probably should have known better."

Ruben was born in Puerto Rico and raised in Brooklyn. His inner-
city neighborhood was diverse, and the mostly Hispanic population
was "full of different kinds of spirituality." His next-door neighbor,
he told me, was a practitioner of Santeria, a religion indigenous to
Africa and the Caribbean. At home, Ruben lived openly and had
never experienced any problems.

"Coming out all depends on how thick your skin is," he said.
"For some people it's really no big deal. But then you'll find people
who let the fear of exposure rule their lives. There are dangers to
going out there and telling people you're a Witch. You have to be
careful. Not every place is Salem, Massachusetts. You have to use
common sense and instinct, and if you think you might have a problem with someone, just forget it and move on. There are still a lot of
dumb and ignorant people out there. Nothing's going to change
them, so why bother trying?"

But there are positive experiences. I met Allison at a New York
City Pagan gathering. Originally from Greenwich, Connecticut, she
was a sophomore at Penn State in Pennsylvania. Initially, she introduced herself as "Silver Willow" and told me that she had been
practicing Wicca for two years. Life at school complemented her
Witch identity because students and faculty were open and accepting. Her family, she explained, was a different story. She had been
raised in Orthodox Judaism. After her parents divorced, Allison's

mother distanced herself from organized religion, but her father remained devout in his Judaic beliefs.

"I didn't think my mother would mind my being a Witch," she said. "She went through a typical midlife crisis and shut out anything that reminded her of her marriage. Judaism was part of that. It was sad to see her lose that, but I think she always felt displeased by Judaism anyway. When I told her about Wicca, she said she didn't care so long as I was happy and taking care of myself. I was relieved, but I wanted to be completely open about myself to everyone, including my dad. I knew he was going to be a challenge."

Allison decided to invite her father up to the Penn State campus one spring weekend. If he saw her life as it was—deeply rooted in nature and wholly benevolent practices—she believed he'd come around. The plan worked.

"When my dad got to campus, I showed him around and then brought him to my room. It was his first time up, and he noticed my pentacle and the goddess statue I have on my desk. I just came out and told him that I was a Witch, but I went on in detail about it, explaining everything about the Wheel of the Year and how worship really revolves around the seasonal cycles. I really made a point to educate him. His acceptance was a slow process. He wasn't thrilled, but he didn't freak out either. A few months after that he asked me why I had left Judaism, and I told him the truth—that I wasn't comfortable in a religion that confined women to specific roles. I still don't think he's happy about it, but he is accepting of me. He actually bought me a book on Wicca a few weeks ago. I think you have to come out into the open as a Witch very positively and very truthfully. You're either completely open or completely closed. I don't think there can be an in-between."

When deciding what route to take, it is important to know the facts and your rights. Witches are legally recognized in the United States. You cannot be denied access to your religion, nor should you be subjected to discrimination. If you want to start a student Pagan group on campus, you will probably have to go through various administrative channels. Again, flat-out denial by your peers is suspect. Is there a valid reason for their unwillingness—budgetary concerns, student government appeals—or is there a general disagreement on the part of your school? A portion of your tuition is dispersed for student activity fees that help foster community on campus. This alone gives you the right to start or organize any group of your choosing. Coming out of the broom closet does, of course, extend beyond the reaches of college life. Do you have a job that might be threatened by the mere mention of the word *witch?* You might have academic aspirations, and going public could very well set you apart from the more clinically reserved side of academe. Just the same, the Witchcraft label can also bolster your popularity in certain liberal settings.

The choice, like the power, is yours.

Coming Out: The Pros and Cons

If you have reservations about coming out, consider the positive and negative aspects and how they will ultimately affect your life before you do. Every choice and decision you make in life will have its repercussions. Some will be good. Some, of course, will be trying. Take refuge in one fact: whatever the outcome, it can only make you a stronger person and, thus, a stronger Witch.

Let's look at the pros.

- Undoubtedly, coming out of the broom closet will make you more comfortable with yourself. You will feel less of a need to hide your thoughts, opinions, and emotions. There are no more secrets to keep concealed.
- With free thought comes confidence. Intellectually and spiritually, you will have harnessed the true essence of your inner self. This will make your magick stronger. It will also solidify your personality.
- No matter how many people disagree with your beliefs, there will be countless others attesting to your courage. You will gain respect—within the Wiccan and Pagan community but also from

those peers, colleagues, and friends who are smart enough to understand the power of free speech, action, and identity.

- When the veil of concealment is lifted, chances are you will be more eager to get out there and connect with your own community. At Pagan festivals or open circles, your presence will be welcomed, and without the threat of exposure cloaking you, new experiences will impart their lessons with greater depth.

The list could go on for a few pages. There is not enough one can say about the wealth of richness you gain when deciding to live as your true self. But what might be an advantageous decision for one person might be wrong for another.

Here are a few cons.

- First and foremost, be prepared for a plethora of different reactions from people when you decide to tell them you're a Witch. Even your closest friends and dearest family members who had no idea will process the information emotionally. People will shock you. The most liberal pal in the bunch might equate Wicca with Satanism. The most conservative might nod and say, "Whatever makes you happy." Just remember that not everyone will rally to support you.
- Even at school and on campus, you will face rejection. Friends will drop you. Roommates will look at you differently. It can depend on how big or small the Pagan population is at your school. A person's own religion is also a factor. What you see as wholly benevolent another might see as flat-out evil. Dealing with rejection is never easy. But, alas, it is a part of life. When all is said and done, you will know who your true friends are.
- Fear will seize you. It's only natural. Coming out is a big step, and staring potential adversity in the eyes can make your knees shake. If you have made the decision to go public, stick with it and rail against the urge to cower down. *Fear nothing.*
- In the event that you become a victim of violence, fight back. You don't have to do this physically. Intellectual war is a far greater strategy. No matter the degree of violence, you are being illegally

targeted. Your property might be damaged or, worse, you might come under harm. Again, don't cower down. Make reports to your resident assistant, campus police, or the local authorities. Nothing should keep you from expressing yourself.

Coming Out: A Few Helpful Hints

- Ground yourself first. Do a lot of soul searching and take the time to understand the consequences of your actions. Pray for strength and guidance. Cast a spell for peace of mind.
- When you are ready, select a few people, friends or relatives, that are closest to you. It may not even be Mom or Dad. Keep the number small and come out to the chosen few. The gradual process works best.
- Keep your facts straight. If someone is confused, you will need to educate him or her on what Wicca is.
- Attend a student Pagan meeting and start networking. If there is no such group, start your own.
- If your parents are an issue of growing concern, be cautious about coming out at the wrong time. Christmas Day, for example, is not necessarily the best day to break the news that you're a Witch. If you really fear a negative reaction, put your feelings to the page. A well-written, heartfelt letter can do the trick.
- Stand your ground. Once you have started the coming out process, there is no going back. Cling to your beliefs and your identity. Don't be ashamed or embarrassed, and don't allow others to intimidate you.

Necessary Lies: Life in the Closet

In the summer of 1999, I took a part-time job at a Manhattan law firm that serviced the fashion and entertainment industries. Actors, models, and designers strutted through the doors on a daily basis. I am not easily starstruck, but one day, a particularly stunning young woman took a seat not far from my desk. She was not a well-known model, yet her chiseled face had graced the covers of five national magazines. She was slowly climbing the steely ranks to the "high fashion" plateau. Her beauty was remarkable. In fact, it was nothing short of miraculous. As she waited to meet with her attorney, she read from the pages of *Mists of Avalon* by Marion Zimmer Bradley. I couldn't help but comment on the book and its clear references to Paganism. Much to my surprise, the young woman eagerly responded, and a conversation ensued. She looked about twenty-five but had just begun her first year of college at a Manhattan university.

"You're eighteen?" I asked, shocked.

"Twenty," she told me. "I came to New York right after high school to work on my career, but now that I'm making money I decided to try my hand at a degree. I'm only taking a few classes. I look a lot older because of the makeup."

For a few minutes, we chatted about the book. She spoke at length about the Goddess and admitted to being fascinated by the Burning Times and the Salem Witch Trials. Of course, I started to wonder. Was she a Witch? Asking such a personal question would have warranted a stern look from my boss, so I closed the door on that part of my mind. She went into her meeting and left me alone. When she emerged an hour later, she approached me with a smile.

"It was really great speaking to you," she said. "I don't know too many people who know a lot about Pagans!" She scrawled her e-mail address on a Post-it and handed it to me. "Keep in touch, will ya?"

A few weeks later, I e-mailed her. She traveled extensively and our cyber-friendship came together sporadically. Eventually, I asked her in a note if she practiced Wicca.

Her reply was simple: "Yeah, but I'm not all that open about it."

As I began *Rocking the Goddess,* I thought a lot about her. By this time, we hadn't spoken in nearly six months and I had no clue as to her whereabouts. I did see a picture of her in a Sunday edition of the *New York Times*'s fashion section strutting her stuff on a runway, but other than that, we had lost touch. I held my breath and dug out her e-mail address. I wrote her a brief note. A week later, she replied. She was in Ibiza, Spain, living the high life. She was returning to New York soon and was thrilled to hear that I was working on a contracted book. We set a date to have lunch.

I met Star (a name she adopted for our interview) at a trendy restaurant in midtown Manhattan. Huddled at our corner table, she emptied her backpack and showed me the various items she carried with her when commuting from photo shoot to photo shoot. There was a copy of *Wicca for the Solitary Practitioner* by Scott Cunningham, a small pentacle, a circular amulet she had purchased while working in Paris, and a tiny chunk of sea salt.

"It's for good luck and protection," she explained. "In this business, you need a lot of both."

Star grew up on the West Coast. She was Jewish, but neither of her parents were devout in practice. They celebrated holidays and subscribed to certain Judaic beliefs. Otherwise, the concept of religion in her home was agnostic, at best. While in high school, Star began her modeling career. With success came swift financial freedom and initiation into the star-studded fast lane. And yet, there was an emptiness inside that Star couldn't comprehend.

"I was living it up. Shuttling from L.A. to New York and Miami, meeting all those high-profile people," she commented. "My face started to show up in magazines and on a couple of billboards. I was the most popular kid in school, too. But there was something about the whole lifestyle that left me feeling empty. I didn't grow up rich, so I couldn't identify with a lot of the other people I was working with. It's a superficial business. The more successful I got, the emptier I felt. Maybe it was a little bit of guilt mixed in with fear. I don't know. But what I wanted was to understand things better, and I wanted to become a spiritual person. I never had that growing up."

Star had heard about Wicca while in high school. Other kids had whispered about the Goddess, about spells, magick, and the lure of the Moon. The day she turned nineteen, star received a gift certificate to Barnes & Noble from a close friend and decided to go shopping. She stopped in the New Age section. Ten books and one month later, Star was secretly calling herself a Witch.

"Everything I had ever believed about the universe and about spirituality was in those books," she said. "I holed up in my hotel room in New York and just read for hours on end. I couldn't believe it. Even when I was a kid, I prayed to the sky and to the winds and even to the Moon, but I never spoke up about it because I figured my folks would put me in therapy. I didn't know what the word *Witch* meant until then. It was empowering for me as a woman, and the Wiccan philosophy really helped me out in my darkest moments. The Goddess became my sanctuary. Through her, I saw things in a different light and started feeling fulfilled again."

But the private epiphany did not extend beyond Star's own mind. She carried her Wiccan accoutrements out of sight and never told a single person she was a Witch. Back home on the West Coast, she cast spells when her parents were out and reserved the nights of the Full Moon as best she could. By all accounts, she had resigned herself to living life in the closet.

"That was a personal choice, and it wasn't motivated by anyone," she said. "For me it's just easier to keep it personal. The more my career grows, the more public my life gets. I have to think about that. I mean, people in this industry are all open-minded and liberal and they would probably get a kick out of hearing me identify myself as a practicing Witch. But then you have to deal with being labeled. I hate labels. The media will do it to you if they can. Look at Melissa Ethridge. When I think of her, I think of a great rock star and artist, but if a reporter mentions her on TV or in a newspaper, the word 'gay' acts as an adjective. You get pigeonholed. That's why so many gay actors don't want to come out of the closet. I'm on the same wavelength as them where Wicca is concerned. If I came out, I would always be referred to as 'the Witch.' That bothers me. What I believe and how I practice it is nobody's business. It shouldn't have anything to do with my work in the public eye."

Star had confided in only three other people about practicing Wicca. Two were childhood friends, the other a family member. She admitted that keeping her spiritual self under wraps was a difficult task.

"I was doing a fashion show in Milan not too long ago, and everything was really hectic backstage. We're all getting our hair done, putting on makeup, and fitting into clothes at the same time. Well, one model bent down and scooped up a piece of her hair that one of the beauticians had chopped off. She gathered the strands and fastened them in a rubber band. When I questioned her about it, she said, 'It's a Pagan thing. Hair is very powerful.' And then she just ran off. Well, she was probably a Witch, too. I really wanted to throw my arms around her and just talk about it, but I backed off. I know I could have made a friend, but it was just impossible. Again, it's the public eye thing. If the word gets out I'll be labeled and put through the mill. That happens a lot, and it's frustrating. I do offer people advice that's Wiccan in nature, but I don't go further than that. Yeah, I feel like I'm not being true to myself, but there's a lot to consider in my case. Coming out for me can actually be more confining than liberating. That's an ugly thought."

Interestingly enough, Star said that Wicca "made the rounds" in the entertainment industry.

"There are a lot of closeted Witches in this business," she .claimed. "Or at least a lot of people who believe in the Pagan philosophy. Anyone who works in films, theater, fashion, or writing is open-minded and thinks very freely. Wicca attracts those kinds of people. If you go into some of the occult shops in L.A. and San Francisco, you'll spot a lot of notable faces."

At the time of our interview, Star was twenty-one years old. She had taken several classes in English literature at a Manhattan university but was not a matriculated student. The college population, however, is where she feels most at home.

"I like learning and going to school, but with my schedule it's very hard to plan a full semester of courses," Star told me. "I like being around people my own age, and I want that B.A. because I know I can't model forever. I felt comfortable in college. There was a small student Pagan group that had advertised a couple of meetings while I was taking class, but I didn't attend any of them. Finding Witches and Pagans in college didn't surprise me. At this age, we're all just beginning to discover who we are. It makes sense that Wicca is big on campuses all over the place."

Star was not the only closeted Witch I came into contact with. There were countless others, and their reasons for deciding to remain private about their identities differed. Parents were a frequent issue. Others feared that telling me their real names would impede their chances of finding good jobs in rather conservative industries—finance, law enforcement, even publishing. A young woman I met online from Duluth, Minnesota, who introduced herself as "Haven-Witch," told me that coming out of the broom closet would surely jeopardize her future. After college, she planned on entering her father's business. It was a successful company that had been erected on the "principles of Christian values." If he found out, HavenWitch explained, he would probably cut all ties to her.

"My father is a devout Lutheran," she wrote. "It was a big part of my growing up and he'd never understand something like Wicca. If he heard someone mention anything about Witchcraft he'd go berserk."

I asked her how she kept it hidden and if she planned on living in the closet for the rest of her life.

"I just lie to people," was her very honest reply. "My mom found a book on Wicca in my room once and I just told her that it was for a class I was taking in history. She believed me, and that was the end of it. As for the rest of my life, well, I really can't say. I'll take it day by day, but I don't ever see myself living openly to my family."

Ray, a student at the University of Michigan at Ann Arbor, also had his own specific reasons for not coming out of the broom closet. In his case, it had nothing to do with religion. His favorite pastime, he explained, was hanging out and baby-sitting for his two nephews. Ray's older brother and his wife, both politically active members of the conservative party, would not be pleased if they knew Ray was practicing Wicca.

"My brother knows that I'm not into Catholicism any more," he said. "He really isn't either and neither is his wife, but they are very set in their ways when it comes to rearing the storybook American family. They believe in the home and doing things the old-fashioned way. I'm really very close to my nephews. I see them five times a week and I don't want to threaten that. Now, if my brother knew that I was hanging out in the Pagan community and going to festivals, he'd freak out. It's too radical for him to absorb. He'd equate it with evil and I know he'd distance me from my nephews. He already doesn't like that I have friends who are gay. Telling him I'm a Witch would create too many problems and I'm not willing to put myself through that. Those kids are my life."

When I mentioned the coming out issue to students who lived openly, I was greeted by replies that ranged from sympathy to hostility. Some understood the weight of the potential consequences. It wasn't an easy decision, they told me, and in no way would they disrespect or even disagree with those who preferred anonymity. But coming out, others claimed, was a necessity as well as a responsibility. Staying "underground" as a Witch was akin to bowing down to the "conservative regime" that perpetually attempts to discredit Wicca as a valid religion. One example was Georgia state representative Bob Barr, who publicly objected to the recognition of Witches and Pagans on military bases. (Interestingly enough, Wicca has since been added to the Chaplain Handbook of the U.S. Army.) Students who shunned the notion of remaining in the closet argued that silence would only foster ignorance, misrepresentation, and a reduction in the legalities that currently protect Wicca and its practitioners from discrimination. Theirs is obviously a valid claim.

Closeted Witches, however, feel that they must balance the demands of their lives with all that coming out represents.

Sexuality and Wicca: Every (Witch) Way

Sex and religion rarely walk on equal ground. In most Western theologies, the human body is as much a temple as it is a tool for sin. Flesh is sacred, but it is also hot, supple, and slippery when wet. Growing up, we were all educated on the evils of sexual indulgence. That first kiss was okay so long as it didn't include a slip of the tongue. Intercourse was the physical mechanism for procreation and not a frantic rise to pleasure. Violating the religious rules meant an extended stay in purgatory or, worse, complete damnation. The really good boys and girls remained virginal until that explosive wedding night, when husband and wife set their stiffening sights on conception, not orgasm. Sex, by most theological accounts, is a bad thing.

Contrary to most other religions, Wicca is complemented by sexuality in all forms. It embraces the ideology of sex as a "life force" but also as means of pleasure between two—sometimes three—consenting adults. Sex is an exploration, an adventure, an education in itself. When desire stirs in the mind, the body reacts. This is only natural. In fact, a resistance to sex and physical attraction is considered *unnatural* because it opposes a very basic human need. Wicca does not recognize the concept of sin, and so there is no "penance" for indulging the body. This is not to say that Witches are promiscuous. There is a very discernible line between sexual exploration and unhealthy gratification. Witches do not host orgies; nor are they swingers or devotees of the S&M scene. Sex, for the Witch, is as much about intellectual stimulation as it is physical enjoyment. To quote the Charge of the Goddess: *All acts of love and pleasure are my rituals . . .*

Thus, homosexuality and bisexuality find a comfortable and very serious place within Wicca. Most young adults struggling with their

SPOTLIGHT
Pantheon, The Auburn University Student Pagan Association
www.auburn.edu/pantheon

An impressive Web site immediately sets Pantheon, the Auburn University Student Pagan Association, apart from so many others. Along with a list of helpful definitions and links are several articles written about Pantheon, which consists of a number of dedicated students. Membership is growing. The site includes information regarding the group's meeting times, events, publicity, and recent news. The Pantheons welcome contact with other students and college Pagan associations.

Located in Alabama, a stone's throw from the "Bible belt," Auburn University has a strong Christian backbone. Religious intolerance has been an issue for members of Pantheon in the past. In fact, a note on the Web site claims that the Burning Times "are not over."

An Auburn student who did not want to be identified offered a glimpse into the group's power and sophistication.

"We're all an intelligent bunch, and we're serious about the study of Paganism and about better informing the public about what the Pagan path means," the student said. "It hasn't been easy for us. Religious intolerance is alive and well, and we've had to fight for our rights. We've been successful, but you always come across those dumb students who make comments and rip down the flyers we put up all over campus. I once saw a student spit on a flyer I had just put up. We deal with it and move on because violence is unacceptable and we won't stoop to that level. We won't be deterred, either. I'm not exactly open about who I am yet, so I want to be careful. But my fears are lessening as the practice of Wicca grows all over the state and country. I think it's even changing on campus. More and more students have been approaching me lately and asking questions. That's a definite positive."

The members of Pantheon serve as examples for all college students facing similar injustices. Their willingness to uphold the right of religious freedom is to be commended and extolled. In addition to maintaining an informative and colorful Web site, the students of Pantheon participate in Pagan festivals, hold on-campus events, and educate their classmates and peers on the past, present, and future of Paganism. In doing so, they are making a notable history of their own.

sexual identities feel at odds with the dominant Western religious traditions because dogma excludes them from the "acceptable" fold. Christianity, Judaism, and Islam outright shun lifestyles that society considers "alternative." What psychological impact does this have on the gay or bisexual young adult eager to retain a connection with spirituality? Are shame, rejection, and hatred true components of an all-knowing, all-loving, all-compassionate God? Indeed, they are not. Wicca views homosexuality and bisexuality as natural and balanced within nature. When invoked, the Goddess and God are feminine and masculine, respectively, but they also encompass the psyche in all its incarnations. Their collective essence transcends the boundaries of gender.

Coming out of the *broom* closet and coming out of the *closet* are often marginal experiences for the gay Witch. In both cases, he or she is preparing to make a journey that will alter the rest of life. The college years often bear witness to these revelations. If you are not exploring Wicca while a student, you are, at the very least, awakening your sexuality and taking it new heights. (Dorm rooms, as we all know, are not only used for studying and sleeping.) Throughout the course of my research, I met a number of interesting college Witches who were grappling with sexuality and spirituality, and happily marrying the two together.

Edina, a twenty-year-old freshman at Georgia Institute of Technology, began studying Wicca after recognizing her own emerging sexuality. She dated a few boys in high school, but it wasn't long before she acknowledged what turned her on the most: girls.

"I was raised a Catholic, so when I realized that I was a lesbian I was very afraid," she said. "I had already distanced myself from the Church, but I feared my family and what they would think. I didn't do anything about it until I got to college. But even while in high school and living at home, I knew that deep down I was still a religious person. I didn't want to lose my connection to a higher being. Well, the Church has its own laws against homosexuality so I knew I didn't belong there. I just started following my own path, which was mostly agnostic. Then I saw an article on Wicca and I started delving further into it. I think it's the only religion that's truthful because it states exactly what all people believe or want to believe—that the body is sexual. There's no shame in having fun safely, and you're not going to be punished for it."

It wasn't long before the "coming out" issue presented itself to Edina.

"At GIT, I met a few other gay and lesbian students, and that certainly helped me. I was out as a lesbian to my friends at school, and to a few of my professors, but home was a different story. My parents started asking questions—why didn't I have a boyfriend or date, and things like that. They didn't know that I dated girls. I came out to them very flatly, and I made it clear that this is who I am and nothing's going to change it. My mom went to speak to our parish priest about it, but I refused to go along. My parents weren't happy but eventually they came around. That was coming out of the closet for me.

"Coming out of the broom closet is a much different story. Practicing Wicca is still very personal to me, so I don't feel like I'm hiding myself from the world. A few people know. My parents don't. I think they can only handle so much. But being gay and a Witch is like a double whammy because you're railing against the norm twice over. Eventually I'll come out of the broom closet too, but for now I'm happy with what I've accomplished. I know who I am, and a lot of my confidence comes from Wicca. It gave me a home when no other religion would."

Dermott, a senior at Lehigh University in Pennsylvania, had a similar experience. Originally from Utah, he was raised in a Mormon home, where homosexuality was "discussed only when someone brought up sinners." He knew from an early age that he was gay. Fearing rejection, he kept his preferences hidden until he got to college.

"First of all, I have to say that I don't think being gay is a choice," he asserted. "I was born this way. I grew up with a lot of men in my house and knew nothing else but straight people. But from the time I was a kid, I knew that I liked guys. So when people ask me about 'choosing' this lifestyle, I tend to get pissed off. I didn't choose it; it chose me, and I'm very comfortable with that. This is what's natural to me."

When he entered Lehigh, Dermott began networking with GLBTU (Gay, Lesbian, Bisexual, and Transgender Union) chapters all over the state. There weren't many openly gay students on campus, but he did make a few close friends. He came out to them.

"I had lived my whole life in a shell and coming out was very liberating," he said. "I was very honest, and my friends respected me for that. One of them suggested that I tell my parents, but the more I thought about it, the angrier I became because their views were all about the Mormon faith, and it taught them that people like me are freaks, perverts, even criminals. I rejected everything about the Mormon church from that point on."

Dermott explained that despite his decided separation from the Mormon church, he sought "some semblance" of a union with the divine. He found a small group of students on campus that had formed an unofficial student Pagan organization called "Whispering Trees." He began attending meetings when time permitted.

"I wasn't actively involved with the group, but it exposed me to the Pagan path," he explained. "I read up on it a lot, and I did a lot of online cruising. Wicca spoke to me the most because it has no dogma and because the Goddess and God recognize diversity within sexuality. I'm gay, but I can still appreciate physical beauty in every person, and that includes women. I'm open-minded about it. The only thing each of us owns is our body, and sexually we should do what we want to do."

Dermott eventually told his mother that he was gay, but her reaction, as he expected, was less than positive. Interestingly enough, he felt that coming out of the broom closet was more challenging than coming out of the sexuality closet.

"I think people are more accepting of homosexuality these days," he said. "But because a lot of people still don't know the facts about Wicca, they freak out when you tell them you're a Witch. One of my friends said, 'Oh, come on. Being gay isn't enough? What's with this spell-casting thing?' The gay Witch thing can definitely isolate you more, and I know a lot of people think of me as being this radical personality, sort of all the way on the other side of the fence. But that's not it. I try to look at it more positively. I've managed to come to terms with my sexuality, and I'm a spiritual person because of it."

HOW DO YOU *ROCK THE GODDESS?*

Jessica R., junior
Washington State University

"There are hundreds of ways to get in touch with the Goddess and God. One thing I've learned from practicing Wicca is that Deity does not discriminate when it comes to ritual. If your intentions are pure and your energy is grounded, anything is possible. My favorite time of year is spring, so I do this Beltane ritual in which I plant new flowers and herbs. I buy small plastic pots and I do a few variations. My mom loves daisies, so last year I planted a few seeds and turned the pot over to her when the first stems came through the soil. I study botany and biology, and when I make things grow I remember how connected I am to Earth. It's a small, quiet ritual—nothing elaborate or along the lines of traditional magick—but it's still good for the soul and good for nature."

Wicca, Dermott said, changed his perceptions about sex altogether. In the past, he hooked up with partners almost blindly. He was confused and slightly hesitant about following his desires because he had not managed to completely extricate himself from the Mormon teachings, which (like all sects of Christianity) strictly forbid same-sex unions.

"Sex is a powerful force. It's magical because it takes us to new heights," he said. "When I have sex with a guy, the motions and the outcome are the same as in heterosexuality. You're doing it because it feels good and because you want to be as close and connected as possible to the person you're appreciating. My sex life is different now that I'm a Witch. There's no guilt involved. I'm not ashamed anymore. The first time I had sex was after I got to college, and I got drunk immediately afterward because I just didn't want to think about it. That happened a few times. Now it's a totally normal and healthy experience for me. I know the difference between love and sex, and you can have both successfully. I don't understand people who are afraid to explore their own bodies because religion has told them it's wrong. If you live honestly and sincerely, I don't think any Supreme Being gives a damn about sexuality."

· 6 ·

The Campus Coven

Night falls cool and clean over the suburbs. The last streak of red slips beneath the horizon, and the campus wakes. At the north end of the five hundred rolling acres, more than a dozen students meet in the wooded clearing behind the dorms—freshmen, sophomores, juniors, seniors. A few have even traveled from neighboring schools. Sidestepping branches and upturned patches of soil, they follow Michelle, the high priestess of their coven, to the designated spot. A cauldron rests on the rutted ground. They form a wide circle around it and watch as a match is struck and then dropped into the hollow center. Flames crackle and rise. The darkness dies.

Silently the members of the coven join hands.

Using the athame, Michelle begins to cast the sacred circle that will act as a boundary between the two worlds. She summons the elements. She points the athame skyward. She lowers her arms and then swoops them in a clockwise direction. The gesture encompasses all those present. Walking over to Max, the high priest, she offers him the athame and watches as it is passes from hand to hand. Kyle, Tony, Dina, Anne, Stacey, Keith . . . one by one they infuse the object with their essence. When it's done, Michelle reclaims the athame and plunges it into the earth.

Soon, the ritual dance ensues. On this eve of the Spring Equinox, the coven pays homage to the God as his power increases with the daylight. As the members move around the circle, they are spinning the Wheel of the Year. Each throws something into the cauldron as a symbol of what has been lost and what shall soon be gained. Old term papers, grade reports, a faded ID card, scraps of clothing, and keys disappear in the hungry flames. Michelle and Max ask the Goddess for clean air and water, good health and personal prosperity. They disengage from the moving circle and stand at its center. Staring straight up, they invite the sliver of New Moon into the ritual. Thus, they draw the Goddess down from the heavens and into the consecrated space. A low chant starts among them; it grows steadily as the minutes tick by. Soon it rises like a crescendo, stirring the leaves and echoing in the woods. Raising energy, the Witches lose themselves in celebration. The exhilaration of free-flowing worship steels them against a sudden drizzle, against the scurry of raccoons and the clink of lights being turned on in the nearby dormitories. The dance quickens. Michelle, her eyes trained above, stands over the cauldron. She shapes the fire with her hands, creating a cone of power that will enhance her psychic abilities. Max goes to her side carrying a glass filled with water. Steadying it, he bends to pull the athame from the earth. Then, grasping the handle, he traces a pentagram on the air. They take sips of the water before passing the glass around to the other coven members.

A crowd has gathered behind the perimeters of the circle. Students have emerged from their dorms and now dot the wooded clearing. They peer through the trees, over one another's shoulders, across the glassy incline. In the eerie firelight, they smile and stare in awe, wishing they too could be a part of the magic.

The Campus Coven: Witches at Work

When I started Campus Coven at my home school, SUNY Purchase College, I worked at making the group informal. We comprised about ten students who got together once a week to discuss alternative spirituality. Sometimes we met in a dorm room or campus apartment. When weather permitted, we took to the rolling acres and settled beneath a shady grove or in the parking lot. A few students were Witches. Some were interested in the Goddess and others were content to simply explore various religious paths. Because a number of the students were uncomfortable with the idea of a public club, we opted to keep Campus Coven private, and maybe even a bit "underground." Our admission policy, however, was not restricted. We admitted any curious observer, and everyone had a reason for joining. My friend Lisa had struggled with the decision to study Wicca formally in her teenage years; now part of a group, she hoped to expand her horizons further. Josh loved mythology and planned on attending graduate school for folklore. I had been involved with the world of Witchcraft since my early teenage years. As a sociology major, I was obsessed with Wicca and Pagan culture and fascinated by the idea of magick.

One spring evening, I actually witnessed a ritual on campus like the one described above. It wasn't as elaborate, but it was nonetheless a group of dedicated students banding together to worship Earth. While writing *Rocking the Goddess,* I witnessed rituals at other schools as well—everything from an outdoor Maypole dance to a cramped, indoor Samhain celebration. Students I spoke to from all over the country had different opinions and definitions about their practices. Most were not involved in covens in the traditional sense. The frequent and very popular method of getting together is via a student Pagan association or Pagan-sponsored club. Under the umbrella of the administration and student government, clubs are supported and often granted financial funding. Dozens of groups, however, meet regularly without constitutions or designated officers and advisors. This method seems to favor students who are not yet ready to publicize their beliefs and practices. Both work to foster community and interest in Wicca and Paganism, and the number of college Witches continues to rise dramatically.

As we have seen, geography sometimes makes a difference. Groups, clubs, and organizations can and do survive on urban and rural campuses alike, but there are benefits and drawbacks to both.

A big city might offer more resources and opportunities in which to network, but in cities like New York and Los Angeles, outdoor rituals are infrequent because space is limited and campuses often encompass several miles and buildings. A rural environment, however, will grant any Witch a deeper connection to nature and solitude. Open fields and rolling acres of land allot room for more stylized practices.

Witch in the City: The Urban College Campus

New York University sits in the heart of Greenwich Village. Bordered by Washington Square Park, it has long attracted an array of students and faculty from every state and countless foreign countries. Claire, a twenty-year-old sophomore from Michigan, came to NYU for a common reason: she wanted to be in Manhattan, to live in the center of a pulsing, liberal community. It was the place she had long dreamed of. Here, she was free to pursue her artistic interests and her passion for architecture. She was also free to explore her "growing obsession with the lure of the Witch." Raised in a Catholic household, Claire discovered Wicca while a senior in high school. She spent hours in the library, devouring books and articles on everything from Egyptian goddesses to Moon rituals. Her curiosities soon led her to the Internet. She began e-mailing Witches in neighboring towns and eventually met up with a few.

"I was always fascinated with mythology," Claire told me. "I grew up with Jesus and the saints, and that was beautiful, but what I really saw was a religion that catered to men and offered women very few opportunities. I just never understood why women couldn't be priests. When I started researching Wicca, I realized how many women were priestesses and that totally intrigued me."

Thin and fair-skinned, Claire did not stand out in a crowd. She dressed simply. She wore little makeup and no jewelry. An inquisitiveness showed in her eyes, and she spoke with confidence. While comfortable with her identity as a Witch, she was "cautious" about living publicly—a result, she would later explain, of small-town rearing. Meeting up with like-minded individuals she had approached in chatrooms while in Michigan taught her a valuable lesson.

"I met up with two women and one guy," she said. "They were great people and answered all of my questions, but I noticed that they were a little fearful of divulging too much about themselves. Wicca still has its stereotypes. People get spooked when they hear the word *witch*. I practiced a lot on my own while still living at home, and that was cool, but it wasn't until I got to college that my spiritual life changed immensely."

As a nervous freshman in a big city, Claire wasn't sure how her fellow students would react to her budding interests in Wicca. All apprehension died away, however, on her first day of classes, when she met a girl who lived two dorm rooms down the hall. The girl was a Witch—and a proud one, at that.

"She just came right out and identified herself as a Witch," Claire explained. "I was kind of stunned. And then a couple of other people in the class spoke up, nodding their heads and mentioning their own interests in Wicca. It was incredible. About ten of us met in the dining hall that same night and spent hours talking about it. We shared the same views and opinions. I felt like I'd come home."

So what were those views and opinions?

"It all had a lot to do with Wicca being a religion for my generation," she replied. "I mean, we all came from different backgrounds and places, but we'd been raised watching MTV and listening to music that was a world away from the things our parents had known. None of us had ever aspired to the societal norm—you know, marriage, kids, and a nice little house in the 'burbs.' We were all eager, I think, to retain to some measure of religiosity in our lives, but we couldn't adhere to so many strict demands and rules—like what Catholicism and Judaism require. Wicca appeals to people of our generation because it's all about growth. When you're a Witch, there's always something more to learn. It never stops, and it's never stagnant."

Claire forged friendships throughout her freshman year, and the

majority of her closest confidantes were Witches. None of them worshipped on the nights of the Full Moon or observed the Wiccan
sabbats, but they met regularly to talk about their spiritual passions.
They recommended books to one another, took trips away from the
city, even invented a goddess guessing game. It was the beginning
of her intellectual initiation into Wicca.

"That's the great thing about the college Wiccan community,"
Claire went on. "Everyone is like-minded, and we're all dealing
with the same issues—classes, grades, professors we don't like.
What links us at the core is that we're in the same place, and that
kind of agreement builds confidence."

Having experienced the pall of too many term papers to write and
professors who demanded too much, I asked Claire how she handled
it all while settling into her new-found Wiccan family. Did practicing Wicca help her at all?

Her face lit up, and she nodded vigorously. "Wicca teaches you,
from the start, that the mind is key to existence. Through the mind,
through meditation and an understanding of the world and the universe, you pick up important lessons. Everything is connected. It
teaches you not to sweat the small stuff. I know that through the
Goddess, I can do my best and don't have to feel guilty if I fail or
don't come out on top. I got through some tough times because of
Wicca. It always helps."

At the end of her freshman year, Claire hit the academic wall.
She had spent more time socializing than studying and was racing
to pass her exams. She had also fallen into a serious relationship
that was coming apart. Her stress level was at an all-time high. One
of her roommates even suggested that she see a counselor. As the
days ticked by, Claire began experiencing panic attacks. Desperate,
she turned to her beliefs in Wicca and began praying to the Goddess.
On a balmy May night, she walked to Chelsea Piers—a stretch of
Manhattan that overlooks the Hudson River—and meditated. She sat
on a bench and put her feelings to the page. By the time she was
done, the Moon had risen above. She concentrated on the silver light.
She drew the energy of the Goddess into her. Calmed, she walked

back to her dorm and there met up with two friends, also Witches. Together, they retired to the student lounge and performed a banishing ritual that neutralized the negativity circulating through Claire's life. They used simple accoutrements: black paper, potpourri, and a lighter in place of a candle. It worked. Claire gained control of her angst and finished out the semester successfully.

During her sophomore year Claire began forming her first coven. It consisted of three other young women from NYU; one was a friend, and the other two lived in the same dorm. Claire organized a time schedule based upon the phases of the Moon. Once a month, the four friends got together, usually in a dorm room, and cast a magick circle. They concentrated on their "inner selves," discussing their spiritual hopes as well as their professional aspirations. Later, they went out into the pulsing city streets and joined a larger community of Witches.

"Being in a city like New York makes it easier," she went on. "Everyone in the Village is a proud freak in his or her own right, and nothing is taboo. Wearing my pentacle while walking down Bleecker Street is no big deal. Chances are you'll see ten other people wearing pentacles in a coffee shop or nightclub. I still tend to be reserved because of how I was raised, but from coming to school in a big city I'm learning that acceptance comes pretty naturally. I don't worry about it a lot."

Claire also pointed out the array of resources the urban environment provides for young Witches. "If you want to meet older people who practice Wicca, you can go to New Moon New York, an open center that holds public rituals. You can find classes being taught in a dozen occult shops. You don't ever have to go out of the way to find candles or tools because everything is within reach. A lot of the time you can find postings from people who are looking for new coven members, or just groups of Wiccans who get together once or twice a month. It's all here, and it's all easy."

Another added perk, Claire explained, is that metropolitan cities all are within reach of the quieter suburbs, where nature can be appreciated without traffic, smog, and crowds. "The woods are really just a train stop away," she said. "If I have some free time and want to get away, I can go into Westchester or Rockland counties, even Long Island and New Jersey. When you're a Witch in New York City, you get the best of both worlds."

Tom and Beth, students at San Francisco State University, do not belong to a coven or the campus-run Pagan group. Both are natives of Tiburon, California. Tom is nineteen, Beth twenty-one. Like Claire in New York, they share the belief that the urban college campus is conducive to growth as a Witch.

"You can find the Wiccan and Pagan community anywhere in San Francisco or Los Angeles," Tom said. "The student Witches here on campus hold meetings and even talk about networking in the greater community, which many do. I don't have any reservations about living openly as a Witch. A lot of that probably has to do with my location."

Beth met many college Witches in her freshman year. Her first exposure to ritual came on the high holy day of Samhain, when she walked a few blocks from campus to a metaphysics shop and joined an open circle.

"A few teenagers welcomed me in, and the older Witches, the high priestesses and priests, spent hours talking to me afterward. Later, when I got back to campus, I stepped right into another ritual that a few students were doing, and I remember thinking, 'How great is this? If I don't want to stay on campus I can always just go into the city and feel the same sense of togetherness.'"

Both Tom and Beth mentioned the high level of activism found in such cities as San Francisco, New York, and Chicago. Covenant of the Goddess, the largest legally recognized organization of its kind in America, has been around since the 1970s. Based in California, it maintains extensive contact links and representatives in every state. The Witches' League for Public Awareness was founded in Salem, Massachusetts, near Boston. Organizations like these serve as a networking resource for Witches, but they also keep abreast of the legal issues that sometimes throng the Wiccan community.

"In a way, I feel safe in a big city like San Francisco," Tom said. "Nothing is taboo, people are cultured, and the older Witches and Pagans kind of look out for us younger ones. If anything should go wrong, like discrimination or violence, I know someone's watching my back."

At the University of Miami, Ricky practices Wicca openly, and over the last two years has found ways to combine his passion for the Goddess with his Latin-American roots. He grew up in Puerto Rico. In high school, he was one of *las brujas* (the Witches), a small group of students who combined Wicca with elements of Catholicism and Santeria. Moving to Miami, he explained, broadened his horizons immensely.

"It's a colorful and funky city, full of music, art, and night life. The population is largely mixed, so there's more *spirituality* here than there is *religion*. So much of Wicca is about creativity— inventing your own spells, finding new ways to invoke the Goddess and God. Being surrounded by creative people is freeing. Here, they see my pentacle and my tattoos and they're like, 'Oh, what's that? Can you tell me about it?' And I always get positive reactions."

But that wasn't the case when Ricky drove cross-country with a group of friends in the summer of 1999. They came to a rest stop in Dayton, Ohio, and Ricky found himself the center of suspicious glances. "The convenience store clerk at the gas station made the sign of the cross when I walked out," he said. "It was like that in most of the small towns. I could never imagine attending college anywhere but a big city. At U of M I made a lot of cool friends who opened up their own minds to Wicca after meeting me. Being a Witch isn't a big deal here. I'm even open about who I am at work— and my boss is a devout Catholic. The point is this: the city is a big place and sometimes getting lost in the fold is good. I've met people who were turned off by Wicca, but I just forget it and move on because I can. Urban colleges are all about diversity."

Because Wicca is an autonomous religion, practitioners are free to invent their own style of worship. The Goddess and God are summoned from within. Location is a secondary factor where magick is concerned, and a connection to nature can be fostered despite the tangle of skyscrapers, cement, and traffic that comprise big cities. Urban environments offer students a large community and many more resources, yet the "city Witch" does face obstacles. Overcrowding in dormitories is one example. Another is the size of the campus itself. Academic buildings are often spread out over several blocks and miles, and finding a patch of shady green could prove difficult.

But no matter a Witch's destination, the Moon always shines like a beacon in the night sky. Magick and mystery are only a breath away.

Witches in the Woods: The Rural College Campus

Imagine a wooded enclave shadowed by evergreens. A breeze sweeps the rutted ground. It is dusk. The sepia light dissipates as day gives way to night. Soon the black visage is pierced by silver, a gentle glimmer that silhouettes the foothills and dips into the valleys. The Moon rises above.

One by one the sounds of the wild riddle the silence: a coyote's bay, the caw of a bird, a grasshopper's chirp. Raccoons skitter through a thicket of leaves. Gnats swarm overhead, their hum as swift and fleeting as the firefly sparks that prick the darkness. Listen to the gentle ripple of the nearby stream: the water seems to whistle as it slips over stone. Thunder booms in the distance. The rainfall is quick, the patter of drops rhythmic and resonant.

Then a rustling starts among the saplings, barely discernible from the whisper of wind in the trees. A small group makes its way along the narrow trail leading to the enclave. It takes but a moment to form the circle, join hands, and begin the rite. Blessed silence. Complete seclusion. Anything is possible. They chant and sing. They dance, laugh, meditate. Detached from civilization, they are guarded by Nature and the elements. Exposure is unlikely. The night could go on forever.

Students at the University of Maine at Orono know the pleasures of this solitude. The large campus is bordered by acres of woodland. In spring and summer, flowers bloom and the vegetation glows like a deep green canvas. Come autumn, leaves litter the ground, a carpet of red and gold. Snow blankets Earth in the winter months, weighing down the evergreens' boughs. The bucolic refuge of rural America—from towns in New England and the Heartland to the Pacific Northwest—has long attracted people of all ages. Here, life flows with an easy beat. There is a calm cadence to the days that city dwellers will probably never know. Caitlin, a twenty-year-old junior at Orono, calls herself a "city girl transplanted in the corn-fields." She was born in Chicago and had never visited the East Coast before arriving at Orono. A hereditary Witch, she learned Wicca from her mother and was initiated into an eclectic tradition at thirteen.

"I didn't know anything but city life," Caitlin explained. "I always lived in an apartment, and I watched my mother cast spells in the living room as traffic screamed from the street. I did the same with lots of success, but in high school I decided I needed a change. When I chose Orono as my college, I thought a lot about the huge changes I'd have to get used to. That frightened me most."

As an entering freshman, Caitlin struggled with her rural sur-roundings. But she quickly found ways to incorporate her Wiccan beliefs with acres of woods and trees. "I had read plenty of books on Wicca, and I'd always laughed when I came across those pages about Witches worshipping under a Full Moon, out in the open. It was fiction to me. You can't really do that in the city. But once I fell into pace at Orono, I started going out to the woods all the time to cast spells and perform rituals. I couldn't get enough of it. It awakens a new kind of Witch in a person. You're right in the middle of Earth, in the heart of the Goddess."

When weather permitted, Caitlin often hiked a mile or so in search of a shady grove. She settled in and worshipped freely. She never gave thought to prying eyes or the rules that applied to dormi-tory living. In the woods, she lit candles and incense. She planted seedlings, cast magic circles, and took long walks. In her sophomore year, she and three other students led a Beltane ritual and fashioned wands from fallen branches.

"I got to know more intimately the meaning of Wicca as an earth-based religion," she said. "Being on a college campus in the country makes all the difference. There's no interference here. No traffic and no buildings or crowds. Surrounded by woods, you're truly experiencing a connection to nature. It's also a close community because the campus is the only center for miles. Students can't go into town and expect to find much. We all stay here, in the dorms or the student lounge, and get to know one another better. That makes for stronger bonds."

But where do students on rural campuses go to bridge the gap between college Wicca and the greater Wiccan community? How do they go about acquiring necessary tools?

"If you're lucky enough to find older Witches who can act as mentors in neighboring towns, that's great," Caitlin offered. "But otherwise, you make connections through the Internet. I don't feel like I need to do that. Everything I need is here, on campus. When you have nature close by, the woods act as your magickal space. What I'm not allowed to do in my dorm room I can always do in the woods. College students also have to be resourceful and find ways to make their own tools—like wands, oils, and candles. We're all on the same budget for four years."

Despite her urban upbringing, Caitlin explained that she couldn't imagine ever living in a big city again. The visceral attachment she feels with rural settings is central to her identity as a Witch. She discovered a wealth of spiritual knowledge as a direct result of choosing a rural college campus. A link to the out-of-doors—the simple attributes of soil, sky, and landscape—brought her closer to the notion of the Witch as one who walks in tandem with Nature.

Darius is a senior at Bennington College in southwestern Vermont. Comprised of nearly six hundred acres and just as many undergraduates, it is a corner of the world that knows firsthand the meaning of seclusion.

"I've been practicing Wicca since I was fourteen," he told me.

"I was raised in a suburb of Arizona that was close enough to Phoenix but still somewhat removed from anything you'd consider 'urban.' High school didn't do much for my identity as a Witch because when you're a teenager you're into Wicca for the cool reasons—the spells, the silver jewelry, anything that will bring you attention. I was more serious about it than others. I was raised Christian, and it didn't really fit into who I am as a bisexual man. Wicca was the religion that welcomed me home. I am a solitary Witch. I never really gave enough thought to the role that nature plays in Wicca because I just figured that if you stare at the Sky and the Moon, the Deities heard you. But all that changed when I got to college.

"I can see the mountains from my dorm room here at Bennington. I can hear the insects buzzing and the birds chirping. The silence is huge. This is a really close-knit campus and a small school, but I kept to myself as a Witch a lot of the time. Everything changed for me as a Witch when I got here. I couldn't believe how much I felt the Goddess and God when I went into the woods and stood under the Moon. I felt the forces of Earth, and I knew they felt me. I was able to experience ritual as never before, and I was never bothered by people or the things I wasn't allowed to do indoors. The space is here for you in the country. The campus really becomes your home. I missed being out of touch with the rest of the world, like the few Witches I knew back in Arizona, but that kind of aloneness allows you to grow as a Witch.

"I really came into my own as a Witch while in college. I was away, and I grew up. That makes the difference. Wicca can be demanding and I don't think any young Witch knows the meaning of magic until she spends time acquainting herself with Earth. You can't do that in the city! To answer your question . . . as for rituals, I performed my own Samhain celebrations the last four years and I love casting spells in the woods during the spring. I don't need the city at all. College Wicca is great on rural campuses. You can definitely rock the Goddess under a clear sky and nothing but silence."

Traditionally, Wicca is tied to the imagery of nature. The God is horned, like the various animals of the forests. The Goddess is often depicted through lunar symbolism and nascent springs of water. History tells us the same. In pre-Christian times, the Witches of Italy were told by Aradia to go into the woods at night, where mysteries were revealed to them beneath the Moon. What does it all mean?

A natural, quiet setting is favorable to meditation and a calm mind-set needed to cast a spell, but it is not mandatory. Over the centuries, Paganism evolved. What was customary or common in ages past may not be as relevant today. Let us not forget that during and after the Inquisition, Witches retreated into the forests of the night to worship in secret, and without fear. Under cover of darkness, cloaked by trees, they were hidden from danger. But fear is no longer a factor for the Witch. Today, Wicca suits every kind of follower, and the Goddess and God dwell in crowded cities and rural back roads alike.

Goddess in the Shadows: The Underground Coven

November 1, 2001

Dear Anthony,

It is the day after Samhain as I write this. A very auspicious time to contact you. The spirits of the dead are still lingering. But this you already know.

You don't know me, but I got your e-mail address through the grapevine, I guess you'd say. Writing a book on college Witches. A good idea. I have seen you before, even stood close to you at one of the recent Wicca gatherings you attended in Manhattan. Dark hair, dark eyes. Your auburn goatee is distinctive. Taking notes furiously as you watched and listened.

My coven name is Mortem. I'm a college Witch. Right now I'm in school in New York, a junior, but I was a student at two other universities before this. I've been practicing Wicca since I was thirteen. I'm writing because I have a story to tell you. I am a member of an underground college coven and we're not like any other coven or campus group you've interviewed. I'm sure of it. There are six of

*us in the coven, all students here in New York, and we were forced
to go underground because of the nature of our magickal practices.
We are real and serious and not some silly little fad. Wicca is our
spiritual pathway, but several things set us apart from being the
usual kinds of Witches. For example, I'm a psychic and a necromancer, and one of our coven members is a vampire who suffers from*

SPOTLIGHT

Massachusetts Institute of Technology, Pagan Student Group
www.mit.edu/activities/psg

One of the liveliest and most accomplished campus organizations in the country, the MIT Pagan Student Group has been in oper-
ation for several years and continues to attract a diversified
following. They hold frequent meetings and invite Witches and Pagans from neighboring communities for lectures and chats. The annual Samhain celebration has grown in popularity and style and is
attended by students from other colleges and universities.

Their Web site lists the names of officers along with answers to
frequently asked questions and a number of valuable Pagan links.
Like most campus-sponsored organizations, MIT Pagan Student
Group operates under a constitution and works hard to uphold
their mission—to negate the negative images cast upon Witches
and Pagans and to bring about a greater sense of fellowship
among students. Membership is open to practitioners and curious
minds alike.

---

*the beginning stages of porphyria. It makes for an interesting mix, I
guess you'd say. We worship the Goddess and God, but we also
bring other rites into the Circle. Dark rites. Not evil, just dark in
nature, like the night and the hour before dawn. Did you know that
the Greeks who worshipped the goddess Hecate resorted to blood-
drinking because it brought them closer to their shadow-selves? I've
always known it. We're a special kind of coven, which is why we're*

not public. But it's our belief that we represent a necessary and real breed of young Witches. Witchcraft isn't all about pretty moonlight and chanting. No, the Goddess requires more than that. The deeper and darker you go, the closer you get to the light. We are all around the same age, all in college, and this makes for a powerful energy field. If you're going to write about college Wicca, you should write about ALL parts of it, and that includes covens like mine. We call ourselves Coven of the Triple Witch.

If you want, you can talk to me further. I believe your book will be important, and I'd like to contribute to it. But only if you are willing to observe one of our rituals in the flesh. I cannot convey to you the meaning of our magick through writing. You have to see it, feel it, experience it. We meet in a squatter tenement over by St. Mark's Place on specific nights, in the basement. Well away from prying eyes. No one knows us. It's dark and abandoned, and it's inhabited by the ghost of a young man who died violently there more than a century ago. If you want, I'll give you the info and you can come see for yourself. We will give you our coven names and speak to you, but our magick is not light-hearted, just so you know. You must agree to come alone—no cell phones or anything like that. None of us will agree to meet you in a coffee shop or on campus like a lot of the others did. We're underground, so everything we do is underground. I know this letter might be strange even to someone like you who has probably heard most of everything by now, but I'm serious and just hope you aren't spooked or anything. Something tells me that you're not that type, the type to be scared easily. You're more intrigued than frightened, I think. Even standing close to you as I once did, I got the feeling that you always want to know more. But be careful because sometimes you go in too deep and that could be dangerous. I might sound a little far out, but I'm not. Enough with me already. Write me back soon if you want to know more. My coven is meeting in a few days if you want to see anything.
Mortem

I looked up from the computer screen and blinked, then shook my head. I had certainly come across a few nefarious college

Witches, but this was a first. A guy with a name like "Mortem." A vampire in the coven. Dark rites and a mention of blood-drinking. In order to get the story, I had to show up at an abandoned tenement all alone, without a cell phone and, presumably, without my pepper spray key chain. What were they going to do, I wondered, strip-search me? Maybe. Initially, it all sounded too contrived and over the top. On the other hand, Mortem had taken the time to construct a three-page letter to get my attention. And then there was the spooky bit about having stood next to me, and the very accurate description he offered.

The notion of the underground coven intrigued me. What exactly did they practice? Why had they been "forced" to take it all underground? The reference to St. Mark's Place in Greenwich Village, I believed, was merely decoration. The street was trendy and funky and cloaked by a dark past. When I was a student at F.H. LaGuardia High School for the Performing Arts, a number of my Goth classmates in the drama department spoke of St. Mark's Place as a haven for vampires and hauntings. I had strolled it countless times, drifting in and out of the tattoo parlors and bargaining with the outside jewelry vendors. I had seen my fair share of interesting characters, but hey, I'm a New Yorker by birth and in this city, anything goes.

I e-mailed Mortem the next day. I explained that his demands were a bit too confining and suggested meeting him elsewhere, perhaps a locale that would shield him from view but still be public enough to provide a safety net for me. Weeks passed. Nothing. The letter lingered on my mind and I had begun to regret not agreeing to the initial demands. I e-mailed him again in late November, this time including my cell phone number should he want to contact me. Just before the Thanksgiving holiday, I got a call at midnight.

"I probably shouldn't be doing this," Mortem said quickly. "I'm not patient when people ask me questions." His tone was surprisingly normal—not a trace of menace in his voice.

"Where do you want to meet?" I asked him.

He suggested one of the murky, run-down streets that parallel the West Side Highway.

I was silent, unhappily weighing my options.

"If that's not good, we could always meet down in the Village," Mortem said. "No matter where we are, you'll be close enough to people."

"I'm not afraid to meet you," I countered. Though of course, I was.

He laughed. "Good. You shouldn't be."

We decided on the small park at the corner of West Houston and MacDougal Streets, known officially as the William E. Passannante Ballfield.

"How will I recognize you?" I asked him.

"You won't. Just be there. I already know what you look like."

The connection broke.

One week later, waiting in my designated spot, I scanned the wide stretch of West Houston expectantly. Traffic was heavy. It was nearly 10:00 P.M. and the crowds were just beginning to thicken. Finally, I spotted two young men crossing the street, coming toward me. One was tall, thin, and typically Goth: pale skin, black eyeliner, and dark pants, shirt, and jacket. The other was also thin and pale, but his hair fell in dreadlocks past his shoulders and he was dressed casually in jeans, a sweater, and raincoat. He smiled and nodded as he came forward.

"Hi, Anthony."

I offered him my hand. I studied him silently, waiting for him to introduce himself.

"Yes, it's Mortem," he said. He gestured toward his taller friend. "This is Sixx."

"What happened to the rest of the coven?" I asked.

"They didn't want to come." As if on cue, he pulled a bent Polaroid from his coat pocket and held it out. There were five people in the picture, including Mortem, Sixx, and three young women. The sixth member had apparently snapped the shot. I studied it closely for a few moments. They were standing in a semicircle around several lit candles. I couldn't make out the walls or floor, but the setting seemed dark. Darker still was Sixx, who stood frozen in time, shirtless, blood dripping from a cut beneath his left nipple.

I leveled my eyes at them. "So you're the vampire?"

Sixx smiled. His canines had been professionally sharpened, and the effect was startling. "Not in the way you're thinking," he replied. "I'm a Pagan first. I worship the Old Ways. That's my spirituality. I'm a vampire because of how I live from day to day."

"And how's that?"

Sixx motioned toward the empty park. We were too close to the street, he said. It was unseasonably warm, so we settled on a nearby bench. I kept thinking back to Mortem's letter, how dark it was and tinged with a hint of menace. His appearance was almost disappointingly normal.

"Not really," he said suddenly—to me, to the night.

"What?" I was confused.

"The way I look," Mortem answered. "You were thinking I look too normal. Not enough craziness. I guess I came off as a little wacky in my letter."

I was stunned, for I had been thinking just that. So Mortem had read my mind. It sent a little chill streaking through me. In the letter he had mentioned being psychic.

I asked them how they had come to practice Wicca.

Sixx had been obsessed with the occult since childhood. He loved fantasy and horror novels and identified with alternative subcultures. A lonely, introverted kid, he spent most of his time in the library and began reading up on magick. He went Goth as a teenager. Then, three years ago, just after turning twenty, he developed the rare physical condition known as porphyria, which basically made him allergic to sunlight. His skin, he explained, had a tendency to blister and scar, and relief came only in the nighttime hours. He slept at dawn and woke in the late afternoon. But instead of infringing upon his personal life, this new routine empowered him.

"I belong in the night and in the darkness," he said dramatically. "I started making my way deeper into the vampire culture of the city. I went to a lot of the old clubs, like Bank and Mother, and started joining in on vampire covens. It wasn't anything evil, just a place for like-minded people to hang out. But it all enhanced my identity as a Pagan."

I was curious about the vampire aspect, and he reluctantly admitted to sometimes drinking human blood "from donors." This wasn't anything vaguely reminiscent of Wicca. It was, rather, a separate connection to a subculture that had been spawned by Dracula fan clubs, horror movies, and Anne Rice novels. But Sixx insisted that it fit into his "Pagan soul." Like Priestess Sepho, he saw Wicca as a religion of the night.

"If you're prepared to say that you practice Witchcraft, you have to accept it in every denomination," he told me. "Blood is powerful. There's no doubt that historically, people used blood in their rituals for healing. In Romania around the turn of the century, it was a common practice for a mother to mix in a teaspoon of her own blood with the milk she then fed to her child. Now, as a Pagan, I mix a lot of different occult traditions, but I'm close to the Wiccan philosophy because it embraces Earth, which I do. When I do rituals or magick, I use my own blood as a sacrifice to appease the darker gods and goddesses, like Hecate and Pan."

Mortem, on the other hand, was more metaphoric about his Wiccan calling. As a child he often experienced "Technicolor" dreams that included prophetic messages. He began having psychic experiences, and "saw the dead" with perfect clarity. He considered himself a Witch in the Wiccan tradition but believed that in order to truly mirror the essence of nature, one had to respect darkness as much as light.

"I was born a Witch," he said. "There's no other way to account for my obsession with the Pagan gods. Believe it or not, I was raised Jewish and my parents are the most simple people you'd ever meet. Wicca was inside me before I was even born."

Mortem presented me with his current college ID card, though objected to publicizing it. Sixx, on the other hand, told me that he had spent a year at New York's New School University and was currently on leave. Their coven came together as a result of the Internet. Mortem, who had voiced his beliefs about magick and ritual to his school's student Pagan group—beliefs that included skyclad practice and experimentation with mind-altering drugs—was incensed by their harsh rejection. It also irked him that lighting candles in his room was illegal. He defected from the group and posted an ad on a Wicca Web site to the effect that college Witches and Pagans needed to band together and rail against the authority denying them religious freedom. He received immediate replies.

"I got about twenty replies in the first week, and I chose the ones I thought were serious," he said. "I also wanted everyone to be within close proximity. All of us in the coven live in the five boroughs."

Coven of the Triple Witch was formed shortly thereafter. All six members agreed on the rules of the coven—which, in essence, had no magickal limits or boundaries. But where to practice their "renegade" form of Wicca was an issue. None of them could do it in their respective colleges and universities. They found an abandoned warehouse in Queens, which worked out only for a short while, though neither Mortem nor Sixx would tell me why the location didn't last. They searched some more and, following the advice of the squatters on and around St. Mark's Place, discovered their current digs: a tenement with a large and unused basement area. There, they practiced their own kinds of rituals.

"And how do those rituals differ from the rituals other Witches are working?" I asked.

"It has to do with the fact that we're all around the same age," Mortem answered. "We're all between twenty and twenty-four, and like I said in my letter to you, that makes for powerful energy. We're all on the same wavelength and there are absolutely no inhibitions. We're a coven, but we're also a siblinghood. None of us would be able to do the things we do magickally if we weren't all in college and struggling through the same phases of life. When we cast a magick circle, it's like we have one mind. Everything comes together."

"So," I said, "you all formed this underground coven because you were tired of being challenged by rules and a higher authority."

"In many ways, yes," Mortem replied. "But I think college students who are discovering Wicca and practicing it are really just conforming to silly campus laws. I've attended the meetings of other campus Pagan groups, and it all seemed to me like a bunch of fluff. A bunch of students sitting around and talking about the Goddess and spells. I think a lot of those same students would really break out of the mundane cycle and start more of a movement if they realized others were doing it. Witches like us."

"A lot of those students are comfortable exploring spirituality within that setting," I countered. "It doesn't make them any less valid."

"It doesn't, but in a way it does," he said. "Think about the whole college experience. You get away from home with the intention of growing up, learning how to live and fend for yourself. You're also forming relationships and making friends. And you're getting into new ideas, like Wicca. This is the only time in life when you're really free to explore things at the maximum level. When you graduate, you go out there into the real world, you get a job and fall into the same routine as everybody else. Now, that won't happen to me or any of my coven members. We're doing the real thing, and we're totally unencumbered by bullshit laws and people telling us that it isn't allowed, it isn't right, you can't do that here."

I mentioned the picture he had showed me. "What kind of a ritual was that? Sixx was bleeding."

"That was an esbat," Sixx told me. "It was a Full Moon ritual about two months ago. We invoked Pan and Hecate, and we drew a crossroads in the middle of the floor. We spent about an hour raising energy. The Deities came, but it's much more powerful when you offer up a sacrifice. Nothing's more powerful than blood, and no, it has nothing to do with vampirism or evil. That's my way of symbolizing my subservience to the gods."

"Who did the cutting?" I asked.

"I was leading the ritual with one of our female coven members," Sixx said. "We did it together."

"And then what happened?"

Mortem smiled. They exchanged glances and chuckled.

"A lot happened," Sixx said. "It was magick, like always. I went into a trance, on a journey through the Underworld. It's impossible to explain in words, but I guess it's a lot like seeing something incredible for the first time—like when people say they're amazed when they first see the pyramids in Egypt. It's indescribable, the feeling."

"What else do you do during rituals?"

"Whatever's necessary," Mortem replied. "We have no boundaries. Sometimes it's frustrating because we have to go through all these extra measures in lugging things to our space. It would be much easier if we could just do it on campus, or in our rooms, but that's impossible."

I pressed for a more detailed example.

"No matter what we do, we start out with darkness," Mortem said. "You have to get through the dark to get to the light. I'm a necromancer, so we hold a lot of séances and commune with spirits. When we invoke the goddess Isis, we use my pet snake and a few chants from the Egyptian *Book of the Dead*. We work with a lot of different deities. Everyone has a specific need. We do research, too. If someone ever witnessed one of our rituals, they'd probably get the idea that it's profane or over the edge because of what we do with blood and herbs. Sometimes we practice skyclad. It all depends on how deep we want to go."

Our conversation continued for a while longer. Sixx showed me the strange scar patterns on his abdomen that he claimed had taken form "invisibly"—not by his own hands but by way of a deity that had "branded" him during a ritual. One looked like a crescent moon; another resembled a woman's profile. Before we parted ways, Mortem reached into his coat pocket and handed me something. It was a blue votive candle.

"I charged it for you this morning," he explained. "It's for protection."

I studied it closely, turning it around in my fingers. Near the bottom, in small script, were two numbers: *6-13*. My date of birth. It seemed like another psychic jolt because I had *surely not* mentioned it to Mortem during our single, brief telephone conversation.

I thanked them and watched as their backs receded down the busy street. From my vantage point, they could have easily passed as college students out for a night on the town. The Witch and the vampire. Was their story singular, I wondered, or were there many others like them—rebelling against the rules, exploring magick and ritual underground? *That's speculation*, I told myself, heading toward the subway station. *That's* a whole other book.

Student Pagan Groups: Starting Your Own

A sponsored, funded student Pagan group or association will require the support of your college or university. In some cases, you may have to go through specific channels, such as student government or the office of student affairs. Once you decipher the method, remember that it may take time to be deemed "official." That should not stop you or anyone from meeting regularly on campus, however. Classrooms are not always in use, and a lounge or corner table in the dining hall can certainly accommodate a night's worth of discussion.

Before addressing your school about starting a group, put together a proposal explaining exactly what you hope to accomplish. Include:

1. **The name of your group.** You may want to choose something stylish and memorable (e.g., "Nemeton" is the name of Boston University's group). Otherwise, the name of your college or university should precede "Student Pagan/Wiccan Association."

2. **Your mission statement.** What is the group all about? Why are you forming it? Is it going to be an "active" group that will hold regular rituals, or is it more of a discussion group? Remember that no matter your intent, the administration will want to see something along the lines of "fostering community and enhancing student life."

3. **Rules and regulations.** Is the group open to anyone on campus? Do you want more advanced students? Is weekly attendance mandatory? Answer these questions, and then explain whether or not you will be appointing officers (president, vice president, etc.). You may also want to pen a "constitution" that will outline the group's policies, such as how long each officer's term will last, the duration of each meeting, and how you will go about promoting

---

HOW DO YOU *ROCK THE GODDESS?*

Corey Z., senior
Case Western Reserve

"The first ritual I ever did was for the Summer Solstice. I was home in North Dakota, and when you're in the middle of nowhere there's no excuse not to utilize nature for everything. I walked into the woods near my house at dusk, but I didn't have any tools or even an idea of what I wanted to do. I just knew that I wanted to worship Earth and the Goddess. I found a branch and drew a big circle in the ground, then collected some leaves and flowers, a couple of stones. I sat there, all alone, and wrote in my journal about what I was feeling and why I had come to this place. I watched the light wane, and it was the most incredible sunset I had ever seen. I stayed there and watched deer run by, and the birds were singing in the trees. When night fell, I wrote my name on a sheet of paper and buried that in the ground. It was the first time I felt like a Pagan—I was living what it all means. I was surrounded by simple things, things I had seen every day. But on that day, nature came alive."

---

yourselves on campus. If you plan on holding rituals, outline the rules and the process, making certain that you do not intend to violate any campus regulations.

4. **Sponsors.** Chances are you will need a faculty member to sponsor the group. If you do not already have a professor in mind,

ask around. Does your school have a religious studies department? If not, the sociology, anthropology, or psychology departments will surely suffice. Your sponsor need not be a Witch or Pagan. He or she should merely express an interest in what your group is determined to accomplish.

5. **Personal information.** Who are you and why are you qualified to run this group? What are your personal stakes and interests? List your year, your major, whether or not you live on campus. Have you ever started a group before? If so, explain how your skills and experience will impact the group you are proposing. Also list any groups you are currently a member of.

6. **Student support.** Include in your proposal a petition or list of signatures from at least five other students who plan on being active members. This will automatically prove that there is interest on campus. When students speak up, the administration listens.

7. **Information.** Along with your proposal, you will want to include some relevant information on Wicca and Paganism. Don't expect everyone to automatically understand the tenets and philosophies of Wicca. Educating any confused parties will undoubtedly work in your favor. Info can be garnered from Web sites, periodicals, and books—all of which are available through your campus library. (If your school does not have a library equipped with Internet access and scores of research materials, stop paying tuition and request a transfer application from the Registrar *right away*.)

Once you submit your proposal to the proper office, begin organizing what you will need for your first official meeting. Draw up flyers, make announcements in classes, head over to the campus newspaper and ask them to run a story. Any new venture needs publicity.

Solitary Sorcery

In the chill blue of dawn, a young woman makes her way home.

Martha thinks of her destination as she threads through a patch of woods bordering the college campus. Just beyond the towering evergreens, the sky is brightening with the first rays of the Sun. The horizon is shot with red, like a splotch of blood. Seagulls caw overhead before diving toward the water's edge. She glimpses the ocean in the clearing of trees and pauses at the edge of the bluff. Smiling, she takes in the waves and scalloped coastline. Her footfalls are silent as she descends the steps leading to the beach.

Autumn has brought an unseasonably cool wind, but she is clothed in a warming sweater and jeans. Her long hair is tied back in a ponytail. A curious passerby would look at her—the wire-rimmed glasses, the inquisitive expression—and see nothing more than a college kid from the nearby university. But Martha knows better. Eighteen years old, she has left her adolescence behind and entered a new realm of life. Gone are the days of curfews, rules, and high school dances. Her parents are more than a thousand miles away. Now, she comes and goes as she pleases and can light up cigarettes in the privacy of her shared apartment. What's more, she can feel the constraints of her teenage years loosening steadily day by day, releasing her into a sense of awareness, knowledge, and occasional self-doubt. Despite the tumult that accompanies discovery, Martha is pleased to be here: in this place where no one speaks her name, this time of faltering confidence and ever-strengthening identity. She is lost and found in the same moment.

She walks slowly along the beach. Her bare feet sink into the cold sand. Inhaling deeply, she closes her eyes and begins the meditation that has become a daily ritual. Calm floods her. She throws her arms out wide, as if eager to embrace the vastness of Nature—Air, Earth, Water, Fire. The elements fill her with their promise of renewal, and with them comes the simple, sacred spirit of the Goddess. She is the newborn cry of Earth and the soothing release of death. She is breath that quenches the heat with rain and unleashes the fury of tunneled winds over the grasslands. Martha knows the Goddess well. She has been giving her praise for years. She remembers huddling in her bedroom back home, lighting a single candle while staring out the window and up at the Full Moon. Now she is free to summon her Witch's power in the open, harnessing the forces that will do her bidding.

Today she hasn't need for a love spell or a banishing ritual. Today, an idle Tuesday in late September, she journeyed to the beach in search of peace. The pressure of the last few weeks has at last caught up with her: difficult classes, tight deadlines, the strange comfort of her new surroundings. Martha wants only to be rid of the angst. Using her hands, she draws a haphazard circle in the sand. Sitting in the center, she reaches into her sweater and grabs hold of the pentacle dangling from a chain at her neck. Raising her voice above the roar of churning waves, Martha begins reciting her solitary prayer. Her words are scattered by the wind, but their meaning grows in momentum as the Sun climbs into the cobalt sky and warms the surf below. She isn't thinking about the long day ahead. Her mind is not occupied by notions of frat parties or boys. That was the old Martha, the girl once at odds with her own imperfect reflection. This, *she tells herself,* is the new me: sated but searching, confident but cautious, a true participant in my own spiritual growth. *In her mind's eye she can see the Sun's light curling around the circle in which she sits. She can feel the Goddess imbuing in her the power of a thousand moonlit nights. How boundless the rush. How palpable the magic. Invoked from the sanctum of her heart, it explodes like a flame and welcomes her home.*

The Witch, Alone: *Solitary Practice*

As Wicca continues to evolve as a religion, so too do its practitioners. More women and men are extending their studies and delving deeper into the meaning and the mind-set of the modern-day Witch. Although some will always prefer a life of complete privacy—if not anonymity—the number of people joining covens and attending workshops and festivals continues to rise. In the previous chapter, we saw the benefits of the college coven or student Pagan group. That kind of community and lively atmosphere builds up self-esteem and creates comfort zones. It can also lead to friendships, relationships, and partners in magick and ritual. But there is an "other side" to Wicca that has little to do with union between the High Priest and Priestess or dancing around a circle while holding hands. The solitary Witch works alone.

Ultimately, every Witch starts out as a solitary. No matter your age, you lit your first candle on your own. Did you buy that book a few years back? Did you execute a search on the Internet or cruise into a chatroom? Indeed, you did. Later, you cast the first spell when your parents weren't home. You developed a strange love for long walks in the woods, a stroll down by the beach at twilight. Night intrigued you. The dark was your friend, magick your intellectual lover. You were alone. Unaccompanied and unparalleled. A solitary Witch.

On campus, you will decide whether or not to practice as a solitary or in a coven. Joining a student Pagan club or organization does not necessarily equate a coven, unless all members are meeting monthly to worship the Full Moon. Many college Witches join covens in neighboring communities or (as we have seen) go underground with their practices. The overwhelming majority, however, prefer the solitary path. Alone, you are free to move about studying Wicca at your own pace. You can construct rituals that suit your needs and personal tastes. It is important to understand that the word "solitary" does not imply a hermit or recluse. Rather, it refers to the Witch or Pagan who practices magick without the aid or kinship of a coven. Does this make magick less powerful? No. Does it mean that a solitary cannot join a group for an occasional ritual? No. Solitaries are still free to craft a spiritual niche, but independence is at the heart of it all.

Private Realms: *Magick Made Simple*

Rainy B. had already been practicing Wicca for three years when she started her college career at Baruch College of the City University of New York. A Manhattan resident, she was familiar with the local Wiccan community and had attended workshops and open circles on a regular basis. She knew teenagers, students, adults, fathers, and mothers who openly proclaimed themselves Witches. In fact, while a freshman at Baruch, Rainy was asked by a Brooklyn-based coven whether she wanted to join as their newest member.

"It was a coven of older people, and I was flattered that they had asked me," she said. "But I decided against it because it just didn't feel right. I had seen dozens of covens and they're a cool community of people, but when you join a coven you have to submit to a number of rules and demands. You have to be present at every gathering. You can't miss a Full Moon. That's okay for some people but I've always been kind of a loner, and solitary Wicca suits me much better. I do it the way I want and how I want."

In terms of magick, Rainy told me that she felt "empowered" by the spells she wrote and created.

"About a year ago I came up with this good-luck spell that uses olive oil, copper, and a few other ingredients, and the results have been amazing. It had been dwelling in my own mind for a long time, but I put it together when I was ready. I didn't ask anyone for help. I went to the library and bookstores and did the research myself. It's really an incredible high when you do something on your own. That's a lot of what solitary practice is about. You learn at your own pace. You can even bring it to a halt if you feel like you need a rest. You can't do that when you're in a coven. For me, magick is very personal and I know that I'm growing as a Witch because I practice solitary."

Urania, a recent graduate of the University of Chicago, was a member of a coven throughout her college years. The coven met in suburban Illinois on a monthly basis, and although she enjoyed the sense of community, she ultimately left to practice on her own. In a telephone conversation she cited the demands of coven life as contributing to her decision.

"There can be a lot of politics when you join a coven. People don't always agree, and I remember a few incidents that were rather negative in the coven I was a member of. I look back on it fondly, though. I'm still very friendly with everyone and I usually join in on their Samhain celebration. But I like my spiritual life much better now that I'm a solitary. It's less stressful, and I'm free to explore other Traditions and network with other covens. Sometimes it can get lonely, but when you want that extra company, you can always find a Pagan festival going on somewhere in the city."

Networking remains an important issue for solitary Witches. New Age and occult shops often publicize weekly or monthly meetings that help better serve their local communities. There are even Wiccan/Pagan dating services and instructional classes for solitary practitioners. If none of these options appeals to you, remember that with solitary practice, you are truly exploring Wicca on your own. There are no degrees to earn, nor is there any formal initiation. Weigh the pros and cons.

Cyber Haven: *Witches Online*

Execute an Internet search using the words *Wicca, Witch, Pagan,* or *Witchcraft* and you will be led through a maze of Web sites and personal home-pages that can number in the hundreds of thousands.

Wicca has grown so much as a culture in the last decade, there is no definitive way to describe the "true" practitioner. Online, Witches host their own chatrooms and message boards, and every one seems

---

SPOTLIGHT

Ohio State University Pagan Student Association

www.acs.ohio-state.edu/students/pagansa

The Ohio State University Pagan Student Association is not a small campus organization. According to their Web site, it is comprised of both undergraduate and graduate students. They are a diversified bunch. Pre-med and English majors aside, other members are studying religion, theater, and anthropology. They also admit recent graduates who still want to be a part of a Wiccan/Pagan community.

"It's a very popular and well-run student club," said a representative from the Office of Student Affairs. "They're organized and very serious about what they want to do, and they're always making plans to improve things with each new semester. Students join the meetings regularly. It's an open forum."

In fact, the PSA is proud to have members of various religious faiths. There are Druids and Witches, but also Christians. The informative Web site lists pages that answer frequently asked questions. It also contains a small glossary of common terms used in the Wiccan/Pagan faiths. Students from neighboring colleges and universities can log on to find the PSA calendar of events (recent discussions include yoga, magick, and making masks) among other helpful links.

---

to have a vision of spirituality that differs from the next. I found a number of sites that branded solitary Witches as "fraudulent" because they did not undergo long-term study with a coven or high priestess. Another claimed that to truly "walk between the worlds," one had to be a Witch through hereditary or direct lineage. The flux of opinions is expected given the millions of people who surf the Internet daily, but online methods can be useful for networking and building connections.

For all its good use, the Internet can also present some very real dangers. If you are living on a campus that is lacking a Wiccan or Pagan scene and feel like you need to make connections, your computer will most likely act as the source of change. Begin by exercising caution. Internet crimes are on the rise, and law enforcement agencies all over the United States have implemented high-level technological resources to combat illegal activity. And, yes—it happens in the Wiccan and Pagan online communities. Bogus retail sites promising low rates and great products represent only one kind of scam. In truth, harm can affect more than just your credit cards. Funky screen names and advertisements may conceal less-than-honorable intentions, and you have to be smart when meeting people in chatrooms or through message boards. Presenting yourself as a young and eager Witch will open the door to a variety of responses—some, of course, will be sincere, but others will come across as flat-out strange. Agreeing to meet your new-found friend outside of the public arena is the biggest—and sometimes the most perilous—mistake. Sure, he may claim to be the reincarnated version of a centuries-old Witch who can brew the elixir of life, but keep any personal information away from the screen. The same goes for covens or groups that post blurbs about recruiting new members. Wicca is not a religion that advertises conversion, so any site that asks you to submit an "application" should hit the cyber highway.

I had heard stories of Witches being duped into bizarre situations, but how high, I wondered, did the danger levels rise? Over the course of several days, I experimented with the online Wiccan and Pagan community, adopting a fake screen name with a typically ordinary profile: *NiteGod, college student, into Wicca, looking to make new connections and meet friends.* The most memorable experience was via a "Wiccan Chathouse" with a slammin' roster of guests. I logged on and was denied access several times because the room was at full capacity. Finally, I got in. Messages and conversational nuggets were shooting onto the screen like bullets. Regulars here knew one another, and they chatted at length about spells and magick. If anyone wanted to know more about me, he or she simply had to click on my name to access the profile. I typed in a "Greetings to all" and then waited.

A few minutes later, I was being hit up for a chat. The user had a "magickal" name. I returned a hello and then clicked for his profile, but he had not provided one.

"Where are you?" I typed in.

"New Jersey. Not far from Manhattan."

"How old?"

"Thirty-eight."

"And you're a Witch."

"Yes. What college do you attend?"

"SUNY Purchase."

"Do you like it?"

"I love it. It's a great place."

"Any Witches up there?"

"Quite a few."

"What's your name?"

"Anthony. Yours?"

"Crow."

"How about your real name?"

"That's been my nickname since I was a kid. I've been practicing for twenty years," he went on. "How about you? What are you interested in knowing?"

I told him that I wasn't really sure. I knew enough about Wicca, but the various traditions sometimes confused me. He was polite in answering my questions and seemed to be genuinely knowledgeable about the Wiccan movement. We chatted for about a half hour. I was about to bid him farewell when he chimed in with an offer.

"I sometimes teach classes about Wicca, if you'd be interested," he said.

"Where? Are you a college professor?"

"No, nothing like that. There's a New Age shop near Montclair, New Jersey, where I teach. A lot of college students come."

"What's the price?" I asked.

"It's fifty dollars for two sessions, and each runs about three hours long."

"What's the name of the shop? Maybe I already know it."

He replied by offering his telephone number. If I wanted any more information, I'd have to phone him.

Well, I thought as I closed out of the room, Crow might have been sincere, but why not offer the name of the shop? I was intrigued. If he was a teacher, what exactly did he teach? He had mentioned a lot of college students coming to his little classes; if so, would he be willing to put me in touch with a few of them? The other possibility was just as simple. Maybe he was a freak who used the Wicca angle to prey on young, curious minds, luring them into some sort of trap. I weighed the options, then reached for my cell phone.

Crow was surprised to hear from me. "I had a feeling about you," he said right away.

"What kind of feeling?" I asked him.

"You just seemed really intrigued by what I was saying. That's a good sign. It means you're serious about your passion for Wicca."

"Can you tell me more about these classes you teach?"

"Well, they're mostly classes for beginners. I start out by exploring the Goddess and God and other deities, and then the second half of the class is about magick and spell-crafting."

"Can you tell me the name of the shop?"

"Tell me a little about yourself first."

I hesitated, not wanting to divulge too much information. "I'm majoring in sociology."

"Sounds good. You would probably need the beginners' class."

"Where can I get more info? The shop, maybe?"

"No," Crow said. "I'd have to meet you first and decide what level of understanding you're at."

The first strike. I asked him, "What colleges do some of your students attend?"

"Mostly colleges in Jersey."

"Like?"

"Give me your phone number and I'll get back to you about when we can meet," he said, eager to turn the conversation around.

"Where would I meet you?"

"I don't get into the city much. Do you ever get into Jersey?"

"Sometimes."

"Maybe you can come to my apartment . . ."

I told him I'd think about it and hung up. It was a strange experience, and I seriously doubted Crow's positive intentions given his suggestion that I—a complete stranger—take a road trip to his apartment. I kept cruising online. I met many interesting people who chatted with me at length about Wicca and offered their help on a purely impersonal level. A few even provided their e-mail addresses should I want to keep in touch. It wasn't all bad.

But when I searched a message board I found something interesting—an ad seeking young Witches for a "private occult study group." I wrote an e-mail to "Merlynna" and received a swift reply.

"We're a small group that originated in Savannah, Georgia, but our members live all over the country. We publish a newsletter and hold an annual meeting. We are 90 percent Wiccan/Pagan, and the others are avid occultists. Along with membership comes a bunch of resources, a lot of them unpublished and otherwise unattainable."

The note went on to say that the group was young, mostly between the ages of twenty and twenty-eight. To apply, I would have to fill out an application that included a request for my social security number. And there was a fee: forty dollars for an eight-month duration. I e-mailed Merlynna a reply, posing a few questions. I never heard from her again.

In the "Witch's Dome" chatroom, I met a married Pagan couple whose profile listed "swinging" as a hobby. The husband-and-wife team claimed to be at their computer together and wrote messages to the effect of: "Seeking inquisitive, sexually experienced, and open-minded male or female for mutual fun." Soon enough, I typed in my own message: "College student interested in exploring the Wiccan scene." I was approached by several people, three of them fellow students. Twenty minutes into the chat session, the horny couple sent me a private message.

"How old are you?" came the first question.

"My early twenties," I replied. "I read your profile."

"Are you interested?"

"That depends. What kind of stuff are you guys into?"

They explained that they were both bisexual, in shape, and really didn't have any limits.

Great, I thought. Porn star Pagans. "Are you into S&M?" I asked.

"We've done it before, yes. But we practice sex magick too."

"Like what?"

"Sometimes we use herbal potions that can enhance orgasms, and for fellow Pagans, we prefer to have sex within the magick circle."

"Where do you host these little trysts?"

"In our home. Strip-at-the-door policy. And you have to bring your own booze."

"Have you ever played around with a college student before?" I asked. "We can be crazy and we have A LOT of energy."

"LOL [laughing out loud]. Yes, the younger ones always do! It doesn't bother us that you're a college student. You're of age. Can you send us face and body picture? Preferably in the nude."

Oh sure, Mrs. Caligula. I'll even provide the whips . . .

A young man who went by the name DawnTreader educated me on the Wiccan and Pagan online culture. He was twenty-six years old and a recent graduate of the Massachusetts Institute of Technology. He considered himself a Pagan who drew from various spiritual traditions, including Native American and Yoruba. For the last two years, he had worked as a Web master and consultant for a number of "alternative" sites.

"More than anything, I think the Internet has brought the Wiccan and Pagan community together in the last decade," he told me. "Thousands of sites are used for networking and provide links to retailers, covens, and study groups. Personally, I think it's the number one way Witches and Pagans connect with one another."

DawnTreader was a solitary, but he had made several friends via his online resources. That was how he initially found work. I asked him if he had ever come face to face with anything disturbing.

"I had one experience that kind of shook me up," he explained. "I was still in college and not very public about my spiritual beliefs. I was a little older than most of the students at MIT, so I felt like

---

HOW DO YOU *ROCK THE GODDESS?*

Anthony Paige, senior
SUNY Purchase College

"Religion is my obsession. It is also my salvation. No other sub-ject holds the power to simultaneously challenge and soothe my mind. When I think of Paganism, I am filled with historical images: of Witches dancing under the Roman Moon, of candles blurring the darkness like fireflies in a windstorm. It's my way of paying hom-age to my ancestors, who until very recently roamed the small towns and villages in the south of Italy. Wicca fascinates me from a sociological perspective. I see young adults my own age se-duced by a faith that grates against the world's technological skin, and I wonder what it's all about. Alone—as I often am—I feel the dark beauty of the night come alive; I hear the wind whispering as it ushers in the dawn. The mystery of the Witch traps me in its web, and I have to write my way free. And so words become my salva-tion too. I honor the Goddess by writing about her—the mystery, the magic, and the devotees who call themselves her children."

---

that set me apart. I spent a lot of time surfing the Net. I met two Witches in a chatroom one night, and we remained in touch for about two weeks before I decided to meet them. When I finally did, they confessed that they were more into Satanism and felt like I should join in their secret little coven. They were completely differ-ent in person than how they presented themselves while we were chatting. Well, I totally disagreed with everything they were saying, and I broke away without saying much. One of them kept e-mailing me for about a month, and sometimes his messages were dark—you know, a lot of drama he thought would scare me.

"In a lot of ways, Wicca is still an underground scene. It's a subculture and can be marginal to other things—the Goths, the vampires, the psychics. Most sites about parapsychology have direct links to Wicca and Paganism. The Internet gives people a chance to create their identities without having to worry about exposure. In one way that's good, but it can also get out of hand. You have to be smart about the people you're meeting. In cyberspace, no group is immune to strange happenings."

For solitary Witches, the Internet remains a vital resource. Well over half of the people I interviewed mentioned online activities as a gateway to education, networking, even enlightenment. Surfing is a good thing: the waves of change come when you ride new currents. Just remember that still waters run deep.

Book Three

●

A WITCH'S
PARTY

●

Independent Study

·8·

College Witches Intercontinental

The following list should act as your own personal directory for networking. The colleges and universities listed have either their own Student Pagan Groups/Organizations/Associations or represent educational institutions from where people spoke to me. In some cases, I have included the names of outside covens comprised of college students. To find more information on a specific group, simply type its name into any Internet search engine, or visit the Web page of that college.

United States of America

ALABAMA
University of Alabama at Birmingham
University of Alabama at Cullman: Circle of the Feathered Serpent
Auburn University: Pantheon

ARIZONA
University of Arizona at Mesa/Phoenix: East Valley Psycho Pagans
University of Arizona at Chandler: Nether-World Society
University of Arizona at Tucson: Arizona Student Pagans

ARKANSAS
University of Arkansas at Fayetteville: Student Pagan Association
University of Arkansas: Student Pagan Association

CALIFORNIA
Palomar College: Pagan Pathways
University of California at Santa Cruz: Pagan Student Union
University of California at Santa Barbara
University of California at Davis
University of California at Berkeley
University of California at Los Angeles: UCLA Pagan Circle
University of California at Riverside: Pagan Student Union
University of South California: Students of Ancient Religions
University of California at San Marcos: Pagan Alliance Network
San Francisco State
California State University at Chico
Standford University
Long Beach, California: Coven of the Dark Goddess
Bakersfield, California: Knights of Luna
Laguna Hills: Coven of the Articulate

COLORADO
University of Colorado at Boulder: Pagan Student Alliance
Colorado State University, Fort Collins: Pagan Student Alliance
University of Colorado at Denver

CONNECTICUT
University of Connecticut: Pagan Organization for Diverse
    Spirituality
Yale University: Student Pagan Organization
Connecticut College
Danbury: Goddess Star Coven (open to all students in the Northeast)
Jewett City: Wiccan Pagan Study Group

DELAWARE
University of Delaware: Students of the Earth
Delaware Technical Community College: Moonwolf Circle

FLORIDA
University of Florida: Pagan Student Union
University of South Florida: United Pagan Allied Network
University of West Florida: Pagan Campus Ministries
Valenica Community College: Wiccan/Pagan Student Association
Florida Community College: Study Group for Pagan College
    Students
Florida State University: Pagan/Wiccan Group

GEORGIA
University of Georgia at Athens: Pagan Students Association
Georgia State University: Pagan Student Association
Georgia Institute of Technology: Student Pagan Community

HAWAII
University of Hawaii at Honolulu
University of Hawaii at Maui

ILLINOIS
Eastern Illinois University: Society for Metaphysical Advancement
Illinois State University: P.R.O.T.E.C.T. (Pagans Reaching Out to
    Educate Campus Together)
Southern Illinois University, Edwardsville: MYSTIC (May You See
    Things in Clarity) Society
University of Illinois at Macomb: Sanctuary Open Circle
Northern Illinois University: Pagan Awareness Association
University of Illinois at Urbana: Pagan Awareness Network
Bradley University: Student Pagans
Goodfield: Coven of the Four Seasons

INDIANA
Indiana University, Bloomington: Earth Religions
Indiana Polytechnic, Fort Wayne: Pagan Student Alliance
Perdue University: Pagan Academic Network
Kokomo: Coven of the Witching Hour

IOWA
University of Northern Iowa: Modern Alternative Religious Society
Grinnell College: Pagan Discussion Group
Marycrest University: PaganCrest
Iowa State University: Pagan Community
University of Iowa: River City Pagan Community
Iowa City: Coven of the Crystal Tower

KANSAS
University of Kansas
Hadam: Coven of the Emerald Fire

KENTUCKY
Murray State University: Student Pagan Association
University of Kentucky at Louisville: Pagan Student Union
Eastern Kentucky University: Pagan Alliance
Bowling Green State University: Pagan Student Union

LOUISIANA
Northwestern State University: Numinous
Tulane University: Alternative Spirituality Discussion Group
Louisiana Tech
University of New Orleans
New Orleans: Coven of the College Stars

MAINE
University of Maine at Orono: Pagan Campus Organization
Colby College: Circle
University of Southern Maine: Pagan Students Association

MARYLAND
Frostburg State University: Pagan Association
St. Mary's College: Circle of the Blue Heron
University of Baltimore County: Pagan Students Association

University of Maryland at College Park: Pagan Student Union
Villa Julie College: Pagan Students Association

MASSACHUSETTS
Boston University: Nemeton, Pagan Student Alliance
Massachusetts Institute of Technology (M.I.T.): Pagan Students
Group
Bridgewater State College: Witches Interactive College Community
Association
University of Massachusetts at Amherst: Pagan Students
Organization
Westfield State College: Crescent Moon Society
Wellesley College: Pagan Students Group
Smith College: Association of Smith Pagans
Harvard University
Salem State College
Salem: College Coven of Pan

MICHIGAN
Eastern Michigan University: Magickal Life
Ferris State University: Earth Spirit
Wayne State College: Full Moon Circle
Michigan Technological University: Deosil
Michigan State University: Wiccan Journey
Michigan State University: Green Spiral
Western Michigan University: Ancient Altars
Central Michigan State University: Open Grove Society
Lansing: Goddess Rising College Coven

MINNESOTA
University of Minnesota, East Bank: University Pagan Society
St. Cloud State University: Pagan Alliance
Bemidji State University: Celebration
St. Olaf's College: Pagan & Alternative Religions Association
Mankato State University: Student Pagan Organization

University of Minnesota at Duluth: Society for Pagan, Paranormal
and Magickal Studies
University of Minnesota, Twin Cities: Society for Pagan,
Paranormal and Magickal Studies
Macalester College: MacPagans
University of Minnesota at Morris
Duluth: Coven of the Brite Blade

MISSISSIPPI
Mississippi State University: Wiccan/Pagan Student Alliance
University of Mississippi at Oxford

MISSOURI
University of Missouri at Rolla: Society of All Paths
Truman State College: Truman Pagan Fellowship
Washington University: Silver Crescent
Southeast Missouri State University: Circle of the Blessed Moon
University of Missouri at Columbia: Sacred Ways of Earth
University of Missouri at St. Louis

MONTANA
University of Montana at Missoula: POWERS (Pagan or Wiccan
Education, Resources & Support)
MSU College of Technology
Montana State University

NEBRASKA
University of Nebraska at Lincoln

NEVADA
University of Nevada at Las Vegas: UNLV Pagans & Wiccans

NEW JERSEY
Rutgers University: Pagan Students Association
Drew University: Neo-Pagan Association

Princeton University
Seton Hall College

NEW MEXICO
New Mexico State University at Las Cruces: Pagan Student Union

NEW YORK
SUNY Purchase College: Mysterious Realm
SUNY Canton: Student Organization of United Pagans
SUNY Oswego: Pagan Students Association
SUNY Albany: Student Pagans
SUNY Buffalo: Alternative Religions Student Association
SUNY Potsdam: Pagan Studies Organization
SUNY Stony Brook
SUNY Brockport
Columbia University: Pagan Student Group
John Jay College of Criminal Justice (CUNY): Guided by Maat
Cornell University: United Pagan Ministries
Marymount College
New York University
Manhattanville College
Manhattan College
College of Mt. Saint Vincent
Pace University
Sarah Lawrence College: Paganna/Agape
Rensselaer Polytechnic Institute: Pagan Association
Colgate University: Alternative Spiritualities
Sienna College
Iona College
Syracuse University: Pagan Student Alliance
Elmira College: Guild of Alternative Spiritualities
New School University
The Cooper Union
St. John's University

New York, New York: Coven of the Triple Witch; Coven of Astara
Scarsdale, New York: Siblings of the Dark Moon

NORTH CAROLINA
University of North Carolina at Chapel Hill: Kallisti
University of North Carolina at Greensboro: Wiccan/Pagan Student
   Alliance
East Carolina University: Pagan Student Association
Haywood Community College: Fellowship of the Earth
North Carolina State University: Society for Paganism and Magick
Western Carolina University

OHIO
Oberlin College: Pagan Awareness Network
Ohio State University: Pagan Students Association
Ohio State Eastern University: Student Pagan Association
University of Dayton: Pagan & Secularist Alliance
Bowling Green University: Pagan Students Union
Case Western Reserve University: PanSpiritual Association
Columbus College of Art & Design: Association of Student Pagans
Kent State University: Neo-Pagan Coalition
University of Toledo: Kindred Spirits

OKLAHOMA
Oklahoma State University: Pagan Students Association

OREGON
Reed College: Reed Pagan Circle
Rogue Community College: Student Pagan Alliance
University of Oregon: Pagan Student Union
Salem: Grove of Dawn College Coven

PENNSYLVANIA
Penn State: Silver Circle
Carnegie Mellon University: Eclectic Studies Group

Lehigh University: Whispering Trees
Indiana University of Pennsylvania: Spirit of the Oak
University of Pittsburgh: Circle of the Ancients
Drexel University: Silver Dragon Circle

RHODE ISLAND
University of Rhode Island: Silver Threads

SOUTH CAROLINA
Clemson University: The Moonrise Group/Alternative Religion
    Discussion
Winthrop University
Sauk Valley Community College

TENNESSEE
Middle Tennessee State University: Student Pagan Organization
University of Tennessee at Chattanooga: Student Pagan Alliance
Rhodes College
University of Nashville

TEXAS
Texas A&M: Pagan Student Association
Rice University: Pagan Student Association
Sam Houston State University: Student Pagan Association
Lamar University: Neo-Pagan Alliance
Texas Technical University: U-Pagan Group
Stephen F. Austin State University: Pagan Student Alliance
University of Texas at Dallas: Student Pagan Association
University of North Texas: Pagan Student Association
University of Texas at Austin: Pagan Student Alliance
Cisco Junior College: Iron Butterfly Study Group and Learning
    Circle

UTAH
Weber State University: Pagan Student Spirit Alliance
Salt Lake Community College: Pagan Student Alliance
University of Utah: Pagan Student Alliance

VERMONT
University of Vermont at Burlington: Pagan Society/Vermont
    Pagans
Bennington College

VIRGINIA
Virginia Tech: Silver Crescent
University of Richmond

WASHINGTON
Washington State University at Seattle: UW Pagans
Eastern Washington University: EWU Pagans
Washington State University at Pullman: UW Pagans
University of Washington: Pagan Alliance
Seattle: Dragonna Blue College Coven

WISCONSIN
University of Wisconsin at Stevens Point: Aurora Boread
Lawrence University: Pagan Organization
University of Wisconsin at Milwaukee: Pagan Student Fellowship
University of Wisconsin at La Crosse: Circle of Pagan and Pagan
    Supporters
University of Wisconsin at Madison: Goddess Spirituality Group

WYOMING
University of Wyoming at Jackson Hole

WASHINGTON, D.C.
Catholic University of America
American University
Georgetown University

ARGENTINA

Universidad de Buenos Aires
Universidad Nacional de Mar del Plata

AUSTRALIA

Flinders University: Pagan Association
Monash University: Alternative Spirituality Club
University of Sydney: PAGUS
University of Australia, Perth: University Pagan Network

BELGIUM

University of Ghent: Pagan Club

BRAZIL

Universidad de Sao Paulo
Universidade do Amazonas

CANADA

University College of the Fraser Valley: Pagan Students Association
University of Victoria: Thorn & Oak/Student Pagans
University of British Columbia: Pagan Students Association
St. John's College: Pagan Society
University of New Brunswick: Sacred Spirits
Mount St. Vincent University: Pagan Society
Mt. Allison University: E.R.O.S. (Earth Religion Organization of
    Students)
McMaster University: Wiccans Together
Trent University: Pagan Circle
Niagara College: Pagan Circle
University of Windsor: Pagans and Like Minds
University of Waterloo: Infinite Circle
Carelton University: Pagan Circle
Concordia University: Pagan Society
University of Toronto: Pagan Society
Ryerson Polytechnic University: Alliance of Pagans
York University: Caer Avalon

DENMARK

Aalborg Universitet
Technical University of Denmark: Paganus
The National Film School of Denmark

GERMANY

Universitaet Duesseldorf
University of Cologne

ITALY

Bocconi Universita: Streghe
American University of Rome
Instituto Giordano
Lorenzo de' Medici School
Istituto Universitario di Architettu ra di Venezia
Universita Cattolica del Sacro Cuore

MEXICO

Universidad di Tijuana: Brujas

NETHERLANDS

Erasmus University, Rodderdam: Olds Gods Unite
Royal Conservatory of Music and Dance: Goddess Arts

PHILIPPINES

Xavier University, Alteneo de Cagayan: Blessed Circle of the
    Almighty
University of Philippines, Manila: Dark Black Coven
De La Salle University: Agla Advoratus

PORTUGAL

Universidade do Porto: Irmandade das Sombras

SCOTLAND

University of Glasgow: The Hearth Moot
University of Edinburgh: Society Mystica

SINGAPORE

National University of Singapore: Divine Blessing Coven
Nanyang Technological University: Children of Isis

SOUTH AFRICA

University of Stellenbosch: Shadow Coven
Rand Afrikaans University, Johannesburg: Moonlight Society

UNITED KINGDOM

University of Bristol: Earth Religions Society
Leeds University: LUU Kabal
University College, London: Union Pagan Society
Leicaster University: Wiccan Focus
University of Greenwich, London: Greenwich Uni Pagans
York University: Pagan Group
Cardiff University
University of Sheffield: Pagan Society
Keele University: Arcana

· 9 ·

Spells for the College Witch

Gods and Goddesses: Who They Are, How They Help

Throughout the annals of Wicca and Paganism, there are countless Gods and Goddesses. Every civilization has its own ties to Earth-based divinity, from Roman and Celtic to Native American and Asian. Following is a list of various deities. It is, of course, not complete, but any Internet search engine will easily expand your curiosities. When invoking a deity for magickal or ritual purposes, remember to follow the Wiccan rede: Harm none, do what you will. Also be certain to thank the deities before, during, and after your work is done.

THE GODDESSES

Aradia: She was a prophet, the daughter of Diana, sent to Earth to teach Witchcraft. There are truly no limits to her power. She will protect and defend. She will grant luck and positive influence. She is the Moon, the Sun, the Stars. Invoke her when performing any spell, ritual, or magickal practice. Summon her for strength.

Lakshmi: (Hindu) A goddess of wealth, she can draw the influences of money and material possessions. She is also associated with good fortune. Invoke her for beauty as well as wealth.

Aphrodite: (Greek) A goddess of love, desire, beauty, sexuality, and sexual rapture. She is often depicted with a swan or a dove. Invoke her for all matters of love and sex, as well as for self-confidence and insight in relationships.

Isis: (Egyptian) The very essence of female divinity, she is a goddess of Earth and the Moon. She aids in magick and motherhood, fertility and knowledge. Invoke her using a symbol of the Crescent Moon.

Venus: (Roman) As a goddess she is almost akin to Aphrodite, but Venus, while still greatly linked to love and sex, is also a deity of virginity and the maiden. She is a protector of women. Her time of year is traditionally the spring. She can be invoked when performing rituals for love, fertility, or relationships.

Freya: (Norse/Viking) A goddess of the Moon and the sea, she is associated with cats and all matters relating to love, fertility, and motherhood.

Makosh: (Slavic) A goddess of Earth, the seasons, fertility, and rebirth. Invoke her for strength using a lock of your own hair and a symbol of the Sun.

Kali: (Hindu) She can be something of a dark goddess, given the frequent image of her blood-speckled body. Dark magick relating to Earth and the seasons are connected to her, but so too is the notion of transformation.

Athena: (Greek) Wisdom is what this stunning goddess stands for. She is a granter of knowledge and courage. She is a fighter, a warrior, and an eradicator of injustice. Invoke her for strength in your toughest battles. Her essence will instill in you a wealth of serious scholarship.

Hecate: A goddess of Witches, Witchcraft, and the Moon, her symbol is the crossroads. She can be quite dark and is known for taking various forms. Her power is immense. Invoke her for healing, when performing spells, or for banishing.

Diana: (Roman) A huntress, Diana roams the woods and all places serene. She can bring forth animals and the whisper of the wind. Her physical beauty, in its maiden aspect, is and has always been, astounding. She is a great champion of women and should be invoked for any women's cause.

Durga: (Hindu) A goddess of Earth and all divine force, she exemplifies the universe in all its shifting patterns. This makes her a granter and a destroyer. She is often invoked in healing rituals and to banish disease.

Cerridwen: (Celtic) A multifaceted goddess, she often takes on all three aspects: maiden, mother, and crone. She is dark and light. Her symbol is the Moon. Thus, she is invoked for most magick and is included in all Wiccan rituals.

THE GODS

Apollo: (Greek) The god of life, Earth, and power. He gives light and is known for truth. High on his chariot, he rides the Sun across the sky. He can be invoked for healing, but is especially beneficial for musicians and artists.

Kama: (Indian) Historically a god of love in Indian tradition, he can be invoked for any matters of the heart and family.

Eros: (Greek) A god of love, attraction, and sexuality, he is physically beautiful and poised with the mythical bow and arrow. Invoke Eros for all matters sexual, but also for aid in love and attraction, and anything to do with the body.

Dionysus: (Greek) Traditionally, he is a god associated with wine and all of the human mysteries. He is a creator but also a destroyer. Just as the wind harvest will have its delicious patch, so too can it unleash a bad taste. This metaphor should be remembered when invoking this great god. His power is infinite.

Osiris: (Egyptian) He is the god of vegetation and the harvest, of abundance and plenty. Summon his aid to bring more positive energy into your life, be it school- or work-related.

Hermes: (Greek) He is a very physical god and is known for his enormous strength and speed. He can be invoked for matters dealing with communication. His winged helmet implies flight, and so many also invoke him for travel.

Janus: (Roman) A god of beginnings, he can be invoked when starting a new project or embarking on a different stage of life. His doorway will open up to knowledge and new rooms. Meditating on this awesome god can also aid you in matters of divination.

Sors: (Roman) A god of good fortune and luck, his essence can bring forth a positive new change in life. Invoke him for that necessary streak of advantage.

Mars: (Roman) The god of war, he is often depicted wearing a suit of armor and trailed by a wolf. When invoked, he aids in difficult situations. He can quell the angst of failing relationships and chase away your enemies.

Agni: (Hindu) Traditionally a god of fire, his form comprises many shapes. He may have several arms and legs, but despite his appearance, he is a deity of power and strength. He is often invoked at Summer Solstice rituals.

Neptune: (Roman) He is the great god of the seas and the oceans. His symbol is water. When invoked, he can bring calm and fluidity to any situation. Students of marine biology should pay him special attention.

Cernunnos: (Celtic) The traditional Horned God, he roams the forests and the woodlands, a great masculine figure crowned with stag horns. In rituals, he exemplifies the hunt in nature.

The list of Goddesses and Gods is much longer and can be more detailed. When researching deities on your own, you may find that any of the above are capable of other great feats as well. If one in particular strikes a cord deep down inside, explore what you feel. It is certainly acceptable to be devoted to one particular God or Goddess.

Wicca, as we have seen, is a special religion because it truly operates without dogma or rules that can confine practitioners. It has a penchant for being eclectic, too. It is not uncommon for Witches to harness or incorporate other spiritual pathways in their practice. Witches in Italy, for example, worship the goddess Aradia, but it is not at all uncommon for them to pay homage to certain Roman Catholic elements. Angels are universal beings, respected and called upon by all cultures and creeds. The saints, no doubt, were extraordinary people who lived and died on Earth. They were touched and filled with divine power. If you think it might enhance a spiritual need, call upon them to aid you.

The archangel Michael is a phenomenal being. He is the captain of the angelic host, the leader of the army of God. He is full of mercy and compassion. He is strength, courage, and will. He battles the forces of evil and, according to biblical lore, will defeat the darkness in the battle of Armageddon. Perhaps more than any of these, Michael is a deeply spiritual being whose presence can be felt at any time. The archangels Gabriel and Raphael are also masters of supreme authority. Gabriel is the angel of truth. Raphael is often viewed as a patron for science, knowledge, and intellectual depth.

Whenever I think about the complex relationship between Paganism and Catholicism, I am reminded of the summers I spent in Italy as a child. Cristina, the quiet, middle-aged woman who had lived next door to us in Venice, was known locally as a "strega." She brewed tonics and knew strange little chants. She always told us that the answers to life's puzzling questions could be found in *"la luna"*—the moon. Without a doubt, Cristina was a Witch. But she was also spiritual in many other ways. If you complained to her about having lost something—an object, a job, even a lover—she would instruct you to put a vase of flowers in your window come the Full Moon. Not just any flowers, but Lilies of Saint Anthony. To receive a positive outcome, you had to pray to the revered saint. Whatever was lost, she promised, would be regained.

Casting spells and performing magick and rituals—each acts as a bridge to knowledge and meaning. Employ whatever positive influences you choose. A sampling of possible spells for the college Witch follows.

To Bring Money and Financial Stability

You will need:

    a needle and thread
    a piece of green cloth
    a dollar bill
    three coins (nickels, dimes, or quarters)
    1 teaspoon of cinnamon
    a small piece of white paper and a pen

On a night when the Moon is in a waxing phase, sit at your desk or some other quiet spot in your dorm room or apartment, and spend a few minutes meditating. This is an easy spell to bring money into your life, so envision exactly what you want to change or improve with regard to your finances. Maybe you want just enough money to get you through the semester. Maybe you want enough to pay off some of those loans. In your mind's eyes, envision the intended goal. When you feel calm and ready, ask the Goddess and God—or any deity of your choosing—for strength and guidance. Use your energy to invoke.

Begin the spell by sewing the piece of green cloth into a little pouch; leave one end open. Continue to envision the goal as you pull each inch of thread toward you and away. Next, take the slip of paper and pen and write down your name and date of birth; fold it up into a tiny square. Lay the dollar bill flat on whatever surface you are facing, then begin folding it over the tiny square on which you wrote your name and date of birth. Carefully press the bill into a small square or rectangle, small enough so that it will fit into the pouch. Continue to let your mind fill the silent atmosphere with positive images. Place the folded bill inside the pouch. Now turn your attention to the coins. Hold them in the palm of your hand and envision them multiplying. Drop them into the pouch. Add the dash of cinnamon, and then seal the open end of the pouch with your needle and thread, making certain the edges are tightly bound.

You now hold in your hand a magickal tool. Ask the Goddess and God or deity to guard your actions and intentions so that they manifest properly and positively. Holding the pouch, meditate again, consecrating it so that it will do your bidding. Carry it in your backpack or in your pocket.

To Aid in Taking Exams

You will need:

  a piece of paper
  a pen

Athena, the goddess of wisdom, is perhaps the best deity for college students. She represents not only courage and strength, but insight and intelligence as well. You need all these attributes to pull through four years of hard work. This is a small spell, but a useful one nonetheless. It should be performed before you begin studying. As always, begin by finding a quiet spot. Meditate and ground yourself. Write the following verse on the piece of paper.

Athena, goddess of wisdom and the divine college
Grant me aid and powerful knowledge
The answers come, clear as glass
By moon and magick so shall I pass!

Also write down the name of the class for which you are preparing to study. Finish it all off by inking in your name and date of birth. Fold the paper and put it away in your pocket, but be sure to carry it with you to class. Keep it hidden on your person, and recite the verse to yourself as often as you need. After you complete the exam, in a private spot outdoors, burn the paper and release the ashes to the wind.

To Bring Success in Love

You will need:

 rose petals
 rainwater

Love spells can be a tricky business. You never want to cast a spell on someone specific because that can violate one's own personal will. But you can harness the forces to bring the power of love into your life—and maybe even connect to that special someone. This spell transcends gender and sexuality. All you need is the desire to make it happen.

When there is a rainfall, leave a mason jar or even a small cup outside. Collect as much of the water as possible. Seal it in the jar and keep it in a cool place. At the next Full Moon, set the jar outside again, in the path of the moonlight for at least an hour. Gather petals from a red rose. As you charge them, raising energy and asking the goddess Aphrodite to aid you, drop the petals one by one into the jar of rainwater. Let it set for a while as you continue to meditate. Later, empty the jar onto the earth, preferably in the shadow of a tree. As the water and the rose petals are absorbed, so too is your desire emitted into the atmosphere. Love will come to you.

To Bring Good Health

You will need:

 a bag of peppermint tea
 an apple
 a cup of warm water
 a plastic knife

Nothing is more important than good health. Living on campus, away from home, chances are that you're not eating as well as you should be. No dining hall cook has ever published a book about those tasty, funky-colored concoctions, so you sometimes have to take matters into your own hands. On a night when the Moon is waxing or full, sit in private and invoke the goddess Cerridwen. Picture her as the triple Goddess, in all three aspects. With the plastic knife, inscribe your name and a pentacle into the apple. Hold the apple in your hands while you meditate, drawing in the positive, healing energies of the universe. If you are dealing with an ailment, concentrate on neutralizing its effects on your body. As you eat the apple, envision it coating you with the Moon's light. Take out the seeds from the core and set them aside. Drink the peppermint tea slowly. When you are done, gather the seeds and charge them. Return them to the earth by casting them in a river or stream; if one is not within easy reach, bury them in the ground. As they germinate and grow, so too will your good health.

To Bring Good Luck

You will need:

a green candle
a sewing needle
a lighter
a pinch of salt

We all need a little good luck once in a while. This spell is meant for the college student who lives off campus or at home, since burning candles (in most colleges and universities) is a violation of residency laws. On a night when the Moon is waxing or full, retire to a quiet, clean space and place your unlit candle in its holder. Ground yourself through meditation. Sprinkle the salt on the floor—around the candleholder and to your right and left. This works to cleanse and consecrate your area. When you are ready, take the sewing needle and carefully inscribe your name and date of birth into the sides of the candle. Work your way around it, from top to bottom. Include a small pentacle or any other symbol that is special to you. Hold the candle in your hands, charging it with energy. Hold it until you feel your pulse beating against the wax. Replace it to the holder and light it. Continue to meditate and visualize the good luck you need. Ask the Goddess and God, or whichever deity you are working with, to manifest your desire positively.

Leave the candle burning in a safe place—put it into a large pot, for example, away from anything that could catch fire. When it is completely burned down and there is no longer a flame, gather the remnants of the wax and cast them to the earth: in a moving body of water or in the ground.

For a Smooth Transition into College Life

You will need:

a pen and paper
creativity

Leaving home and beginning your life anew in a strange place is no small feat. It is undoubtedly exciting, but so too does it usher in feelings of fear, angst, worry. Maybe the issue of friends concerns you—will you meet people and forge positive relationships? Will you be able to handle the heavy workload? Every question is valid when you are readying yourself for college. In fact, once you walk out that door and step onto campus as a resident, nothing will ever be the same. Fortunately, the Goddess and God can help.

Once you have decided on the college you will attend, perform this very simple and personal spell. Begin by making a copy of your acceptance letter, then set it aside. Shortly before leaving for school, gather together your thoughts—every fear, concern, excitement— and put them to a new page. Craft a meaningful letter of your own to the Goddess and God, and don't hold anything back. Summon the power of stability, the strength of the God through nature. Draw a pentacle on every corner of the sheet of the paper. When you are done, fold your letter over the copy of the acceptance letter. Take the neat little square and put it away for safe keeping. Don't let anyone see it.

When you arrive on campus, make certain to put the letter under your mattress or in your own dresser drawer. Reflect on it whenever the going gets tough. It is your mind and heart and all of your emotions. It is your psyche, and as a Witch you are forever linked to the Goddess. In due time, you will see the "old" you and come to understand how you have changed and grown with the help of your magick.

To Bring Protection

You will need:

salt
2 red ribbons, each 12 inches long
a mirror

On the night of the New Moon, clean off your desk and sprinkle a dab of salt over it. Set the mirror before you so that you can see your own reflection. In meditation, invoke the goddess Aradia. Envision a circle of white light spiraling around you and infuse it with protection against all enemies and negative vibes. As you do so, braid the two red ribbons together, chanting the words: "I am guarded, I am safe. Beloved Aradia is in this place." When you get to the end, knot both ribbons together and wear this around your wrist or on your person. The acting of knotting and braiding brings protection. Once charged and consecrated, this will act as a strong magickal tool.

Spells are prayers. When you cast a spell, you are asking the Goddess and God for aid, but you are changing consciousness by way of your own will. Remember that the power lives within you. As you develop your own abilities, your mind will mature and you will begin to write and create your own magickal formulas. The more personal your creation, the more powerful the result.

· 10 ·

Rocking the Goddess

American popular culture has embraced the Witch in all her incarnations. She is remembered as a victim of hysteria and brutality, and as a figure of mystery and rebellion. Her image is burned onto the collective mind-set of every generation. Undoubtedly, she has survived centuries of slander without ever truly disappearing. Our history books take schoolchildren back to the Salem Witch Trials and, more recently, the feminist movement of the 1960s. Today, the modern Witch lives at the forefront of religious and political contemplation, sewing the threads of freedom, education, and enlightenment. She is here to stay.

As a country, the United States thrives on what the media deems as "hot." Well-known Witches have written books and made the publicity rounds on television, but there are many prominent non-Witches and Pagans who have stepped up and voiced their support for Wicca and Goddess spirituality as a whole. While promoting their feature film *Practical Magic,* actors Nicole Kidman and Sandra Bullock commented frequently on the serious nature of Witchcraft in America. Cybil Shepard thanked the Goddess out loud in an acceptance speech at the 1997 Emmy Awards. Olympia Dukakis is yet another example of a public figure who has shown support for Goddess-based spirituality; she has spoke publicly about the "female essence of divinity." Who among us has not heard the "rumor" about rock star Stevie Nicks? Once a member of the 1960s hippie movement, she has shadowed her lyrics with pseudo-Pagan elements. New Age guru Deepak Chopra speaks of the universe as contingent upon "Mother Earth" and has written about the benefits of Native American spirituality. Writer Erica Jong penned a book titled *Witches,* in which she shone a spotlight on various goddesses, spells, and magick. In her classic novel *Mists of Avalon,* Marion Zimmer Bradley enthralled readers with a fantastical saga about a Pagan world. The Goddess has also seeped into the writings of Gabriel Garcia Marquez, Isabel Allende, and Alice Walker. In her Mayfair Witches saga, best-selling author Anne Rice explored Witchcraft and sorcery throughout several centuries.

On the college front, students are undoubtedly finding more acceptance via campus organizations, professors, and classes. The University of California at Santa Barbara offers a graduate degree in religion that does not fail to explore Wicca. In the United Kingdom, Bath Spa University has taken a bold step to foster a connection between Pagan culture and the academic world; they offer a New Age and Pagan Studies Programme to graduate students. And, as we have seen, television can entertain anyone who doesn't feel like leaving the house. Turn on *Charmed, Angel,* or *Buffy* and you're sure to find the Witch strutting her stuff on screen.

No matter a person's age, the Witch still holds the power to seduce, amaze, and enchant. You need not be a practitioner of Wicca to experience its magick. Browse the bookstores, the Internet, the very people you call friends. We have all felt the mystery. Is there not a Witch in every one of us?

The Charge of the Goddess

Listen to the words of the great mother;
She who of old was also called among men
Artemis, Astarte, Athene, Aphrodite,
Isis, Diana, Cerridwen
And by many other names:

Whenever ye have need of anything,
Once a month, and better it be when the moon is full,
Than ye shall assemble in some secret place
And adore the spirit of me,
Who am Queen of all witches.

There shall ye assemble,
Ye who fain to learn sorcery
Yet have not won its deepest secrets;
To these will I teach things that are yet unknown.
And ye shall be free from slavery;
And as a sign that ye be really free,
Ye shall be naked in your rites;
And ye shall dance, sing, feast
Make music and love,
All in my praise.
For mine is the ecstasy of the spirit,
And mine is also joy on Earth;
For my law is love unto all beings.
Keep pure your highest ideal;
Strive ever towards it;
let naught stop you or turn you aside.
For mine is the secret door which opens upon the Land of Youth,
And mine is the cup of the wine of life,
And the Cauldron of Cerridwen,
Which is the Holy Grail of immortality.

I am the Gracious Goddess,
Who gives the gift of joy unto the heart of man.
Upon Earth, I give the knowledge of the spirit eternal;
And beyond death, I give peace and freedom
And reunion with those who have gone before.
Nor do I demand aught in the sacrifice;
For behold,
I am the mother of all living,
And my love is poured out upon the Earth.

Hear ye the words of the Star Goddess;
She in the dust whose feet are the hosts of heaven,
And whose body encircles the Universe.
I who am the beauty of the green Earth,
And the white Moon among the stars,
And the mystery of the waters,
And the desire of the heart of man,
Call unto thy soul.
Arise, and come unto me.
For I am the soul of nature, who gives life to the Universe.
From me all things proceed,
And unto me all things must return;
And before my face, beloved of Gods and men,
Let thine innermost divine self be enfolded in the rapture
of the infinite.
Let my worship be within the heart that rejoiceth;
For behold,
All acts of love and pleasure are my rituals.
And therefore let there be beauty and strength,
Power and compassion, honor and humility,
Mirth and reverence within you.

And though who thinkest to seek for me,
Know thy seeking and yearning shall avoid thee not
Unless though knowest the mystery;

That if that which though seekest
Theee findest not within me,
Though wilt never find it without me.
For behold,
I have been with thee from the beginning;
And I am that which attained
at the end of desire

—Doreen Valiente

The Charge of the God

Listen to the words of the Great Father,
Who of old was called Osiris, Adonis, Zeus,
Thor, Pan, Cernunnos, Herne, Lugh
And by many other names:

My Law is harmony with all things.
Mine is the secret that opens the gates of life
And mine is the dish of salt of the Earth
That is the body of Cernunnos
That is the eternal circle of rebirth.
I give the knowledge of life everlasting,
And beyond death I give the promise of
Regeneration and renewal.
I am the sacrifice, the father of all things,
And my protection blankets the Earth.

Hear the words of the dancing God,
The music of whose laughter stirs the winds,
Whose voice calls the seasons:

I who am the Lord of the Hunt and Power of the Light
Sun among the clouds and the secret of the flame,
I call upon your bodies to arise and come unto me.
For I am the flesh of the earth and all its beings.
Through me all things must die and with me are reborn.
Let my worship be in the body that sings,
For all acts of willing sacrifice are my rituals.
Let there be desire and fear, anger and weakness,
Joy and peace, awe and longing within you.
For these too are art of the mysteries
Found within yourself,
Within me all beginnings have endings,
And all endings have beginnings.

—Janet and Stewart Farrar

Pagan Music: Beat of the Earth

SEVEN 13

www.coven13.com

www.seven13band.com

Amanda Adams founded Seven 13 four years ago. A musician since childhood, she earned her B.A. from the University of Massachusetts and her M.A. from Harvard. She plays piano and flute, but those fortunate enough to hear Seven 13 will find themselves immersed in much more than just dual instrumentation. Musically, Seven 13 is an experience. Four of the band's seven members are Pagan, and their unique sound draws from many different esoteric influences.

"Our music is a bridge between the two worlds," Amanda explained. "It's part classical, part modern rock. But it also goes much deeper than that. It definitely mirrors life in every capacity and emotion. The darker overtones are a theatrical representation of our music, but our message as a band is independent and subjective. Our fans tell us all the time that our music takes them on a journey. It's healing. It's hopeful. It's about all positive walks of life."

Seven 13's first CD, *Book of Shadows*, was a triumph of sound and synergy. Their second, *Unleashed*, far exceeds any listener's expectations. The band is based in Boston but has performed around the United States, including two New York City hot spots.

LOREENA MCKENNITT

www.quinlanroad.com

If you haven't yet experienced her brilliance, use this book to slap yourself broadside in the head. The Canadian-born Loreena McKennitt has emerged as one of the entertainment industry's most innovative talents. She writes, composes, and produces her own music for an ever-widening legion of fans. There is no official word on whether or not McKennitt herself is a practicing Pagan, but somehow it doesn't matter. Her lyrics are like a tapestry, weaving tales that resonate with both the light and the dark in nature. Her most recent CD, *The Book of Secrets,* explores the ancient fertility practices of pre-Christian Europe in "The Mummer's Dance." Her previous projects all touch upon the mysterious, the enigmatic, and the magical. Undoubtedly, there is a Pagan influence that runs throughout McKennitt's body of work.

MUSIC FOR THE GODDESS
www.musicforthegoddess.com

Wendy Sheridan began Music for the Goddess in 1998. The band comprises six members and got its start performing at Pagan festivals like the Mid-Atlantic Starwood gathering and others in their home state of New Jersey. Wendy and her husband, Rich, are Pagan. They are raising their daughter in the shadow of the Goddess. The band draws heavily on Pagan and Wiccan influences to create original, imaginative sounds. Their first CD, *Goddess Mandala,* is filled with the sounds that make their music special and different.

"We're certainly eclectic and modern," Wendy explained. "We combine a number of musical elements to put out the best work possible. Our music is a direct connection to the Goddess. Most of us in the band are Pagan, and what we do spiritually helps our music. We've performed for young audiences and the response has always been positive."

Oftentimes, Wendy offers her advice to younger fans.

"I always tell college students interested in Wicca and Paganism to think their spiritual paths through. Unless it speaks to your heart, the magick isn't going to work. They need to take their time dealing with the many powerful forces that are alive within them."

In the meantime, kicking back with Music for the Goddess isn't such a bad idea.

MURDER OF CROWS
www.murderofcrows.net

Since 1997, Murder of Crows has been rocking the Seattle, Washington, music community. Their music can best be described as "dark rock," but it is nonetheless intelligent and thought provoking.

The catch phrase on their Web site reads: *We're just like the kids next door . . . if you lived near a graveyard.* The band credits its success to an all-Pagan membership and lots of support from the Wiccan and Pagan community. Their first LP, *Under the Flesh,* earned them the "Best Goth Rock Album of 2000" Award from Wrapped in Wire, a music Web site.

Anyone listening to Murder of Crows for the first time will be seduced by their unique sound. It is not for the faint of heart, but deep and shadowy lyrics will provoke a sense of wonder and, maybe, a pinprick of that good spooky stuff.

The Wiccan Web

The following Web sites are useful sources of information when researching Wicca and Paganism. There, are of course, countless others, but I have surfed through all of these and found them to be among the best.

The Witches Voice	www.witchvox.com
Old Ways	www.oldways.com
WLPA	
(Witches League for Public Awareness)	www.celticcrow.com
Path Path	www.paganpath.com
Sun Dragon Wicca Page	www.wiccan.com
Wicca info	www.pagans.org
Wicca in the U.K.	www.wiccauk.com
Gerald Gardner info	www.geraldgardner.com
The Wicca Box	www.thewiccabox.com
The Magick	www.magicwicca.com
The Pagan Web	www.thepaganweb.wm
The Witches Web	www.witchesweb.com
Modern Wicca	www.modernwiccan.com
Pagan Resources	www.pagansunite.com
The Dance	www.thedance.com
Wyld Wytch	www.wyldwytch.com
The Cyber Witch	www.cyberwitch.com
Pagan Power	www.paganpower.com
Solitary Wicca	www.solitary-pagan.com
Wicca Women	www.wiccawomen.com
Italian Witchcraft	www.strega.net
	www.strega.com
	www.strega.org
Paranormal info	www.theshadowlands.net

In the forests of the night, mystery waits.

I am standing on the rutted ground of an unknown place. Darkness envelops me. I feel as if I have awakened from a deep sleep that has transported me beyond the realm of dreams. There is no fear. Held within a womb of shadows, I can breathe. I peer through the veil and make out the silhouette of trees: black and green bark, leaves trembling in the first rush of wind. Blades of grass brush against me as I take a step forward. The silence is immense.

Looking up, I catch a glimpse of the sheltering sky, my eyes tracing over white clouds that drift by like smoke. Stars blink through the canopy of indigo. A familiar scent welcomes me—of burning oak and straw, of wet soil freshened by rain. Somewhere in the distance, water is moving. I can hear the thin trickle of a stream. It grows louder as I walk, a billowing whisper, a breath echoed from afar.

It is calling my name.

"Yes," I say. "Who are you?"

"Come," the voice replies.

The trail beneath my feet leads the way. I need not glance down. Pinpricks of light riddle the darkness and a hidden force draws me farther into the forest. A serpent uncoils itself from an overhead branch, its sheen as bright as silver. The thick body moves gently along my arms and shoulders before vanishing into the air.

"Come . . ."

I reach a crossroads. The owl perched above the fork flutters its wings, then rises up, frozen in motion. I look to my left and right. I smile, recognizing the personal items that are strewn along both paths: dozens of books, pens, paper, keys, even the cup that once sat on my desk. Symbols of knowledge. Tokens of the past bidding me farewell. Now I understand. One phase of my life is finished, it has reached its pinnacle, and I am ready to move on. The crossroads is a test, for I know that any path will lead to the same destination. All I have to do is believe. Destiny is subservient to my will.

"Come . . ."

I turn right. I do not look back. Above, long saplings are coming loose, shivering pink and crimson against the sky's brightening path. I move faster. Mist rises from the flanking underbrush and quickly takes shape: a transparent image of a woman, her hair pulled back, her arms opened wide. She hovers there, stunning and breathless, demanding recognition. A single tear streaks my face, resting above my lips like a crescent moon.

"Come . . ."

I have reached the shimmering heart of the forest. I can hear it, thudding. I can hear the voices chanting in unison, speaking the words that will resurrect a mystery.

"Whenever you have need of anything, and better yet if the Moon is full . . ."

They stand before me, a circle of Witches in the grove. I am ushered past them and into the center, where the ground seems to float in between the worlds of spirit and form. I know what I must do. I have come here of my own free will. I have read and spoken, written and received. I have loved and hated, failed and triumphed. I have pierced Nature's soul and embraced the beautiful unknown. And so I have beheld the truth.

What begins in mystery ends in ecstasy.